Palgrave Studies in Victims and Victimology

Series Editors
Pamela Davies, Department of Social Sciences,
Northumbria University, Newcastle upon Tyne, UK
Tyrone Kirchengast, Law School, University of Sydney,
Sydney, NSW, Australia

In recent decades, a growing emphasis on meeting the needs and rights of victims of crime in criminal justice policy and practice has fuelled the development of research, theory, policy and practice outcomes stretching across the globe. This growth of interest in the victim of crime has seen victimology move from being a distinct subset of criminology in academia to a specialist area of study and research in its own right. *Palgrave Studies in Victims and Victimology* showcases the work of contemporary scholars of victimological research and publishes some of the highest-quality research in the field. The series reflects the range and depth of research and scholarship in this burgeoning area, combining contributions from both established scholars who have helped to shape the field and more recent entrants. It also reflects both the global nature of many of the issues surrounding justice for victims of crime and social harm and the international span of scholarship researching and writing about them.

Matthew Davis

Identifying Victims of Human Trafficking

The Legal Issues, Challenges and Barriers

Matthew Davis
Wolverhampton, UK

ISSN 2947-9355   ISSN 2947-9363   (electronic)
Palgrave Studies in Victims and Victimology
ISBN 978-3-031-61740-9   ISBN 978-3-031-61741-6   (eBook)
https://doi.org/10.1007/978-3-031-61741-6

Cover illustration: Raggedstone/Alamy Stock Photo

This Palgrave Macmillan imprint is published by the registered company Springer Nature Switzerland AG
The registered company address is: Gewerbestrasse 11, 6330 Cham, Switzerland

If disposing of this product, please recycle the paper.

Contents

1

Identifying Victims of Human Trafficking: The Legal Issues, Challenges and Barriers

1   Introduction

> Our fight against human trafficking is one of the great human rights causes of our time.
> —Former US President Barack Obama

There are many global crime issues which take place transnationally across borders as well as internally within countries. These include terrorism, money laundering, trafficking of firearms and human smuggling. This book focusses on one of these prevalent global crime problems, human trafficking. All countries are either directly or indirectly affected and have recognised the prevalence of such occurrences in their own nations. Human trafficking is a hugely interesting but complex subject which has many layers of discussion associated with it, raising many issues of how and where the crime takes place and its detrimental impact on vulnerable people. The study of human trafficking contains many facets of interdisciplinary scholarly analysis which must be unpacked to start to comprehend the size and scale of the problem

© The Author(s), under exclusive license to Springer Nature Switzerland AG 2024
M. Davis, *Identifying Victims of Human Trafficking*, Palgrave Studies in Victims and Victimology, https://doi.org/10.1007/978-3-031-61741-6_1

by making sense of the crime, alongside the detrimental impacts trafficking has on victims. Due to the cross-border nature of organised crime, these crimes pose a significant issue for States to combat on their own. Therefore, cooperation between States is essential to identify non-State actors perpetrating these crimes, identify and protect victims and bring offenders to justice through effective prosecution and successful convictions.

States have international legal obligations to combat transnational organised crime.[1] The *United Nations Transnational Organised Crime Convention (UNTOC)*[2] was drafted in the year 2000. This international legal instrument was signed by 143 States in response to increasing threats of international terrorism, acts planned by sophisticated non-state actors in one country who were well financed and resourced and planning to execute acts of terror in another nation.

As part of UNTOC there are three additional, but less formal agreements called Protocols. There is one Protocol on the smuggling of humans[3] and one Protocol on the trafficking of firearms.[4] A third Protocol was created to specifically address and define human trafficking.[5] This is the *Protocol to Prevent, Suppress and Punish Trafficking in Persons, Especially Women and Children.*[6] All three Protocols supplement the United Nations Treaty Convention against Transnational Organised Crime.

In addition to numerous international and national legal instruments, the recently announced *UN Sustainable Development Goals (SDG)* outline a number of targets for the world to meet by 2030.[7] One such target is to combat organised crime including human trafficking and modern slavery.[8] This target seeks to eliminate all types of trafficking and exploitation,[9] end violence and torture against children, combat forced labour and child labour,[10] and promote gender equality within productive employment[11] and peaceful and inclusive societies by providing access to justice for all by building effective, accountable and inclusive institutions at all levels.[12]

The challenge of abolishing modern slavery remains a precarious one given the huge scale and hidden nature of the problem. It has been estimated that in 2021 there were more than 49.6 million people around the world who were victims of modern slavery.[13] The UN has reported that between 2017 and 2018 "a total of 74,514 victims of trafficking were detected in over 110 countries."[14] The world has seen many global emergencies which facilitate the increased number of people migrating which arguably makes people more vulnerable to trafficking. For example, the ongoing Syrian conflict which started in 2011 and is continuing today has seen millions of Syrians displaced. More recently in 2021, Taliban militants were installed as the new Government in Afghanistan resulting in many people fleeing seeking asylum in other countries. The result of people fleeing their host countries due to existing wars and new conflicts has been highlighted by UN Secretary-General, Antonio Guterres:

> Approximately 2 billion people live in conflict-affected countries. Refugees were at the highest number on record in 2021 and forced displacement is continuing to grow, exacerbated by the war in Ukraine.[15]

On 24 February 2022, Ukraine was invaded by Russia. Shortly after the start of the conflict Europol[16] issued an early warning notification alerting EU countries that displaced people from Ukraine and arriving in the EU are at risk of trafficking and exploitation,[17] with women and children at particular risk.[18] The priority for States to identify Ukrainians as trafficked persons[19] was stressed at the time with the intention of vulnerable Ukrainians being protected from organised crime groups. It has been highlighted that there are a host of vulnerabilities specific to asylum seekers and refugees.[20]

The theme of 'vulnerability' is a crucial characteristic to understand when discussing the risk of individuals being targeted by traffickers. Traffickers will often identify who they believe as vulnerable people because they are often easier to deceive and take advantage of. They do this by tricking the victim who is from an unstable or poor social circumstance or poor economic situation to improve their life by tricking them into exploitation with the promise of money, alcohol or drugs. This deceitful method of manipulation makes vulnerable people have a greater dependency from their trafficker for survival. When vulnerable individuals are exploited, it can often compromise their ability to recognise themselves as a victim:

A common factor of trafficking is that the trafficker will present a scenario in which the potential victim can improve the quality of their life and that of their family. Vulnerable people are often targeted as they are seen to be easier to coerce into a situation where they can be manipulated.[21]

Human trafficking is a violation of an individual's liberty and autonomy. But not only this, but as the US Secretary of State further argues, "human trafficking is an affront to our foundational values -that everyone is created equal and has the unalienable rights of life, liberty, and the pursuit of happiness. It erodes our communities, weakens the rule of law, and undermines our national security."[22] The twin approach of combatting human trafficking from a crime control perspective whilst maintaining a victim-centred approach by identifying victims leading to protection and support from the State is a difficult balance to strike. It remains an ongoing challenge, given the advancement of specific political, policy and legislative priorities governments have outlined in their manifestos which makes them ultimately accountable to their electorates at the end of the Parliamentary term.

Regardless of specific political intentions, trafficked victims require protection from the State where they are exploited. As Anne Gallagher advocates, "while there seems to be general agreement on the need for victim protection, the precise contours and limits of that protection have not yet been firmly established."[23] Detection and identification are crucial for victims to get the services and support they require to start the recovery from the trauma they have endured. This book will identify the main issues and challenges associated with the identification of trafficking which will discuss complex issues showing the practical difficulties associated with the detection of potential victims, leading to victims being positively identified by a State. The importance of ensuring that identification remains a priority is examining international legislation, obligating States to create identification procedures[24] to guarantee services and support after identification to survivors. Article 4 European Convention on Human Rights (ECHR) prohibits slavery and forced labour.[25] The consequence for States is that they have obligations to make specific provisions in their domestic criminal law prohibiting slavery and forced labour, investigate and identify situations of potential trafficking and compensate victims of trafficking.

The UN Model Law on Trafficking in Persons accepts that any approach to protecting and identifying survivors "strike a balance between fulfilling victims' basic and immediate needs upon fleeing a situation of exploitation and a Government's need to regulate the dispensation of services and benefits."[26] It has been widely accepted that victims have rights and entitlements which are enshrined in international law. The way in which responsibilities afforded to survivors of foreign nationality play out within domestic law and policy will be highlighted and examined extensively throughout this book.

As acknowledged already, human trafficking is not only a global crime, committed by transnational organised crime groups, but fundamentally it is a human rights violation against an individual. The most effective way of committing to protecting the rights of survivors is through the effective identification of survivors. In the UK, the importance of proactively identifying victims of Modern Slavery and supporting survivors to recover and reintegrate back into society remains one of the UK's priorities.[27] To facilitate effective detection of trafficking and successful identification, it is crucial to understand how the crime starts through deception and how the coercive methods of traffickers keep victims controlled in a cycle of exploitation making it hard for victims to escape.

It has been seen that "trafficking organisations prefer to recruit victims in lower income countries, where the size of the vulnerable population is larger, and exploit them in higher income countries, where profits are higher."[28] Any individual who is part of a vulnerable social group could in theory be at risk of trafficking. Vulnerable groups include forcibly displaced persons, asylum seekers, refugees and internally displaced persons (IDP).[29] Millions of people affected by war and displacement, climate change[30] and extreme poverty are deemed vulnerable, exposing them to the risk of being trafficked if they have not already been so. At the end of 2022, there were estimates of 108.4 million forcibly displaced persons in the world. Of those, there were 5.4 asylum seekers and 35.3 million refugees.[31]

When traffickers employ various methods of recruitment through deception and keeping victims in exploitative conditions through coercion, victims are limited in their freedom of movement, liberty and freedom of association. In many cases, the right not to be subjected to torture and/or cruel, inhuman and degrading treatment is also violated.

As there are many groups of vulnerable persons, it is often difficult for trafficked victims to be distinguishable from other vulnerable groups such as economic migrants, asylum seekers, smuggled persons and refugees. Victims also face challenges self-identifying themselves as victims given the manipulation and psychological damage traffickers inflicted on them. In these situations, the victim requires the help of someone else to detect the behaviour and identify them as a potential victim.

The true extent of the number of trafficked victims in the UK is unknown. However, what is known are the reasons why identification is important for the perspective of victims. The process of identification does have its limitations of specific benefits such as the regularisation of a legal immigration status, but the process does advance other benefits, services and support:

> Whilst a decision that a person is a victim of modern slavery does not guarantee that the individual will be able to stay in the UK, it has substantial consequences for an immigration application also affects the welfare benefits to which the person is entitled.[32]

The increased numbers of detection and identification of victims offer greater opportunities for trafficked persons to escape the exploitative environment and access essential help and support to start the long journey of recovery from their traumatic experiences. For this to happen, the State must carry out their positive obligations to identify, protect and provide help and support effectively. When States fail in their obligations victims may "be at real and immediate risk of re-trafficking if not afforded proper support and protection."[33] The importance of authorities screening foreign nationals who appear in the UK to assess their reasons for being in the country in a timely manner and without delay cannot be underestimated here. This provides an opportunity (if required) for the individual to be referred to the National Referral Mechanism (NRM). Moreover, in international law there is an obligation to strengthen border controls so that the detection of trafficking can take place.[34] However, it has been advocated that a rights-based approach to border control is required.[35] This view is justified by the fact that identifying victims can be a complex and lengthy process. The risk is that if screening is not done quickly, the higher the risk of the person being exploited.

The Subtle Differences Between Human Trafficking and Human Smuggling

It can be argued that it is easy to confuse human trafficking and human smuggling and vice versa. An example is the small boats issue where people are being smuggled from France to the UK in small boats. The perpetrators are referred to as 'traffickers' when in fact they are 'human smugglers.' The misuse of terms is deeply unhelpful to define what the act really and difficult to come up with workable solutions if policymakers and legislators are devising policy on trafficking when in fact the small boat issue is specifically about smuggling. For clarity and understanding the following criminal acts are defined. Human smuggling can be described as:

> Smuggling of migrants shall mean the procurement, in order to obtain, directly or indirectly, a financial or other material benefit, of the illegal entry of a person into a State Party of which the person is not a national or a permanent resident.[36]

There are significant differences between the two acts and have different purposes. For example, human smuggling is considered a crime against the State (or a violation of State Sovereignty), whereas human trafficking is regarded as a crime against the individual perpetrated by an abuser and exploiter, giving rise to human rights violations being committed against the person including the person's freedom and integrity. The purpose of smuggling is to move one person from one country to another illegally because the person who has no legal status being in that country and is considered 'illegal.' Offenders of human smuggling can be prosecuted under Section 25[37] and Section 25A[38] Immigration Act 1971. The transaction between the smuggler and the individual ends when that person enters the border illegally. In contrast, a trafficked victim can be moved internationally across borders, but victims do not need to cross a border to be recognised as a victim. Internal trafficking where a victim is moved within a state can take place and therefore the crossing of a border is not needed for trafficked victims to fall within the legal definition. Exploitation can happen when someone enters the country illegally or if someone has legal status being in that country. Consent is a relevant issue and one which distinguishes between the two acts. In smuggling the individual is consenting to travel across the border illegally. In cases of human trafficking, consent is not obtained from the victim and their means of escape[39] and freedom are severely restricted either by physical means or psychological behaviour or indeed a combination of both methods. International law does not consider that either a child or adult can consent to being trafficked. There are situations whereby one act of being smuggled can often lead to trafficking. For example, a typical scenario may occur where "a person who has voluntarily gone into an arrangement under which he is smuggled into the UK and agrees to work for a period without pay to repay back those who transported him may well also not be a victim of trafficking, despite the fact that this person is in debt bondage to his minders for a defined period. However, a combination of debt bondage plus force, coercion or menaces is highly likely to result in the individual being a victim of trafficking."[40]

The two acts can often be confused. Therefore, the language used to describe each act needs to be precise and clear to avoid confusion. Language used is key to understanding the issue. Teresa May, "I must say there has been some loose talk about people smuggling and human trafficking, and using the two terms in the same breath as if they are the same—they are not; they are two separate crimes."[41] The difference between what each person is entitled to as a smuggled person is different to a trafficked person, and the State has different responsibilities and duties to a trafficked victim.

Often the word trafficking and smuggling are used by various people including politicians who then conflate one crime with the other. The terms are being used interchangeably. There are several distinct differences between the two.

The overlap between the two acts has significant issues for individuals as they can be exploited despite being referred to as smuggled previously, especially in cases where people experience delays in receiving decisions about their asylum application, as their choices in order to survive are significantly restricted, pushing them into making riskier decisions leading them into exploitative environments.

As seen, traffickers can profit from the services and work from victims whilst smugglers profit from the service they are providing to others. This does not mean that the two criminal actions are mutually exclusive. An individual can become trafficked who had previously been smuggled. This can arise because of the nature of the illegal status of that person who had freely chosen to be smuggled from Point A across the border into Point B. This act makes them vulnerable in the receiving State, because of the lack of rights and entitlements arising out of the crime against the State. This vulnerability exposes a smuggled person to the real risk of being exploited because of the lack of legal status attached to that individual. In some cases, the individual is subjected to debt bondage whereby the person has to repay the cost of travel of being smuggled and made to pay off their debt and exploited in doing so.

This conflation between smuggling and trafficking has been reflected in a legislative perspective from the UK's Nationality and Borders Act 2022 which will be examined in the next chapter. It seeks to make it less easy to be recognised as a victim of trafficking as a direct fear that economic migrants are using modern slavery avenues of protection as a way of gaining entry and residence into the UK.

One thing is for certain that from a broader international perspective, "States now recognise that trafficked persons have special rights and that the State owes a particular duty of protection and support to those persons."[42]

Different Types of Human Trafficking

There are many types of human trafficking. It has been reported that "as new forms of exploitation emerge, boys and men account for a greater share of detected victims."[43] These new forms of exploitation include forced criminality[44] and mixed types of exploitation. Where females are detected, it has been evidenced that they are subjected to greater violence than male victims with traffickers abusing victims of both genders for longer periods.[45] Key types of exploitation which have been identified amongst identified victims globally illustrate the nature and most common forms of exploitation:

Trafficking for forced labour – 38.8%
Trafficking for sexual exploitation – 38.7%
Trafficking for mixed forms of exploitation – 10.3%
Trafficking for forced criminality – 10.21%
Trafficking for forced marriage – 0.9%
Trafficking for exploitative begging – 0.7%
Trafficking for illegal adoption – 0.3%
Trafficking for removal of organs – 0.2%[46]

The ability to spot a victim involved in a specific type of trafficking may be compromised by what method of exploitation the victim is subjected to. There are a host of different types of forced labour exploitation. The share of victims is mostly found in agriculture and the fishing industry. Domestic work and cleaning services are also popular alongside street selling and construction. Lesser popular environments are within the entertainment industry, mining, catering and hospitality sectors and a small percentage have been to exist within nursing and the garment industry.[47]

It has been seen that human trafficking for criminal exploitation where the victim[48] is forced to carry out acts which are considered "unlawful or antisocial (e.g. Begging or prostitution) or directly criminal (e.g. producing drugs, acting as a drug mule or property-related street crime)"[49] are more difficult for the identified as a victim, rather than an offender committing a criminal offence.[50] Some of these examples can be seen through the phenomenon of 'County Lines Exploitation' in the

UK involving vulnerable children being manipulated and then coerced into trafficking drugs from inner city suburbs across to other counties to towns and regions described as more affluent and provincial. The punitive prosecutorial approach against vulnerable people does nothing to advance the interest of their victim status and shows that where the criminal justice system fails to adopt a victim-centred approach to tackling the global and national issues surrounding trafficking by failing to acknowledge that some offenders are indeed victims of crime themselves.

There are also a host of reasons associated with the various types of trafficking as to why an individual may become at risk of being trafficked in the first place. Recognised identified vulnerabilities include "poor socio-economic status, lack of educational and work opportunities, child sexual and other forms of abuse, a history of sexual assault/rape, community or gender-based violence, a background of state persecution/torture, health conditions as well as learning disabilities and disability, natural disasters and pandemics."[51]

The Challenges Associated with Self-Identification and the Imporatnce of Identification of Victims

Victims of trafficking experience many types of harm and abuse, often before a trafficking experience occurs. Modern slavery has been acknowledged as a huge facilitator where victims are either experiencing harm within an exploitative environment or where survivors have expressly testified to trained professionals providing help and support to victims after they have escaped exploitation. Identification becomes extremely challenging when individuals present themselves to agencies but have difficulty disclosing their experiences and asking for help, partly because of a loss of autonomy and agency resulting from the impact of abuse and harm from traffickers, but also due to physical injuries, and psychological problems which are difficult to see without further discussion and evaluation.

An important issue to acknowledge is the impact of trauma which can often affect the ability of victims to self-identify or for agencies to recognise a victim of trafficking during the identification process. Many trafficked victims suffer from Post-Traumatic Stress Disorder (PTSD) after being trafficked and exploited, making it challenging for them to discuss their experiences. The symptoms associated with PTSD can be summarised as the following:

> Re-experiencing traumatic events as intrusive thoughts, flashbacks and nightmares, avoidance of reminders or triggers of the trauma, negative alterations in cognition and mood – this may lead to a victim to have strong beliefs about self-blame, guilt, shame or fear of others.[52]

The consequences of victims experiencing PTSD can be seen in a variety of ways when coming into contact with agencies who have the opportunity of recognising them as victims. Firstly, PTSD can affect the ability of some victims to be credible and reliable in terms of disclosing their abusive experiences. It also may impact their ability to "narrate a detailed and coherent account of their traumatic experience."[53]

Secondly, the impact of trauma has the ability to affect a victim's consistent version of events and the victim's testimony may be different given the inability of the victim to remember such events or the thought of recalling them has negative psychological effects such as retriggering past traumatisation. The evidence provided by the victim may be different from previous evidence raising the issue of whether decision makers not believing the victim. Regardless of whether the person is a victim the disclosure of such experiences will be difficult for some victims to recount. In addition, "victims of trafficking may not tell the truth and may even lie for a number of different potential reasons connected to their experience as victims of trafficking."[54]

Evidence from expert medical professionals is important and may be required to corroborate statements made by the victim. This supporting information can be identified as independent and provide evidence that the victim has been subjected to abuse which has brought on mental health conditions such as PTSD.

In conclusion, despite the difficulties victims may have experiencing PTSD because of traumatic abuse and exploitation, the overarching question for the decision maker who decides whether the person is a trafficked person or not is "whether the person is likely to be a victim of trafficking; it is not whether the person is telling the truth about what has happened to them prior to discovery."[55] The Home Office Modern Slavery Guidance provides that when making a decision "they must weigh the strength of the evidence presented, including the credibility of the claim, and use common sense and logic based on the particular circumstances of each case."[56] Consequently, there is no burden on either party to prove that he or she is a victim of trafficking or not.

In addition to the impact trauma has on identification, there are a host of additional reasons why it is difficult for agencies to identify victims in a number of environments. From a criminal justice perspective, it is an onerous task for the police to have the responsibility of spotting the signs that someone may be trafficked. Moreover, it has been found that police are not aware of who a victim is or have an idea of who a typical victim is, leading to mistakes when dealing with individuals.[57]

It has been acknowledged that there is a lack of awareness of the criminal justice system not being aware of this phenomenon and consequently can lead to situations that have been prosecuted at the expense of being treated and protected as a victim of crime because of them being trafficked for exploitative purposes.

The dangers of misidentifying a victim of human trafficking and being identified as a criminal rather than a victim of crime can be seen from the of *R v O*.[58] This case in February 2008 involved a woman (who was later identified as a 16-year-old child) who stated that her nationality was Nigerian but admitted presenting a Spanish identity card to UK passport control and pleaded guilty at trial. Before the trial, her legal representatives were informed by the Poppy Project[59] that she could potentially be a victim of human trafficking as she had stated to them that she ran away from being a prostitute. However, this information was not acted upon, and therefore no referral was made to the NRM under obligations set out by Article 10 Council of Europe Convention on Action Against Trafficking in Human Beings.[60] Despite the UK not ratifying this at the time of this case, the UK had obligations under Article 18 Vienna Convention on the Law of Treaties to 'refrain from acts which would defeat the object and purpose of the treaty.' Furthermore, the CPS had guidance to follow regarding 'Suspects in a Criminal Case who might be Victims of

Trafficking or Slavery.'[61] The victim had been let down by the defence counsel representing her as it was held that:

> No steps were taken by the defence to investigate the history. No consideration was given by the defence as to whether she might have a defence of duress. The possibility that she might have been trafficked was ignored. There is nothing in the transcript to suggest that any thought had been given to the State's possible duty to protect her as a young victim.[62]

It was further advocated by the court that "defence lawyers must respond by making enquiries, if there is before them credible material showing that they have a client who might have been the victim of trafficking, especially a young client. Where there is doubt about the age of a defendant who is a possible victim of trafficking, proper inquiries must be made."[63] One case where the UK had ratified the CofE Convention by the time the case came to court was the victim in *R v L and Other Appeals*.[64] In this case, the Poppy Project advocated for a woman from Uganda who had been arrested for using a forged passport when applying for a National Insurance number. She was then charged and convicted of the offence. Whilst in prison, a psychiatrist instructed by the Poppy Project concluded that "there was powerful evidence that the appellant fell to be treated as a victim of international trafficking for sexual exploitation in forced prostitution. She was suffering from complex post-traumatic stress disorder with severe trauma."[65] She was then referred to the NRM where the UK Border Agency believed that she was a victim of trafficking and gave the survivor a Conclusive Grounds Decision confirming her victim status. Nevertheless, throughout the trial there was no attempt by her solicitor to investigate the matter further or refer to the NRM. By the time the case came to the appeal, the judge acknowledged the view held by the prosecutors that "that if the actual facts had been known at the time when the decision to prosecute had been made, the case would not have proceeded."[66] Furthermore, "on the basis of the facts which are now known, if this appellant had been prosecuted, an abuse of process argument would have been advanced with a realistic prospect of success,"[67] and allowed the appeal, quashing the conviction. This case illustrated several important issues on how victims who have their victim status disregarded are then poorly treated in the criminal justice system. It shows "serious incompetence or substantial ignorance. Ample opportunities arose for the appellant to be correctly identified as a victim of human trafficking, which would have spared her the traumatic experience of being convicted and sentenced as a criminal, and instead provided her with the support afforded to victims."[68]

A similar determination was made in two late cases, *R v THN*,[69] and *R v T*.[70] In the former case, a child victim of trafficking had pleaded guilty to producing a controlled drug, Class B. It was held that "the Crown accepted that had the evidence which was now available been available at the time when the original decision to prosecute the appellant was made, on the basis of the public interest test in the context of trafficked children, there would have been no prosecution."[71] In the latter case of a child who had been sentenced to 2 years in a young offenders' institute after being found guilty under Section 6(2) Misuse of Drugs Act 1971 for cultivating cannabis. It was held that "no proper consideration was given to the question whether the appellant had been the victim of trafficking."[72] There was eventually a positive CGD, but "this decision did not reach his solicitors until April 2013, and it was not provided to the Crown by those representing the appellant until 14 April 2013"[73] which was further into the later stages of trial proceedings.

In summary, these cases raise the important issues of identification and the awareness within the legal profession (amongst defence solicitors, the CPS and judges) to be alert to the fact that a defendant may be a potential victim of trafficking whilst observing Article 26 of the ECAT relating to the non-prosecution of trafficked victims.

These issues are not insurmountable and can be easily remediable by greater awareness through effective training throughout the legal profession.

We have already looked at how individuals have been recorded as trafficked victims in UK Government statistics. As we know, many victims are trapped in silence away from the public where they are living a life of exploitation in a cycle of trauma and abuse. Furthermore, the "misperceptions of who is likely to be a victim, how victims should behave and where they come from can all hinder victim identification."[74] Given the intrinsic issues many victims experience in this environment, it is important to acknowledge how difficult self-identification is. What I mean by self-identification is how victims portray themselves as victims of crime and acknowledge that they are being exploited, and in some cases have committed criminal offences as part of their exploitation. Some individuals may not self-identify because they do not trust authorities[75] that they will be believed, which prevents them from accessing services and support as trafficked victims.[76]

Some victims may not know or comprehend the level of exploitation which they are being subjected to due to the manipulation of their exploiters. This relationship between the exploiter and the exploited victim represents a complex dynamic which in some cases will result in the victim relying on their exploiter(s) for their survival such as accommodation or to satisfy a drug and/or alcohol problem.

To assist us with understanding what the main challenges of self-identification are, we need to revisit the legal definition of human trafficking set out in Article 3(a) UN Trafficking Protocol. We already know that there are three elements to the legal definition. Firstly, there is the act, secondly there is the 'means' and thirdly we know that the purpose must be to exploit that person. In terms of understanding self-identification further, we need to narrowly focus our attention on the means aspect of the definition. Here, we are analysing the actions of the trafficker and the specific impacts that those actions have directly on the victim which specifically keeps that victim trapped in an exploitative situation and an environment whereby it is extremely difficult to leave.

We will see how the Illegal Migration Act 2023 will facilitate this fear even greater when we look at the impact this legislation will have on trafficked victims in the UK in Chapter 3.

Identifying an 'Ideal Victim'

A logical question to pose from the outset is, 'Who is a victim of human trafficking?' From a legal perspective seen from the Explanatory notes of *Council of Europe Convention on Action against the Trafficking of Human Beings (ECAT)*,[77] a victim is defined as "anyone subjected to a combination of elements (action, means, purpose)."[78] But what are these elements and how do they operate in practical situations of trafficking? To answer this question, we need to examine the legal definition of human trafficking. There is a legal definition agreed in international law and adopted by States within the United Nations. Human trafficking is defined as:

> …the recruitment, transportation, transfer, harbouring or receipt of persons, by means of the threat or use of force or other forms of coercion, of abduction, of fraud, of deception, of the abuse of power or of a position of vulnerability or of the giving or receiving of payments or benefits to achieve the consent of a person having control over another person, for the purpose of exploitation.[79]

By understanding what the crime entails makes the understanding of who a victim of this crime is. We have already seen the subtle differences and confusion with another type of irregular migration, human smuggling. The Organisation for Security and Co-operation in Europe (OSCE) goes further by acknowledging the importance of identification by defining a victim as:

> …any natural person who has been subject to trafficking in persons, or who the competent authorities including the designated non-governmental organisations where applicable reasonably believe is a victim of trafficking in persons, regardless of whether the perpetrator is identified, apprehended, prosecuted or convicted.[80]

Identifying how victims may be classified as fitting within a construed victimhood can be problematic. Assuming who may or may not be a victim is extremely subjective without knowing all the information about the person's present circumstances or the past traumatic events the individual has experienced. Nils Christie identifies an ideal victim as "a weak person in comparison to the offender, engaged in morally sound or ordinary, everyday behaviour when the crime happened, and having no criminal history; the ideal victim's perpetrator is perceived clearly as the big and bad person, with an ideal offender being unknown to the victim and in no personal relationship to her."[81] Christie identifies 4 'ideal victim' attributes:

(1) The victim is weak. Sick, old or very young people are particularly well suited as ideal victims.
(2) The victim was carrying out a respectable project- caring for her sister.
(3) She was where she could not possibly be blamed for being – in the street during the daytime.
(4) A condition for being an ideal victim is thus that you are powerful enough to make your case known and successfully claim the status of an ideal victim.[82]

A second model portrays an ideal victim "as a 'pure victim' as a woman who adheres to traditional gender roles, is passive, non-violent, and emotionally dependent on her abuser."[83]

A third view offers several characteristics of a trafficked victim who is "(1) a woman or girl trafficked for sex; (2) law enforcement assesses her to be a good witness; (3) she cooperates fully with law enforcement investigations; and (4) she is rescued instead of escaping from the trafficking enterprise."[84] These views are simplistic especially where views such as regarding victims as "young women or girls, or alternatively, as young boys, to position victims as prototypically weak and helpless. Furthermore, these victims are construed as respectable, and passive-agents (and thus blameless) exploited by diametrically opposed ideal offenders."[85] It is not necessarily the case that all victims are weak but are unable to physically leave the environment because they have no other place to go. They may be involved in criminal activity under duress from their trafficker. There are a host of internist and extrinsic reasons why trafficked victims find it difficult to self-identify as victims and therefore do not fit within the ideal victim standard. These challenges will be addressed later in the chapter.

There are further issues associated with stereotyping what an ideal trafficked victim looks like. Incorrect perceptions from the public and those working in frontline agencies as to who is a trafficked victim may prevent more individuals being correctly identified as victims if they do not conform to Christie's theory ideal victim definition. It may also lead to situations where individuals are being ignored or misiden-tified as another type of person from a vulnerable group, for example, a smuggled person, asylum seeker or refugee. It is only through careful evaluation and assessment of a victim's experiences and circumstances an accurate determinative status will be arrived at. As acknowledged, "an understanding of the trafficking process could help erode certain biases about the 'ideal' victim and thus enable more effective identification of victims."[86]

Identifying a victim separately from any crime in which they have committed is very difficult. The distinction between a victim and offender is very thin and, in some cases, individuals can find themselves being a victim and an offender at the same time. Genuine victims who are made to commit crimes as part of their exploitation find themselves at a disadvantage when Governments seek to demonise the NRM system they essentially created when they make statements as to how the process is being taken advantage of and undermined by non-genuine people who are in fact criminals. The effect has been the risk of victims not being adequately protected by the system which has been designed and imple-mented to shield them by recognising a person's story of exploitation, rather than wishing to cast doubt and take the view that a victim is really an offender in disguise. Treating every migrant suspiciously is not productive and shows that the focus must be on maintaining a strong and robust identification system with the emphasis on deciding whether the individual has indeed been trafficked or not. Every potential victim of trafficking has the right to be referred and not suspected of criminality from the outset. A failure to accept this undermines the whole system of detection from the outset, referral into the NRM and positive identifi-cation at the end, opening a gateway for the victim to receive help and support for the survivor to recover from their exploitation.

Alongside the responses to removing exploited individuals and identi-fying them as victims of trafficking from the NRM, there is an obligation on States to criminalise the offence and prosecute offenders. In 2022, the Crown Prosecution Service (CPS) in the UK "prosecuted 405 defendants on trafficking charges, a decrease from 466 defendants in 2021. Courts convicted 282 traffickers in 2022, a decrease from 332 in 2021."[87] The issue of prosecutions and the prosecution of victims will be exten-sively examined later in Chapter 6. We now turn to how the issue of immigration has been 'politicised' by politicians and some aspects of the electorate and how this behaviour has negatively impacted on more trafficked victims less likely to being identified in the UK. This 'politicalisation of immigration' compromises, overshadows and hides the true criminal nature of trafficking in the UK along with its victims. This will be examined in the next chapter.

Notes

1. The UN has defined organise crime comprising of 'a group of three or more persons that was not randomly formed; existing for a period of time; acting in concert with the aim of committing at least one crime punishable by at least four years' incarceration; in order to obtain, directly or indirectly, a financial or other material benefit.' See Article 2(a) UN Convention against Transnational Organised Crime 2000 (2225 UNTS 209).
2. UN Convention against Transnational Organised Crime 2000 (2225 UNTS 209).
3. Protocol against the Smuggling of Migrants by Land, Sea and Air, Supplementing the UN Convention against Transnational Organised Crime (UNGA Res. 55/25).
4. Protocol against the Illicit Manufacturing of and Trafficking in Firearms, Thie Parts and Components and Ammunition, Supplementing the UN Convention against Transnational Organised Crime (UNGA Res. 55/25).
5. Trafficking in persons under Article 3A "shall mean the recruitment, transportation, transfer, harbouring or receipt of persons, by means of the threat or use of force or other forms of coercion, of abduction, of fraud, of deception, of the abuse of power or of a position of vulnerability or of the giving or receiving of payments or benefits to achieve the consent of a person having control over another person, for the purpose of exploitation. Exploitation shall include, at a minimum, the exploitation of the prostitution of others or other forms of sexual exploitation, forced labour or

services, slavery or practices similar to slavery, servitude or the removal of organs."

6. Protocol to Prevent, Suppress and Punish Trafficking in Persons, Especially Women and Children, Supplementing the UN Convention against Transnational Organised Crime (UNGA Res. 55/25).

7. See 'UNODC and the Sustainable Goals,' September 2023, https://www.unodc.org/documents/SDGs/SDG_website_u pdate_09.2023.pdf.

8. See the Sustainable Development Goals (SDGs), where the global community has committed to ending modern slavery among children by 2025, and universally by 2030 (Target 8.7).

9. Article 8.7.

10. Article 16.2, 8.7.

11. Article 8.

12. Article 16.

13. International Labour Organisation & Walk Free Foundation, 'Global estimates of modern slavery: Forced labour and forced marriage,' International Labour Office (ILO), Geneva (September 2022) at 2, https://www.ilo.org/wcmsp5/groups/pub lic/@ed_norm/@ipec/documents/publication/wcms_854733.pdf.

14. Office for Democratic Institutions and Human Rights (ODIHR), 'Guidance—Addressing Emerging Human Trafficking Trends and Consequences of the Covid-19 Pandemic,' at 5.

15. United Nations, 'The Sustainable Development Goals Report 2022,' at 2.

16. The European Police Office (Europol) is a European Union Agency for Law Enforcement Cooperation which support Member States in preventing and combating all forms of serious international and organised crime, cybercrime and terrorism.

17. Europol Press Release, The Hague, March 2022 Ref. No.: 2022-340 Europol Operations Directorate Operational and Analysis Centre European Migrant Smuggling Centre, March 2022, https://www.europol.europa.eu/cms/sites/default/files/docume nts/Early_Warning_Notification__War_in_Ukraine_%E2%80% 93_refugees_arriving_to_the_EU_from_Ukraine_at_risk_of_expl oitation_as_part_of_THB.pdf.

18. European Commission, 'A Common Anti-Trafficking Plan to address the risks of trafficking in human beings and support potential victims amongst those fleeing the war in Ukraine,' at 1 https://home-affairs.ec.europa.eu/system/files/2022-05/Anti-Tra fficking%20Plan_en.pdf.

19. The Council of Europe Group of Experts on Action against Trafficking in Human Beings (GRETA) stress the importance of detecting potential victims and traffickers under Article 10 Council of Europe Convention on Action against Trafficking in Human Beings in their 'Guidance note on addressing the risks of trafficking in human beings related to the war in Ukraine and the ensuing humanitarian crisis.' 4 May 2022 at 4 https://rm.coe.int/ guidance-note-on-addressing-the-risks-of-trafficking-in-human-beings-r/1680a663e2#:~:text=The%20Guidance%20Note%20a ddresses%20a,co%2Dordination%20and%20data%20collection.

20. There are many vulnerabilities which make some people more susceptible to trafficking. For a deeper understanding more about vulnerability to trafficking in persons, see The Inter-Agency Coordination Group Against Trafficking in Persons (ICAT), 'Addressing Vulnerability to Trafficking in Persons,' Issue Brief 12/ 2022, https://south.euneighbours.eu/wp-content/uploads/2022/ 08/icat_issue_brief_12_vulnerability_to_tip_published.pdf.

21. Home Office Modern Slavery: statutory guidance for England and Wales (under s49 of the Modern Slavery Act 2015), 9 October 2023 at 13.6, https://www.gov.uk/government/public ations/modern-slavery-how-to-identify-and-support-victims/mod ern-slavery-statutory-guidance-for-england-and-wales-under-s49-of-the-modern-slavery-act-2015-and-non-statutory-guidance-for-scotland-and-northe.

22. A. Blinken US Secretary of State, US Trafficking in Persons Report 2023 at 4.

23. A. Gallagher, "The International Law of Human Trafficking" (Cambridge University Press, 2010) at 276.

24. For example, Article 10 ECAT.

25. P. Southwell, M. Brewer, B. Douglas Jones QC, "Human Trafficking and Modern Slavery Law & Practice" (Bloomsbury Professional, 2020) at 402–403.
26. UNODC Model Law on Persons, UN Sales No.09.V11 (2009) at 21.
27. HM Government Modern Slavery Strategy, 2014 at 24.
28. D. Hernandez & A. Rudolph, "Modern Day Slavery: What Drives Human Trafficking in Europe?" (2015) European Journal of Political Economy, 38, 118 – 139 at 134.
29. Any of the above groups could be at risk due to war/conflict, natural disasters or climate change (climate refugees).
30. The UNODC reports that in 2021, 23.7 million people were internally displaced because of climate change. See UNODC, 'Global Report on Trafficking in Persons 2022,' at X.
31. UNHCR Global Trends Report–Forced Displacement in 2022.
32. R (on the application of TVN) v SSHD [2021] EWHC 3019 (Admin) at 2.
33. See R (TDT) v SSHAD [2018] EWCA Civ 1395 at para 40.
34. Article 11(1) UN Protocol to Prevent, Suppress and Punish Trafficking in Persons, Especially Women and Children, Supplementing the UN Convention against Transnational Organised Crime (UNGA Res. 55/25).
35. M. McAdam, "Who's Who at the Border? A rights-based approach to identifying human trafficking at international borders," (2013) Anti-trafficking Review, 2, 33–49.
36. Article 3(a) Protocol against the Smuggling of Migrants by Land, Sea and Air, supplementing the United Nations Convention against Transnational Organized Crime, General Assembly resolution 55/25 of 15 November 2000.
37. Section 25 Immigration Act 1971 for assisting unlawful immigration to the UK.
38. Section 25A Immigration Act 1971 for knowingly helping asylum seekers to enter or arrive in the UK depending upon the circumstances of the attempted facilitation.
39. It has been acknowledged that some traffickers will offer small freedoms to help maintain control and reduce the risk of escaping

from the exploitative environment but have consequences associated with these privileges. See R (on the application of TVN) v SSHD [2021] EWHC 3019 (Admin) at para 94.

40. R (on the application of TVN) v SSHD [2021] EWHC 3019 9Admin) at para 13.

41. Illegal Migration Bill, 729: debated on Monday 13 March 2023, https://hansard.parliament.uk/Commons/2023-03-13/debates/ 97D4F67E-2C1B-44CB-B860-DD9024958EEF/IllegalMigra tionBill#contribution-1C16679A-5EAD-4D46-9BA9-9D2E38 92403D.

42. A. Gallagher, "The International Law of Human Trafficking" (Cambridge University Press, 2010) at 279.

43. UNODC, 'Global Report of Trafficking in Persons 2022,' at XI.

44. Forced criminality will be examined in Chapter 6 which discusses the challenges of identification where victims are coerced into committing criminal offences under duress by traffickers.

45. UNODC, 'Global Report of Trafficking in Persons 2022,' at XII and XIII.

46. UNODC 'Global Report on Trafficking 2022,' at XV.

47. See UNODC 'Global Report on Trafficking 2022,' at 37 which details the percentage of victims found from 89 cases which resulted in a conviction against traffickers who exploited 890 victims over a period of 2012 and 2020.

48. It has been found that the majority of victims are male who are forced to commit these offences. See UNODC 'Global Report on Trafficking 2022,' at 39.

49. C. Villacampa & N. Torres, "Human Trafficking for Criminal Exploitation: The Failure to Identify Victims," Eur J (2017) Crim Policy Res, 23, 393–408 at 393.

50. This issue will be discussed in far more detail in Chapter 6 when we examine the prosecution of trafficked victims for offences committed under duress from traffickers.

51. J. Hunt, R. Witkin, C. Katona, 'Identifying human trafficking in adults,' BMJ, 22 December 2020, https://www.bmj.com/content/ 371/bmj.m4683.

52. Home Office Modern Slavery: statutory guidance for England and Wales (under s49 of the Modern Slavery Act 2015) 9 October 2023 at 13.12, https://www.gov.uk/government/publications/modern-slavery-how-to-identify-and-support-victims/modern-slavery-statutory-guidance-for-england-and-wales-under-s49-of-the-modern-slavery-act-2015-and-non-statutory-guidance-for-sco tland-and-northe.

53. Home Office Modern Slavery: statutory guidance for England and Wales (under s49 of the Modern Slavery Act 2015) 9 October 2023 at 13.20, https://www.gov.uk/government/publications/modern-slavery-how-to-identify-and-support-victims/modern-slavery-statutory-guidance-for-england-and-wales-under-s49-of-the-modern-slavery-act-2015-and-non-statutory-guidance-for-sco tland-and-northe.

54. R (on the application of TVN) v SSHD [2021] EWHC 3019 (Admin) at para 34(ii).

55. R (on the application of TVN) v SSHD [2021] EWHC 3019 (Admin) at para 32.

56. Home Office Modern Slavery: statutory guidance for England and Wales (under s49 of the Modern Slavery Act 2015) 9 October 2023 at 14.85, https://www.gov.uk/government/publications/modern-slavery-how-to-identify-and-support-victims/modern-slavery-statutory-guidance-for-england-and-wales-under-s49-of-the-modern-slavery-act-2015-and-non-statutory-guidance-for-sco tland-and-northe.

57. See C. Villacampa & N. Torres, "Human Trafficking for Criminal Exploitation: The Failure to Identify Victims," (2017) Eur J Crim Policy Res, 23, 393–408 at 406.

58. R v O [2008] EWCA Crim 2835.

59. The Poppy Project was an organisation who provided housing support to trafficked victims who had been sexually exploited.

60. Under Article 10, each Party shall provide its competent authorities with persons who are trained and qualified in preventing and combating trafficking in human beings, in identifying and helping victims, including children, and shall ensure that the different authorities collaborate with each other as well as with relevant

support organisations, so that victims can be identified in a procedure duly taking into account the special situation of women and child victims and, in appropriate cases, issued with residence permits under the conditions provided for in Article 14 of the present Convention.

61. This guidance has been consistently updated by the CPS. See https://www.cps.gov.uk/legal-guidance/modern-slavery-human-trafficking-and-smuggling.
62. R v O [2008] EWCA Crim 2835 at para 25.
63. R v O [2008] EWCA Crim 2835 at para 26.
64. R v L and other appeals [2013] EWCA Crim 991.
65. R v L and other appeals [2013] EWCA Crim 991 at para 74.
66. R v L and other appeals [2013] EWCA Crim 991 at para 74.
67. R v L and other appeals [2013] EWCA Crim 991 at para 74.
68. J. Elliott, "(Mis)Identification of Victims of Human Trafficking: The Case of R v O," (2009) International Journal of Refugee Law, 21(4), 727 at 740.
69. R v THN [2014] 1 All ER.
70. R v T from R v L and other appeals [2013] EWCA 991.
71. R v THN [2014] 1 All ER at para 45.
72. R v T from R v L and other appeals [2013] EWCA 991 at para 54.
73. R v T from R v L and other appeals [2013] EWCA 991 at para 54.
74. OSCE, "Trafficking in Human Beings: Identification of Potential and Presumed Victims A Community Policing Approach,' SPMU Publication Series Vol. 10, at 45.
75. A. Farrell, J. McDevitt, R. Pfeffer, S. Fahy, C. Owens, M. Dank & W. Adams, "Identifying Challenges to Improve the Investigation and Prosecution of State and Local Human Trafficking Cases" (NIJ: Washington, DC, 2012) 107.
76. E. Cockbain & H. Brayley-Morris, 'Human Trafficking and Labour Exploitation in the Casual Construction Industry: An Analysis of Three Major Investigations in the UK Involving Irish Traveller Offending Groups,' (2017) Policing (advance articles) 14.

77. Council of Europe Convention on Action against Trafficking in Human Beings, 2005, accessed at https://rm.coe.int/168008371d.
78. Council of Europe Treaty Series No. 197, Explanatory Report to the Council of Europe Convention on Action against Trafficking in Human Beings (2005) at para 100.
79. Article 3(a) Protocol to Prevent, Suppress and Punish Trafficking in Persons, Especially Women and Children, supplementing the United Nations Convention against Transnational Organized Crime, General Assembly resolution 55/25 of 15 November 2000.
80. OSCE, 'Trafficking in Human Beings: Identification of Potential and Presumed Victims A Community Policing Approach' June 2011 at 11.
81. N. Christie, 'The ideal victim,' et al. E. Fattah (Ed.) "From Crime Policy to Victim Policy: Reorienting the Justice System" (Palgrave Macmillan, 1986) at 17–30.
82. M. Duggan, "Revisitig the Ideal Victim" (Policy Press 2018) at 12 and 14.
83. J. Davies, E. Lyons & D. Monti-Catania, "Safety Planning with Battered Women: Complex Lives/Difficult Choices" (Sage Series on Violence against Women, Thousand Oaks, 1998).
84. J. Srikantiah, "Perfect Victims and Real Survivors: The Iconic Victim in Domestic Human Trafficking Law," (2007) Boston University Law Review, 87, 157 at 187.
85. M. Wilson & E. O'Brien, "Constructing the Ideal Victim in the United States of America's annual trafficking in persons report," (2016) Crime Law Soc Change, 65, 29 at 43.
86. C. Villacampa & N. Torres, "Human Trafficking for Criminal Exploitation: The Failure to Identify Victims," (2017) Eur J Crim Policy Res, 23, 393–408 at 406.
87. US TIP Report 2023, https://state.gov/reports/2023-trafficking-in-persons-report/united-kingdom/.

2

The Present Politicalisation of Immigration in the UK—A Barrier to Identifying More Trafficked Victims

1 Introduction

It is important to remember that the discussion on identifying potential victims of human trafficking takes place in a highly charged political discussion on legal immigration, illegal migration and irregular migration. The following chapter will examine numerous aspects associated with immigration within the time of the period after the pandemic, through 2022 and into 2023. The reason for the focus on this timeline is due to the increased migratory travel which resulted after Covid-19 restrictions were lifted, the invasion of Ukraine by Russia in 2022 and the political pressure on the Government to stop the small boats from France travelling to the UK via the English Channel. These events coincided with the legislative implementations of the Nationality and Borders Act 2022 and Illegal Migration Act 2023. This period is crucial to understand the impact the events had on the identification of trafficked victims alongside other aspects of migration which were taking place simultaneously.

The pandemic restricted the ability of people to travel across borders due to the ban on international movement. Worldwide travel restarted after the pandemic which has substantially increased. In the year ended

M. Davis, *Identifying Victims of Human Trafficking*, Palgrave Studies in Victims and Victimology, https://doi.org/10.1007/978-3-031-61741-6_2

June 2022, there were an estimated 70 million passenger arrivals into the UK and in the following year to June 2023, this figure had nearly doubled to 125 million.[1] Global events have also affected the numbers of people entering the UK through protection routes offered by the UK Government. The invasion by Russia of Ukraine on 24 February 2022 resulted in the UK Government introducing three refugee schemes for Ukrainian nationals to come to the UK from March 2022. The first was the Ukraine Family Scheme (for Ukrainians to join existing family members in the UK), the second was the Ukraine Sponsorship Scheme, otherwise known as the 'Homes for Ukraine' Scheme and the third scheme was the Ukraine Extension Scheme where Ukrainians who had an existing right to be in the UK could have their immigration status extended. All three schemes led to 179,500 arrivals into the UK.[2]

Additionally, the number of visas granted by the UK Visa and Immigration Department has increased. Visas for work, study, sponsorship licensing for work and study and family-related visas all increased from June 2022.[3] The above are all examples of legal migration which the UK relies on to service the economy (work visas) and benefits the individual (through a study visa or reuniting with family members.) The net migration figure (the difference between those coming into the UK and those leaving the UK) has substantially increased in recent years. In 2019 the net migration figure was 219,000,[4] in 2021 it increased to 488,000[5] and it rose again to 606,000 in 2022 and 672,000 in the year ending June 2023.[6] This can be explained by the increased movement of people after the pandemic. The most popular reasons for people to come to the UK are for either work, study or for humanitarian reasons.

Alongside legal migration, there is the facilitation of illegal migration by organised crime groups which takes place through fraud, deception, smuggling and trafficking. It is a significant issue and is currently unclear as to the scale and nature of the problem which is required to be combatted in the UK due to the sophisticated methods criminals employ to move people across borders illegally. The types of persons involved in illegal migration can be classed into four groups:

1. Persons with a legal immigration status through a valid visa, but then is regarded as an overstayer when the visa expiry date expires, and the person continues to stay in the country.
2. A person who has an irregular immigration status and stays irregular without being detected.
3. A person who has an irregular immigration status and then is detected as being illegal by the State sometime later.
4. A person who is irregular and is rescued and identified as irregular by the State after processing. This situation can be seen in small boats being used by smugglers to move persons across the English Channel. It is likely that some of the people are claiming asylum and wish to do so once on shore in the UK. This will be discussed below.

Illegal Migration—The Small Boats Issue in the UK

On 13 December 2022, the Prime Minister, Rishi Sunak named 'Stopping the boats' as one of his 5 main priorities the Government will pursue.[7] The issue of small boat crossings started to emerge in 2018 after a small number of people recorded as having entered the UK via this route was 299. This increased to 1849 in 2019 and increased to 8466 in 2020.[8] Official Statistics show that for the year ending December 2022, there were 45,755 people detected arriving in small boats.[9] This was 60% higher than in 2021 when 28,526 arrived in the UK via this method.[10] Since January 2018 until March 2023, 71% of nationalities of people making this journey were from Syria (7%), Afghanistan (13%), Iraq (15%), Albania (15%) and Iran (21%).[11] National statistics stated that "90% of small boats arrivals (around 40,000) claimed asylum or were recorded as a dependent on an asylum application."[12] What is interesting is that whilst there appears to be roughly the same number of boats crossing the English Channel for the period 2021–2022, there are more numbers of people per boat making the journey.[13] This illustrates that there is a strong demand for the service, provided by smugglers which feed into the smuggler's business model. Moreover, smugglers can take advantage of the increased demand from people, taking the opportunity to make more profit by putting more people onto boats to make more money despite similar numbers of boat crossings the year before. As of 13 November, 27,284 people had crossed the English Channel in 2023[14] showing that the numbers have fallen compared to 2022. At the time of writing, which is the first quarter of 2024, numbers are starting to rise with official numbers due to be released by the Government.

Asylum in the UK

Alongside the issues and problems associated with combatting illegal migration, the UK has an impressive historical global reputation for offering asylum to vulnerable people from conflict areas and to those fleeing persecution in their own country. The 1951 UN Refugee Convention states that a refugee is a person who:

> …owing to a well-founded fear of being persecuted for reasons of race, religion, nationality, membership of a particular social group, or political opinion, is outside the country of his nationality, and is unable to or, owing to such fear, is unwilling to avail himself of the protection of that country.[15]

In 2022, there were 81,130 asylum applications which is still lower than the highest number of applications seen in 2002 which was 84,132.[16] In between 2002 and 2022, there has been a low of 17,916 asylum applications, 32,733 in 2015 and 50,042 shortly after the pandemic in 2021.[17]

As of June 2023, there were 215,000 cases in the system comprising of people awaiting an initial decision, people awaiting an appeal decision and those who have had their asylum application refused and awaiting deportation.[18] At the end of December 2022, there were 132,182 applicants were awaiting an initial decision on their asylum claim.[19] The UK Prime Minister, Rishi Sunak has pledged to reduce the backlog of 80,148[20] asylum applications by the end of 2023.[21] There are significant delays for people receiving their initial decision raising considerable concerns about them being at risk of exploitation during this wait especially because of the wait for them to have the right to work and the access to financial support.[22] More asylum seekers are being housed in disused barges such as the Bibby Stockholm or RAF Wethersfield but most are being placed in hotels. The UK Government is looking to end this policy at the end of January 2024.[23]

As of June 2022, it was found that "74% of cases had been pending for more than six months, 32% had been pending for between six months and one year, 33% had been pending for between one and three years, 8% of the total had been pending for between three and five years and 1% which had been pending for more than five years."[24]

Consequently, the rights and entitlements of trafficked victims can be somewhat overlooked given the distractions and headlines the above issue has compromising a balanced acceptance of the issues and can be a barrier for the State to resolve them in a rational and effective manner whilst the State acknowledges and adheres to a victim-centred approach.

At the end of March 2023, there were 112,294 asylum seekers receiving support.[25] Despite the large numbers, it has been reported that many number of people who have been granted asylum (and classed as refugees) and are destitute have increased. The Big Issue Magazine found that there has been a 140% increase in destitution with as many as 1000 asylum seekers potentially being homeless at Christmas in Birmingham which costs councils money as well as additional numbers of refugees in Glasgow having to be supported through accommodation and benefits.[26] The consequences of the above are that many refugees are at risk of exploitation given the exposure of being homeless which cannot be mitigated due to increased pressure and strain on public resources.

2 Extent of the Problem in the UK

This section will examine the current process of how potential victims of trafficking are formally identified in the UK. Where identified trafficked victims do not have a legal right to be in the UK, the statutory guidance issued by the UK Government ensures that a Competent Authority must consider whether a grant of leave is suitable so that non-EEA and EEA nationals regularise their immigration status.[27]

There are a host of intrinsic reasons and pressures from traffickers as to why individuals find it difficult to identify themselves as trafficked victims. The impact victims experience at the hands of their exploiters through a range of methods can have determinative consequences on their ability to either escape from their exploitation or self-identify themselves. The degree to acknowledging and understanding the role deception, coercion and control play in keeping victims trapped alongside the mental health consequences of these behaviours have on victims is crucial to learn and appreciate so that States and organisations can appreciate that the trauma trafficked victims experience because of psychological abuse played out within an exploitative environment.

Examining the environments where there is an increased opportunity for public authorities, third sector organisations and the State to identify trafficked victims. There are a host of challenges authorities have in meeting their responsibilities to refer potential victims of trafficked victims for help and support. A State has a legal obligation to punish the offending of slavery and forced labour[28] and it also has a moral obligation to protect victims from exploitation and the best way they can satisfy this obligation is to identify victims. It remains in the interest of the State to help identify more victims so that more traffickers can be prosecuted for victims to obtain justice for the wrongdoing committed against them. This 'top-down' approach can often be compromised by the issue of immigration where victims may be regarded as criminals due to their irregular status within the UK, making them at risk of not being treated as a victim of crime through exploitation, but as an illegal immigrant. There are also significant issues within the process of how individuals go through the formal process of being identified as trafficked in the UK which must be understood. A 'grassroots' approach would be more beneficial to assist individuals so that their rights and access to support are promoted during the identification stage. Where victims choose to leave their exploitative situation, identification becomes a time of the essence to prevent the risk of that individual being re-trafficked if safeguarding measures are not taken for the benefit of the person.

One way in which we can answer the question of what the extent of the problem of detection of victims in the UK can be understanding the numbers of people who have been identified in accordance with the legal obligations the UK signed through the Council of Europe Convention on Action Against the Trafficking in Human Beings which obligated States to train competent authorities to process referrals and identify victims of trafficking, allowing them access to services and support.[29] The UK fulfilled this obligation by creating the National Referral Mechanism (NRM) in 2009.

Process and Approach to Identifying Victims in the UK

Decisions are either made by the Single Competent Authority (SCA)[30] or the Immigration Enforcement Competent Authority (IECA)[31] which considers foreign national offenders who are detained either in prison or in an immigration removal centre people. The process of identifying victims of human trafficking is as follows.

The first decision given to a victim is the Reasonable Grounds Decision (RGD). The decision maker must be satisfied that there are reasonable grounds to believe that the individual is victim of human trafficking,[32] based on the evidence available to them provided in the NRM referral form. This may include evidence such as "eyewitness testimony, medical or expert reports, travel records, police investigations, general evidence such as Country Reports, or supporting evidence of the person's exploitation the First Responder provides, such as observed modern slavery indicators."[33] The RGD is based on a low factual threshold.

The victim should receive this decision within 5 days of a referral being made to the Competent Authority. If this decision is positive, then the potential victim has a 30-day reflection and recovery period which entitles the individual to access help and support.[34] If the individual is a foreign national, then that person cannot be removed from the UK. The individual must then wait for a Conclusive Grounds Decision (CGD). This is a decision based on the balance of probabilities which is higher than the standard of proof attached to the RGD. There is no timeframe for a CGD to be made.[35] The decision maker must be satisfied that "based on the evidence available, modern slavery is more likely than not to have happened."[36] When a positive CGD has been made, the individual is recognised as a victim of trafficking and entitled to at least 45 days of support during which a Recovery Needs Assessment is made, identifying what needs the victim requires.[37] In situations where a person receives a negative CGD, then the individual receives 9 days of move-on support.[38]

The UK Government publishes annual figures on the number of individuals entering the National Referral Mechanism.[39] A comprehensive review on the nationalities, gender, age group, types of exploitation, and the First Responder organisations[40] who referred the individuals alongside the figures on the decision which include the number of NRM positive and negative Reasonable Grounds Decisions (RGD) and Conclusive Grounds Decisions (CGD) are included.

In 2021 there were "12,727 potential victims of modern slavery were referred to the NRM in 2021, representing a 20% increase compared to 2020 (10,601)."[41] It can be established that there is a weak link between people making the journey to the UK in a small boat and being referred into the NRM. It has also been reported that "of the 83,235 people that arrived in the UK on small boats between 1 January 2018 and 31 December 2022, 7% (6,210 people) were referred to the NRM. Most of these individuals (5,897 or 95%) also had an asylum claim lodged."[42] However, it can be established that those people making the journey via small boat and referred into the NRM will also make a claim for asylum. Despite a delay in people receiving a Conclusive Grounds Decision,[43] there is also evidence to suggest that people who are small boat arrivals going through the NRM will have a positive decision, identifying them as victims of trafficking.[44]

In 2022, there were 12,350 foreign nationals referred into the NRM which accounted for 73% of all referrals made in that year.[45] It has been reported that there were "17,905 NRM referrals in 2022/23 which is just over 32% higher than 13,542 in 2021/22. It has been seen that the police made almost 21% of all NRM referrals received in 2022/23."[46]

In terms of referrals by nationality, the most common individuals were Albanian (27% of all referrals) followed by UK nationals (25%). The third most common nationality was Eritrean (7%), followed by Sudanese and Vietnamese (both 5%).[47] Since the end of December 2022, the number of referrals from UK nationals has now exceeded those from

Albania. UK nationals accounted for 25% of all potential victims with Albania dropping to second with 205 of all referrals.[48]

National Referral Mechanism and Duty to Notify statistics are published quarterly and annually. The statistics for 2022 show: 16,821 Reasonable Grounds Decisions were issued—12,959 by the Single Competent Authority, of which 87% (11,273) were positive, and—3862 by the Immigration Enforcement Competent Authority, of which 92% (3572) were positive.[49]

It is reported that it is taking as long as 500 days for NRM referral decisions to take place.[50] Official statistics from the Home Office cite that on average it took 543 days to reach a Conclusive Grounds Decision in 2022[51] and in the first three months of 2023, it was 566 days, compared to 449 days the year before.[52] Despite the UK Government Guidance stating that RGD should be made within 5 days where possible,[53] "the average (mean) number of days has gone from 18 in January to March to 40 days in April to June 2023 for the single competent authority. For the immigration enforcement trafficking body this has gone from 19 to 30 days."[54] Statistics show that in 2022, "6,189 conclusive grounds decisions were issued – 5,756 by the Single Competent Authority, of which 91% (5,163) were positive, and – 433 by the Immigration Enforcement Competent Authority, of which 93% (353) were positive."[55] It has been reported that there has been a drop in delays in the Single Competent Authority from "756 days in January to March to 599 days in April to June 2023. However, the immigration enforcement trafficking body has seen a steady increase since reporting started at the beginning of 2022, and this is now up to 359 days for a conclusive grounds decision."[56]

The present situation is as follows. Regarding referrals, there is a 10% drop in referrals compared between July–September 2022 and July–September 2023.[57] Positive Reasonable Grounds Decisions have remained stable over the past few years with 9 out of 10 decisions being positive.[58] However, the proportion of positive RGD has dropped to 44%.[59] This can be due to the impact and effect that legislation (the Nationality & Borders Act 2022 and Illegal Migration Act 2023) has had on decision making.[60] The average wait for a RGD is now

47 days, compared with 21 days from April–June 2023.[61] The proportion of negative Conclusive Grounds Decisions being made by the Single Competent Authority (SCA) has increased with the number of negative decisions from Immigration Enforcement Competent Authority (IECA) remaining a lot higher than the SCA.[62] Delays in receiving decisions are a significant issue. For the period July–September 2023, it took 530 days for individuals to receive a decision which is higher than from April to June 2023 which was 430 days.[63]

Approximate numbers of people in the UK who are being exploited are an understatement as to the true figure of victims of modern slavery and human trafficking. Whilst there may not be much significance as the existing numbers found from the Government, it does raise the question of how effective the measures taken by the Government to address the issues of identification (because of the time it takes for decisions to be made) alongside the combatting of the offence from a crime control perspective. Often in examining this issue a victim-centred approach and a crime control approach are actions which are not mutually exclusive and an effective set of measures for detecting and rescuing victims, protection of victims during NRM referrals together with supporting victims afterwards must fit alongside law enforcement objectives of charging offenders, with prosecutors securing convictions under the Modern Slavery Act 2015.

Many victims of trafficking report the difficulty of receiving decisions in a timely manner. It has been reported that "during the fourth quarter of 2022, the average conclusive grounds decision took 642 days and of the 16,938 NRM referrals during 2022, 76% (12,907) were still awaiting conclusive grounds determinations at the end of the year."[64]

On the face of it, it can appear that the increase of trafficked victims in the UK is either a positive or negative situation to be in. Positively, the reporting and disclosure of increased number of individuals being identified via the decision makers within the NRM can suggest that awareness and detection of victims are improving every year. However, conversely and from a negative angle, the higher number of victims convey that the UK has an increasing problem with combatting the crime, and that there are many more victims because of the social and economic policies over the past decade (such as the austerity policies of the Government) which have pushed more people into exploitation who then have not yet been recognised by the public, nor referred through the NRM and consequently been formally identified. On balance, both comments are indeed correct. Upon reflection, the greater media attention the crime has received, alongside the additional and improved training of individuals within organisations who are likely to encounter victims as part of their work has steadily increased and give opportunities for victims to escape their exploitation. It is therefore likely that this situation has filtered into a situation with higher referrals through the NRM with more modern slavery advocates assisting and supporting victims through the NRM referral and identification process. Many services are under pressure to keep up with demand with the largest provider of services, the Salvation Army who stopped taking new referrals in December 2022.[65]

Perception by the UK Government that the NRM System Is Being Abused

There has been a frequent perception from the UK Government about the abuse of the NRM system with the process being taken advantage of by individuals who do not have genuine claims for seeking that they have been trafficked. The Government believes that the system of referrals is being abused by victims who are not genuine and trying to use the laws to stay in the UK and/or escape criminal liability by claiming to be victims of modern slavery:

> ...a growing number of pregnant Albanian women who pay criminal gangs to smuggle them into Britain are falsely claiming to be sex trafficking victims to gain asylum.[66]

Furthermore, in March 2021, the Home Office released a press release from the previous Home Secretary, Priti Patel arguing there was "an alarming rise in people abusing our modern slavery system by posing as victims in order to prevent their removal and enable them to stay in the country."[67] Later in 2022, Chris Philp MP described the modern slavery laws (Modern Slavery Act 2015) as "one of the biggest loopholes in our immigration system."[68] This does not appear to be the case. Statistics used in annual reports showed that in 2022, 9 out of 10 NRM referrals resulted in a positive grounds decision.[69] The rise in small boats does not mean that many are seeking to take advantage and abuse the NRM system as the figures show that only a small fraction of those people are going through the NRM:

> …of the 83,236 people who came to the UK on a small boat between 1 January 2018 and 31 December 2022, 7% (6,210 people) were referred to the NRM.[70]

Unfortunately, the rhetoric surrounding the legitimacy of those wishing to be referred and identified by the NRM now highlights how the issue of identification is now being distracted into arguments as to whether victims are genuine or not. Therefore, the focus on protection is being lost and becoming a secondary issue because there is greater suspicion towards individuals seeking to be referred into the NRM and be recognised as victims. The use of words such as 'genuine' and 'legitimate' alongside phrases including 'gaming the system' deflect from the issue of maintaining a consistent victim-centred approach. Having a predetermined idea of who an ideal victim of trafficking is, is not helpful and suspicion around nationality remains a danger whereas UK victims are not subjected to such scrutiny. One person's determination of who they believe a victim of trafficking should look like and behave like will sometimes be different from someone else's perception.

The Status & Effectiveness of a NRM Decision

As we will see later in the book, it is often the case that victims of trafficking are exploited by traffickers and made to carry out criminal offences as part of their exploitation. Victims are then arrested, charged and prosecuted for these offences at the expense of being identified as a trafficked victim. In some circumstances, victims may be referred to the NRM whilst they have been charged after the issue of identification as a trafficked victim becomes apparent. The basis of this section is to outline the present situation regards this issue to understand the significance of an NRM for caseworkers and those working in the criminal justice system.

The case of *DPP v M*[71] considered the admissibility of an NRM decision made by the Single Competent Authority as evidence at a criminal trial to establish whether the defendant who had been charged with an offence as part of their exploitation could rely on the statutory defence, together with knowing how much evidential weight should be given to a positive NRM decision. Whilst there is no guidance on the admissibility of NRM decisions prosecutors argued that the evidence was of non-expert nature but can be used in a trial. It was held that the NRM decision could be used in the trial alongside other evidence to meet the evidential burden on the behalf of the defendant raising a Section 45 statutory defence. However, this position has significantly changed as a consequence of the case of *R v Brecani*.[72]

The Implications of the Brecani Decision

The nature of positive CGDs has been that they have been used in appeal cases for trafficking victims who had committed criminal offences under duress.[73] However, the ruling of *Brecani* reversed this alongside the decision made in *DPP v M*. It was decided that although the decision of whether an individual is a victim of trafficking is one for the jury,[74] the evidence of an NRM decision made by caseworkers in the SCA are not considered to be experts.[75] Caseworkers in the SCA do not meet the 'expert evidence' requirements set out in Criminal Procedure Rules under Rule 19 in criminal trials.[76] Consequently, they cannot offer expert evidence in a trial of this nature as to whether an individual has been trafficked or not.[77]

This is a significant blow for rights of victims having convictions quashed on appeal and for stopping criminal cases from continuing when the issue of whether an individual may or may not be a victim of trafficking.

However, it was stated that decision makers at the Single Competent Authority (SCA) are "not experts but that the SCA's decision on conclusive grounds can be potentially admissible in appeal matters."[78] Additionally, it was highlighted that there may be circumstances where "a suitably qualified expert could give evidence which is outside of the knowledge of the jury, particularly to provide context of a cultural nature."[79] Therefore, this person must have the qualifications, skills and experience of working with victims to offer this expert evidence to the jury to inform them accordingly.

In conclusion, defence lawyers acting for victims face a significant challenge in getting cases dropped by the CPS because of the ruling in *Brecani* which favours prosecutions against trafficked victims for criminal offences. Despite the significance and worth for victims to get a positive CGD to obtain services and support, it may (because of *Brecani*) reduce the number of NRM referrals being made if the chances of them being used as part of the statutory defence are not likely to be successful, or at best, significantly reduced. This is because the Section 45 defence will be more difficult to succeed without the NRM decision being admitted and therefore because of this the defendant will not be able to discharge the evidential burden. The previous system of writing to the prosecution to ask for them to review the decision to prosecute on the basis that it is not in the public interest to continue has been overtaken by the case of *Brecani*. It also does nothing to advance the abuse of process argument and therefore favours prosecutions and disadvantages victims from seeking protection from punishment. If a prosecution fails to give reasons why a positive CGD has not been followed,[80] there will be a chance that defendants could be successful upon appeal, but this negates the protection afforded to victims and exposes them to punishment in the short term.

3 Conclusion

It has been seen that despite the wait for individuals to receive an NRM decision, the probability of them receiving a positive decision is high. The issue is the wait for them to get this decision and the dangers posed to them during this period where they are having to wait. It may be that they are at a greater risk of either being re-trafficked or returning back to their exploiters if not adequately protected and supported during this time. The delays in decision makers also put increased strain and pressure on charities and third sector organisations experiencing delays in taking new potential victims going through the NRM creating a backlog behind them, leading to increased risks of harm and levels of continued exploitation or re-trafficking if they cannot access support and protection.

Conclusively, the main issues for the UK combatting and protecting victims are ensuring that more prosecutions take place, issuing foreign victims with residence permits and protecting children from county lines exploitation.

The UK has appointed Eleanor Lyons as a new Anti-Slavery Commissioner as required under the Modern Slavery Act 2015 on 11 October 2023.[81] This would ensure accountability and oversight over the UK Government's policy and legislative responses to combatting trafficking in the UK and protecting and assisting victims.

Human trafficking is a growing phenomenon and takes place within a growing migration crisis occurring across many parts of the world. Despite the number of trafficked victims being recorded in the UK, the true extent of the scale of trafficking in streets, communities, towns, cities and countries remains unknown. This book examines the pertinent and present-day challenges of detecting and identifying foreign trafficked victims. International victims of trafficking require the destination State to protect them from further abuse and exploitation and are often having increased difficulty in being recognised as genuine victims of abuse. This is often down to the politicalisation of immigration within the UK seen through the hostile environment migrants are exposed to daily in the UK. This book will examine the structural political, legislative and social aspects which affect victims' circumstances and their inability to be more likely to be identified because of their increased vulnerabilities placed upon them by these structural aspects. There are a host of different factors at different levels which influence a lack of adequate detection and identification.

The book will identify and examine the civic society environments where the difficulties of detection and identification of victims (both UK and foreign victims) exist or are simply overlooked. At present, much has been written about measures to combat human trafficking from a crime control perspective. However, this perspective, although important is isolationist and is therefore not enough to understand the nuances of human trafficking which directly impacts victims. This book advocates that a victim-centred approach to the issue of identification is required by States which will satisfy not only their legal obligations to trafficked victims, but also their moral obligations. The issue of immigration has become heavily politicised in recent years, creating challenges for a host of foreign nationals being recognised and having their rights observed by the UK Government. Understanding present attitudes to immigration in the UK and the reason behind some hostility is crucial to acknowledging how policies have been created to deal with this issue which has led to undesirable consequences for trafficked victims.

It has been estimated that 'in 2016 there were more than 40.3 million people around the world who were victims of forced labour, debt bondage, forced marriage, slavery and slavery like practices and trafficking.'[82] Between 2017 and 2018, the UN reported that 'a total of 74,514 victims of trafficking were detected in over 110 countries.'[83] The importance of proactively identifying victims of Modern Slavery and integrating victims back into society remains one of the UK's priorities.[84]

The pandemic in 2020 severely impacted different groups of people significantly in the UK in different ways, with 'evidence showing that he pandemic has increased vulnerability to modern slavery all over the world, as many of the underlying drivers of modern slavery have worsened across many countries during the pandemic, such as poverty, inequality and unemployment.'[85] This provided an opportunity for traffickers to profit from illegal forms of migration via lockdowns and take advantage of restrictions on internal travel within borders. This resulted in victims being trapped in exploitation.

It has been evidenced that migration plays a significant role in the facilitation of human trafficking.[86] Migration can include both legal and illegal forms of movement and can include both transnational journeys as well as trafficking within borders, often referred to as 'internal trafficking.' These established migration routes alongside refugee corridors which are being seen as common in past years have been researched as draws for organised crime groups to exploit by taking advantage of peoples' vulnerabilities. This research provides a strong link between the movements of persons on one side and the prevalence of exploitation by organised criminals on the other.

Covid has had on the economic and social way of life which was disturbed during the pandemic.

Where authorities within States miss the opportunity to identify a potential victim, exploitation is allowed to continue with impunity by traffickers. Where authorities misidentify vulnerable individuals as smuggled persons or economic migrants at the expense of trafficked victims or asylum seekers fleeing persecution, foreign nationals experience both discrimination through 'secondary victimisation' by police, border staff and other arms of the State. Whilst trafficked victims experience human rights violations from traffickers of organised crime groups they are referred to as non-state actors, they can often experience further human rights violations due to their human rights by the failure of the State to correctly identify and protect them as a victim of crime like any other citizen. Consequently, vulnerable individuals who are exploited can often become hidden in plain sight. This book seeks to bring the issues invisible victims of crime have by drawing them out of the shadows of society into the light so that they can be recognised as victims and importantly protected from further exploitation. The following chapters outline and examine these issues in considerable detail.

The following chapters set out many issues which affect the issue of self-identification and identification of victims. These challenges will be highlighted and examined in detail in the next chapters.

Notes

1. UK Government National Statistics, 'Summary of Latest Statistics,' 24 August 2023, https://www.gov.uk/government/statistics/immigration-system-statistics-year-ending-june-2023/summary-of-latest-statistics.
2. UK Government National Statistics, 'Summary of Latest Statistics,' 24 August 2023, https://www.gov.uk/government/statistics/immigration-system-statistics-year-ending-june-2023/summary-of-latest-statistics.

3. See UK Government National Statistics, 'Summary of Latest Statistics,' 24 August 2023 at 4–5, https://www.gov.uk/govern ment/statistics/immigration-system-statistics-year-ending-june-2023/summary-of-latest-statistics.

4. T. Hall, A. Manning & M. Sumption, 'How Different Types of Immigration Contribute to Net Migration in the Long Term and What Levels of Net Migration the UK Might Expect in Coming Years,' 16 October 2023, Figure 5, https://migrationobservatory. ox.ac.uk/resources/reports/why-are-the-latest-net-migration-fig ures-not-a-reliable-guide-to-future-trends/#:~:text=Net%20migr ation%20has%20been%20unusually,pandemic%20(ONS%2C% 202023).

5. See Provisional Figures from the Office for National Statistics, 'Long-Term International Migration, Provisional: Year Ending December 2022,' 25 May 2023 at 15, https://www.ons.gov.uk/ peoplepopulationandcommunity/populationandmigration/intern ationalmigration/bulletins/longterminternationalmigrationprovis ional/yearendingdecember2022. Please note that the ONS adjust the figures usually 6 months later to take account of new data. Please see latest statistical bulletin here https://www.ons.gov.uk/ peoplepopulationandcommunity/populationandmigration/intern ationalmigration/bulletins/longterminternationalmigrationprovis ional/previousReleases.

6. See 'Net migration was unusually high in the year ending June 2023, driven primarily by an increase in international student numbers and high demand for workers in the health and care sector,' The Migration Observatory University of Oxford report from 9 August 2023, https://migrationobservatory.ox.ac.uk/res ources/briefings/long-term-international-migration-flows-to-and-from-the-uk/.

7. HM Government, UK Communication Plan 2023–24, https:// communication-plan.gcs.civilservice.gov.uk/the-prime-ministers-priorities/.

8. See G. Sturge, 'Asylum Statistics,' House of Commons Library, 12 September 2023 at 32, https://researchbriefings.files.parliament. uk/documents/SN01403/SN01403.pdf.

9. The most common type of small boats used in Channel crossings are described as inflatable dinghies.
10. UK Government Official Statistics, "Irregular Migration to the UK, Year Ending December 2022," 23 February 2023, https://www.gov.uk/government/statistics/irregular-migration-to-the-uk-year-ending-december-2022/irregular-migration-to-the-uk-year-ending-december-2022.
11. The Migration Observatory at the University of Oxford, 'People Crossing the English Channel in Small Boats,' 21 July 2023, Figure 1, https://migrationobservatory.ox.ac.uk/resources/briefings/people-crossing-the-english-channel-in-small-boats/.
12. Office for National Statistics, 'Long-Term International Migration, Provisional: Year Ending December 2022,' at 6, https://www.ons.gov.uk/peoplepopulationandcommunity/populationandmigration/internationalmigration/bulletins/longterminternationalmigrationprovisional/yearendingdecember2022.
13. Official Statistics show that in 2020, there were on average 13 people per small boat, in 2021 there were on average 28 people and in 2022, there were on average 41 people per boat. See UK Government Official Statistics, 'Irregular Migration to the UK, Year Ending December 2022,' 23 February 2023 at 6, https://www.gov.uk/government/statistics/irregular-migration-to-the-uk-year-ending-december-2022/irregular-migration-to-the-uk-year-ending-december-2022#:~:text=There%20were%208%2C633%20arrivals%20in,2019%20and%203%20in%202018..
14. N. Eardley & S. Francis, 'How Many People Cross the Channel in Small Boats and How Many Claim Asylum in the UK?,' BBC News, 16 November 2023, https://www.bbc.co.uk/news/uk-53699511.
15. Article 1(A)(2) Refugee Convention relating to the Status of Refugees Adopted on 28 July 1951 by the United Nations Conference of Plenipotentiaries on the Status of Refugees and Stateless Persons convened under General Assembly resolution 429 (V) of 14 December 1950.
16. G. Sturge, 'Asylum Statistics,' House of Commons Library, 12 September 2023 at 5, https://researchbriefings.files.parliament.uk/documents/SN01403/SN01403.pdf.

17. See G. Sturge, 'Asylum Statistics,' House of Commons Library, 12 September 2023 at 11, https://researchbriefings.files.parliament. uk/documents/SN01403/SN01403.pdf.

18. See G. Sturge, 'Asylum Statistics,' House of Commons Library, 12 September 2023 at 15, https://researchbriefings.files.parliament. uk/documents/SN01403/SN01403.pdf.

19. See The Migration Observatory at the University of Oxford report on 'The UK's Asylum Backlog,' at Figure 1, 5 April 2023 https://migrationobservatory.ox.ac.uk/resources/briefi ngs/the-uks-asylum-backlog/.

20. These are referred to as 'legacy cases' in the Home Office Official Statistics 'Statistics Relating to the Illegal Migration Act,' 15 September 2023, https://www.gov.uk/government/statistics/statis tics-relating-to-the-illegal-migration-bill.

21. A. Gentleman, 'Record Asylum Backlog Deals Another Blow to Sunak's Immigration Pledges,' The Guardian, 24 August 23, https://www.theguardian.com/uk-news/2023/aug/24/record-asy lum-backlog-deals-another-blow-to-sunak-immigration-pledges#: ~:text=He%20promised%20to%20stop%20the,by%20the% 20end%20of%202023..

22. Paragraph 360 from Part 11B of the Immigration Rules explains that asylum seekers may apply for permission to work if they have not received an initial decision on their claim within 12 months but this will only be considered if that delay was through no fault of the applicant.

23. Home Office, 'Home Office to Exit First 50 Asylum Hotels by the End of January,' https://www.gov.uk/government/news/home-off ice-to-exit-first-50-asylum-hotels-by-the-end-of-january.

24. J. Tyler-Todd, G. Sturge, C.J. McKinney, 'Delays to Processing Asylum Claims in the UK,' House of Commons Library, 20 March 2023 at 3, https://researchbriefings.files.parliament.uk/doc uments/CBP-9737/CBP-9737.pdf.

25. Home Office, 'Official Statistics Relating to the Illegal Migration Act,' 15 September 2023, https://www.gov.uk/government/statis tics/statistics-relating-to-the-illegal-migration-bill.

26. R. Muthiah, 'Human Trafficking Survivor Was Granted Asylum. Then She Was Evicted Straight into Homelessness,' The Big Issue, 6 November 2023, https://www.bigissue.com/opinion/ref ugee-homelessness-ria-human-trafficking-survivor-jcwi/.
27. Modern Slavery: Statutory Guidance for England and Wales (under s49 of the Modern Slavery Act 2015) and non-statutory guidance for Scotland and Northern Ireland, Section 7.15 and Section 15.194.
28. Article 4 European Convention on Human Rights. See the important case of Siliadin v France, Application No: 73316/01, 26 July 2005 for the application of Article 4 in a trafficking case.
29. Article 10 Council of Europe Convention on Action Against Trafficking in Human Beings, 16 May 2005. Please note that being identified as a victim of trafficking in the UK does not regularise their immigration status and that leave to stay in the UK under the right to services and support under Article 12 and is based only on the willingness of victims to either cooperate with law enforcement in an investigation or to seek compensation from their trafficker(s).
30. NRM relating to children cases are also decided by the SCA.
31. On 8 November 2021 the Home Office created a new body, the Immigration Enforcement Competent Authority (IECA), for the stated purpose of identifying victims of modern slavery.
32. Home Office Modern Slavery Guidance for England and Wales and Non-Statutory Guidance for Scotland and Northern Ireland, October 2023 at 14.52, https://assets.publishing.service.gov.uk/media/651e9cf17309a1000db0a8af/Modern_Slavery_Statutory_Guidance__EW__and_Non-Statutory_Guidance__SNI__v3-5_.pdf.
33. Home Office Modern Slavery Guidance for England and Wales and non-Statutory Guidance for Scotland and Northern Ireland, October 2023 at 14.53, https://assets.publishing.service.gov.uk/media/651e9cf17309a1000db0a8af/Modern_Slavery_Statutory_Guidance__EW__and_Non-Statutory_Guidance__SNI__v3-5_.pdf.

34. Support can include accommodation, health services and legal aid, facilitated by the Salvation Army who has the Government contract awarded to them under the 'Modern Slavery Victim Care Contract' (MSVCC).

35. Home Office Modern Slavery Guidance for England and Wales and Non-Statutory Guidance for Scotland and Northern Ireland, October 2023 at 14.424, https://assets.publishing.service.gov.uk/media/651e9cf17309a1000db0a8af/Modern_Slavery_Statutory_Guidance__EW__and_Non-Statutory_Guidance__SNI__v3-5_.pdf.

36. Home Office Modern Slavery Guidance for England and Wales and Non-Statutory Guidance for Scotland and Northern Ireland, October 2023 at 14.431, https://assets.publishing.service.gov.uk/media/651e9cf17309a1000db0a8af/Modern_Slavery_Statutory_Guidance__EW__and_Non-Statutory_Guidance__SNI__v3-5_.pdf.

37. Home Office Modern Slavery Guidance for England and Wales and Non-Statutory Guidance for Scotland and Northern Ireland, October 2023 at 8.27, https://assets.publishing.service.gov.uk/media/651e9cf17309a1000db0a8af/Modern_Slavery_Statutory_Guidance__EW__and_Non-Statutory_Guidance__SNI__v3-5_.pdf.

38. Home Office Modern Slavery Guidance for England and Wales and Non-Statutory Guidance for Scotland and Northern Ireland, October 2023 at 8.27, https://assets.publishing.service.gov.uk/media/651e9cf17309a1000db0a8af/Modern_Slavery_Statutory_Guidance__EW__and_Non-Statutory_Guidance__SNI__v3-5_.pdf.

39. Official Statistics, Modern Slavery: National Referral Mechanism and Duty to Notify statistics UK, End of Year Summary 2022.

40. First Responders are agencies trained to recognise the indicators of modern slavery and able to make referrals to the National Referral Mechanism (NRM). First Responders include the police, local authorities and some non-governmental organisations including Barnado's, Kalayaan, NSPCC, Migrant Help, Refugee Council and The Salvation Army.

41. L. Williams, 'What the Latest Stats Tell Us About Modern Slavery in the UK,' Modern Slavery & Human Rights Policy and Research Centre, 8 March 2022, https://modernslaverypec.org/latest/2021-nrm-stats.
42. UK Government Official Statistics, 'Irregular Migration to the UK, Year Ending December 2022,' 23 February 2023 at 11, https://www.gov.uk/government/statistics/irregular-migration-to-the-uk-year-ending-december-2022/irregular-migration-to-the-uk-year-ending-december-2022#:~:text=There%20were%208%2C633%20arrivals%20in,2019%20and%203%20in%202018.
43. 76% (2,047 people) of small boat NRM referrals in the latest year, or 70% (4,373) of all small boat NRM referrals since 2018, are awaiting a Conclusive Grounds Decision. See See UK Government Official Statistics, 'Irregular Migration to the UK, Year Ending December 2022,' 23 February 2023 at 12, https://www.gov.uk/government/statistics/irregular-migration-to-the-uk-year-ending-december-2022/irregular-migration-to-the-uk-year-ending-december-2022#:~:text=There%20were%208%2C633%20arrivals%20in,2019%20and%203%20in%202018.
44. The majority (85%) of Reasonable Grounds Decisions for small boat arrivals since 2018 have been positive. Of the Conclusive Grounds Decisions issued, 85% were positive. See UK Government Official Statistics, 'Irregular Migration to the UK, Year Ending December 2022,' 23 February 2023 at 12, https://www.gov.uk/government/statistics/irregular-migration-to-the-uk-year-ending-december-2022/irregular-migration-to-the-uk-year-ending-december-2022#:~:text=There%20were%208%2C633%20arrivals%20in,2019%20and%203%20in%202018.
45. Modern Slavery & Human Rights Policy & Evidence Centre, 'Explainer: The Illegal Migration Act Modern Slavery Provisions,' 11 September 2023 at 7.
46. 'Modern Slavery and Organised Immigration Crime Programme Annual Report 2022/23,' at 13.
47. Home Office, Modern Slavery: National Referral Mechanism and Duty to Notify Statistics UK, End of Year Summary 2022

at Section 2.4, https://www.gov.uk/government/statistics/mod ern-slavery-national-referral-mechanism-and-duty-to-notify-sta tistics-uk-end-of-year-summary-2022/modern-slavery-national-referral-mechanism-and-duty-to-notify-statistics-uk-end-of-year-summary-2022#:~:text=In%202022%2C%20the%20NRM%20received,the%20preceding%20year%20(12%2C706)..

48. Home Office Modern Slavery: National Referral Mechanism and Duty to Notify Statistics UK, Quarter 3 2023 – July to September, 3 November 2023, at 3.4, https://www.gov.uk/gov ernment/statistics/modern-slavery-national-referral-mechanism-and-duty-to-notify-statistics-uk-july-to-september-2023/modern-slavery-national-referral-mechanism-and-duty-to-notify-statistics-uk-quarter-3-2023-july-to-september.

49. Home Office, Modern Slavery: National Referral Mechanism and Duty to Notify Statistics UK, Quarter 4 October–December 2022, Data tables 17 and 18.

50. See Independent Anti-Slavery Commissioner, 2022 at http:// www.antislaverycommissioner.co.uk/news-insights/iasc-says-home-office-should-be-stripped-of-responsibility-for-modern-slavery-victims/.

51. UK Home Office (2023), 'Modern Slavery: NRM and the Duty to Notify UK Stats, End of Year Summary 2022,' at Section 3.2, https://www.gov.uk/government/statistics/modern-slavery-nat ional-referral-mechanism-and-duty-to-notify-statistics-uk-end-of-year-summary-2022/modern-slavery-national-referral-mec hanism-and-duty-to-notify-statistics-uk-end-of-year-summary-2022#:~:text=In%202022%2C%20the%20NRM%20receive d,the%20preceding%20year%20(12%2C706).

52. UK Home Office (2023) 'Modern Slavery; NRM and the Duty to Notify UK Stats, Quarter 1 Jan – March 2023,' https://www. gov.uk/government/statistics/modern-slavery-national-referral-mechanism-and-duty-to-notify-statistics-uk-january-to-march-2023/modern-slavery-national-referral-mechanism-and-duty-to-notify-statistics-uk-quarter-1-2023-january-to-march.

53. UK Government Statutory Guidance Modern Slavery: statutory guidance for England and Wales (under s49 of the Modern

Slavery Act 2015) and non-statutory guidance for Scotland and Northern Ireland, 24 July 2023 at 7.6, https://www.gov.uk/gov ernment/publications/modern-slavery-how-to-identify-and-sup port-victims/modern-slavery-statutory-guidance-for-england-and-wales-under-s49-of-the-modern-slavery-act-2015-and-non-statut ory-guidance-for-scotland-and-northe#the-national-referral-mec hanism-decision-making-process.

54. S. Lenegan, 'More Delays, More Refusals, No 'Bad Faith': The Latest Trafficking Statistics,' FreeMovement, 22 August 2023, https://freemovement.org.uk/more-delays-more-refusals-no-bad-faith-the-latest-trafficking-statistics/. Data taken from tables 19 to 21 and 31 to 33, accessed at https://www.gov.uk/government/sta tistics/modern-slavery-national-referral-mechanism-and-duty-to-notify-statistics-uk-april-to-june-2023.

55. Home Office, 'Modern Slavery: National Referral Mechanism and Duty to Notify statistics UK, Quarter 4 2022–October to December 2022', Data tables 20 and 21.

56. S. Lenegan, 'More delays, More Refusals, No 'Bad Faith': The Latest Trafficking Statistics,' FreeMovement, 22 August 2023, https://freemovement.org.uk/more-delays-more-refusals-no-bad-faith-the-latest-trafficking-statistics/. Data taken from tables 19 to 21 and 31 to 33, accessed at https://www.gov.uk/government/sta tistics/modern-slavery-national-referral-mechanism-and-duty-to-notify-statistics-uk-april-to-june-2023.

57. Home Office Modern Slavery: National Referral Mechanism and Duty to Notify Statistics UK, Quarter 3 2023 – July to September, 3 November 2023, at 1, https://www.gov.uk/govern ment/statistics/modern-slavery-national-referral-mechanism-and-duty-to-notify-statistics-uk-july-to-september-2023/modern-sla very-national-referral-mechanism-and-duty-to-notify-statistics-uk-quarter-3-2023-july-to-september.

58. Home Office Modern Slavery: National Referral Mechanism and Duty to Notify Statistics UK, Quarter 3 2023—July to

September, 3 November 2023, at 4.1, https://www.gov.uk/gov ernment/statistics/modern-slavery-national-referral-mechanism- and-duty-to-notify-statistics-uk-july-to-september-2023/modern- slavery-national-referral-mechanism-and-duty-to-notify-statistics- uk-quarter-3-2023-july-to-september.

59. Home Office Modern Slavery: National Referral Mechanism and Duty to Notify Statistics UK, Quarter 3 2023—July to September, 3 November 2023, at 4.1, https://www.gov.uk/gov ernment/statistics/modern-slavery-national-referral-mechanism- and-duty-to-notify-statistics-uk-july-to-september-2023/modern- slavery-national-referral-mechanism-and-duty-to-notify-statistics- uk-quarter-3-2023-july-to-september.

60. This issue will be examined in Chapter 3. It relates to how the threshold for a positive Reasonable Grounds Decision changed which has led to a reduction in the number of positive RGD. This guidance has since changed in July 2023.

61. Home Office Modern Slavery: National Referral Mechanism and Duty to Notify statistics UK, Quarter 3 2023—July to September, 3 November 2023, at 4.1, https://www.gov.uk/gov ernment/statistics/modern-slavery-national-referral-mechanism- and-duty-to-notify-statistics-uk-july-to-september-2023/modern- slavery-national-referral-mechanism-and-duty-to-notify-statistics- uk-quarter-3-2023-july-to-september.

62. Home Office Modern Slavery: National Referral Mechanism and Duty to Notify statistics UK, Quarter 3 2023—July to September, 3 November 2023, at Figure 9, https://www.gov.uk/government/ statistics/modern-slavery-national-referral-mechanism-and-duty- to-notify-statistics-uk-july-to-september-2023/modern-slavery- national-referral-mechanism-and-duty-to-notify-statistics-uk-qua rter-3-2023-july-to-september.

63. Home Office Modern Slavery: National Referral Mechanism and Duty to Notify statistics UK, Quarter 3 2023—July to September, 3 November 2023, at 4.3 data table 31, https://www.gov.uk/gov ernment/statistics/modern-slavery-national-referral-mechanism- and-duty-to-notify-statistics-uk-july-to-september-2023/modern- slavery-national-referral-mechanism-and-duty-to-notify-statistics- uk-quarter-3-2023-july-to-september.

64. US TIP Report 2023 found at https://www.state.gov/reports/2023-trafficking-in-persons-report/united-kingdom/.

65. The Salvation Army was awarded the contract to provide support to victims going through the NRM as part of the Victim Care Contract (VCC). In 2021, the Modern Slavery Victim Care Coordination (MSVCC) contract worth £280 million includes 'Places of Safety' provision which a three day provision for individuals rescued from exploitation to decide whether they wish to enter the NRM.

66. T. Ward & S. Fouladvand, 'Human Trafficking, Victims' Rights and Fair Trials,' (2008) The Journal of Criminal Law, 82(2) at 147.

67. Home Office, press release, 'Alarming Rise of Abuse Within Modern Slavery System', 20 March 2021, https://www.gov.uk/government/news/alarming-rise-of-abuse-within-modern-slavery-system.

68. S. Tobin, 'Ex-justice Minister Criticises Lawyers over Modern Slavery Claims,' The Law Society Gazette, 17 August 2022, https://www.lawgazette.co.uk/news/ex-justice-minister-criticises-lawyers-over-modern-slavery-claims/5113454.article.

69. US TIP Report 2023, https://www.state.gov/reports/2023-trafficking-in-persons-report/united-kingdom/.

70. M. Gower & G. Sturge, 'Modern Slavery Cases in the Immigration System,' House of Commons Library Research Briefing, 8 March 2023 at 6.

71. DPP v M [2020] EWHC 3422 (Admin).

72. R v Brecani [2021] EWCA Crim 731.

73. See case of SG [2018] EWCA Crim 1824, R v AAD, R v AAH, R v AAI [2021} EWCA Crim 106 and AAJ [2021] EWCA Crim 1278.

74. R v Brecani [2021] EWCA Crim 731 at 40.

75. R v Brecani [2021] EWCA Crim 731 at 54.

76. R v Brecani [2021] EWCA Crim 731 at 47.

77. R v Brecani [2021] EWCA Crim 731 at 53 and 54.

78. CPS Guidance, 'Modern Slavery, Human Trafficking and Smuggling' 6 July 2022 at 20.

79. R v Brecani [2021] EWCA Crim 731 at 58.
80. See Article 4 obligations in investigating claims of modern slavery thoroughly in R v Brecani [2021] EWCA Crim 731 at 64 and 65.
81. 'Home Secretary Announces New Independent Anti-Slavery Commissioner,' https://www.gov.uk/government/news/home-secretary-announces-new-independent-anti-slavery-commissioner#:~:text=Eleanor%20Lyons%20will%20take%20up%20the%20role%20to%20help%20combat%20modern%20slavery.&text=Eleanor%20Lyons%2C%20the%20current%20Deputy,response%20to%20this%20devastating%20crime.
82. International Labour Organisation & Walk Free Foundation, 'Global Estimates of Modern Slavery: Forced Labour and Forced Marriage,' International Labour Office (ILO), Geneva (2017) at 9.
83. Office for Democratic Institutions and Human Rights (ODIHR), 'Guidance—Addressing Emerging Human Trafficking Trends and Consequences of the Covid-19 Pandemic,' at 5.
84. HM Government Modern Slavery Strategy, 2014 at 24.
85. O. Hesketh & O. Johnstone, 'Impact of the Covid-19 Pandemic on Modern Slavery,' Modern Slavery & Human Rights–Policy & Evidence Centre, Modern Slavery PEC Policy Brief 2021-4, November 2021, at 4.
86. D. Hernandez & A. Rudolph, 'Modern Day Slavery: What Drives Human Trafficking in Europe?' (2015) European Journal of Political Economy, 38, 118–139.

3

Contextual Issues Associated with the Detection and Identification of Victims of Human Trafficking

1   Introduction

The last chapter introduced the global crime problem of human trafficking and how the identification of victims takes place within a mix of various connected issues which can at times overshow the identification of the crime and the victims the crime affects. This chapter examines a number of issues entwined within a broader context of political and legal aspects which create barriers for more trafficked victims to be identified. It will identify the main immigration policies which have been implemented over the past two decades which seeks to understand the difficulties foreign victims face because of being present in the UK due to their status of being either illegal, an asylum seeker or a refugee. It is often the case that even where positive identification takes place, this does not mean that a survivor automatically has the right to legally stay in the UK. It will be seen what the challenges of regularising a foreign victim are despite being recognised as a survivor. This can have serious implications for victims, i.e. the risk of being re-trafficked if they are not able to seek welfare and accommodation. The discussion on the responses of the UK Government cannot be dealt with without examining the impact of Brexit. This will be examined along with new legislation, namely the

M. Davis, *Identifying Victims of Human Trafficking*, Palgrave Studies in Victims and Victimology, https://doi.org/10.1007/978-3-031-61741-6_3

Nationality & Borders Act 2022 (NABA 2022) and the Illegal Migration Act 2023 (IMA 2023). It will be seen that the above policies and legislation have either had or are likely to have a detrimental and serious impact on survivors, leaving many with no path to being positively identified by the State.

2   UK Political and Policy Aspects

Whilst the fight against transnational crime remains problematic for many countries to combat, the current Conservative Government has acknowledged that there is much more to do within the UK to combat human trafficking and to protect victims. Home Affairs Committee Chair, Dame Diana Johnson MP acknowledges "while Britain took an important step in the fight against trafficking with the introduction of the Modern Slavery Act in 2015, the Home Affairs Committee will investigate what more needs to be done to prevent this crime, prosecute exploiters and protect victims."[1] This shows that fighting trafficking and protecting survivors is a work in progress.

The Hostile Environment Policy in the UK

As discussed in the last chapter, combatting modern slavery and human trafficking takes place within a politically charged environment with divisive attitudes towards immigration amongst some parts of the electorate. Successive governments have felt pressured to address concerns about immigration for decades. The intention has been to take a deterrent approach by dissuading as many migrants as possible from coming to the UK or for migrants already here in the UK making it as uncomfortable as possible. This has been done to seek the approval of an anti-immigration section of the voting public.

A significant policy aimed at addressing the concerns of both legal and illegal immigration can be the hostile environment policy in the early 2010s. The legacy of the hostile environment policy can still be felt today because of the legislative impact it had which will be discussed shortly. As part of this policy the UK Government carried out several initiatives that indirectly impact the ability of foreign victims to self-identify themselves as victims of human trafficking. The hostile environment policy was one of the most notable policy announcements former Prime Minister Teresa May made when she was Home Secretary in 2012. She said that "foreign nationals believe that they can come here and overstay because they are able to access everything they need."[2] Specific legislation was passed which made it extremely difficult for foreign nationals who did not have the right to be in the UK (regardless of how or for what purpose they were in the UK) to work and access benefits, hold a driving licence, open or manage a bank account, acquire housing[3] or to access healthcare through the NHS.

The hostile environment policy coincided at the same time as when the human rights violations associated with modern slavery were being pushed up the political agenda given the increased media attention in newspapers and on television, especially when the crime involved the abuse of children. Furthermore, immigration was fast becoming a leading part of the Conservative manifesto in 2015 with David Cameron committing himself to reducing the net migration figure in the tens of thousands, not hundreds of thousands.[4] This pledge was offered as a means of the Conservative Party continuing to signal themselves as the political party of law and order to the electorate.

However, the origins of the hostile environment were not a product exclusively to the Conservative Government. It can be seen that a decade before the Conservative policies came into force, there were many hostile environment practices being brought through legislation, suppressing the needs of migrants who had come to the UK. These will be identified and summarised below.

The Asylum and Immigration Appeals Act was passed in 1993. Before then, there was no domestic asylum legislation since the UK ratified the 1951 Refugee Convention in 1954. The first legal instruments relating to asylum and incorporating a procedure for dealing with asylum applications in the UK were the Immigration Rules. Prior to this refugees had equal access to mainstream statutory services with assistance from community services including access to accommodation, health services,

employment advice and child and adult education.[5] The 1990s repre-
sented the start of "four main deterrence policies which have been
systematically pitched against people seeking asylum – dispersal, detention, deportation and destitution."[6] The tangible emergence of a hostile
environment can start to be seen from The Immigration and Asylum
Act 1996 which sanctioned benefits to late asylum claims, demonstrating
a deterrent and restrictive approach towards asylum seekers. Refugees
were becoming more visible within society because of the way they were
treated such as the availability and use of food vouchers accepted by local
authorities and charities.

The Immigration and Asylum Act 1999 signalised the creation of the
National Asylum Support Service (NASS). This contributed further to
the visibility of refugees being signposted to and helped by public, private
and increased voluntary support services.

The Labour Government's plan on immigration included the policy to
create an "increasingly uncomfortable environment for illegal migrants
by denying then the benefits and privileges of life in the UK."[7] This
coincided with the Immigration, Nationality and Asylum Act 2006
which sort to ensure that the immigration status of applicants was being
checked and approved by State services and the private sector. This also
included universities who were obligated to disclose to the Home Office
the information of student lecture absences.

The Conservative–Liberal Democrat coalition government was
formed in 2010. The middle part of this decade signalised the start of a
more visible anti-immigration rhetoric. This changed from being termed
as 'uncomfortable' to becoming more toxic in nature, a hostility narrative
towards encompassing the criminalisation of asylum seekers and demonising people and organisations where checks on asylum seekers did not
take place. The introduction of 'Operation Vaken' included "billboard
vans bearing the slogan, 'Go home or face arrest' sent into mixed ethnic
communities of six London boroughs in the summer of 2013 to test
whether 'illegal migrants' would deport voluntarily if warned of a near
and present danger of being arrested."[8] From a legislative perspective,
the Immigration Act 2014 and the Immigration Act 2016 make it even
harder for migrants to live and settle in the UK. The Immigration Act

2014 has required banks to stop opening bank accounts for undocumented migrants where they believed that a person was illegally in the UK. They also have the obligation to notify the Home Office. Likewise, Landlords must check the immigration status of an individual as part of their vetting processes and if required, notify authorities of someone who they suspected of being illegally in the UK.

The Immigration Act 2016 has consequences for authorities and businesses. For example, the law punishes landlords who have reasonable cause to believe that they have left a property to an undocumented illegal migrant, a crime which is punishable for up to 5 years.

Despite Theresa May saying that the justification for the hostile environment policy is to ensure "fairness asserting that most people in the UK think that it is not fair for irregular migrants to continue to exist as everybody else does,"[9] there are no clear aims or objectives which can be measured against the hostile environment, evaluating its success or failure. It has been admitted that the "Home Office does not have in place measurements to evaluate the effectiveness of the hostile environments, or of the impact of the provisions brought in by the Immigration Acts of 2014 ad 2016."[10] The House of Lords Library Briefing Report[11] states that the "system was put in place to deter illegal immigration and to prevent people who didn't have the right to be in the country to access public services. It's in the country's interests to have a secure immigration system in relation to these cases."[12] There are numerous consequences for migrants which have directly impacted on them, especially the vulnerable and young people who are disproportionately affected. The UN Special Rapporteur states that the "policy is destroying the lives and livelihoods of ethnic minority communities with hospitals, banks, and private residences being turned into border checkpoints."[13]

One of the main reasons why migrants wish to come to the UK is to work. As part of the asylum screening process asylum seekers are prevented from working for a minimum of 12 months whilst waiting to hear about their asylum application. This time limit before working can be reduced to 6 months and justified on the basis that asylum decisions are taking so long.

Recently, we can see the rhetoric of maintaining a strong law and order narrative in the present problem of migrants crossing the English

Channel in small boats. The current Conservative Government led by Rushi Sunak has outlined this as one of his main priorities in his administration. This focussed approach can also be seen as an opportunist by the Conservative Party to show their credentials as a Government serious on reducing overall levels of immigration. The people who are making this journey to gain entry into the UK have legitimate claims of persecution in their home countries and will go on to claim refugee status in the UK and be awarded asylum protection.

One direct consequence of the hostile environment policy is the serious impact felt by vulnerable individuals of foreign nationality who are coerced and pushed into more exploitative situations within riskier, perilous environments.[14] One could argue that a lesser of two evils were presented to these individuals. On the one hand, they may have found themselves being exploited and coerced into committing criminal offences as part of their exploitation, and on the other, if they came into contact with the State (police or immigration officials) with no legal immigration status they could find themselves being detained and possibly deported. In cases of conviction, they may also be deported. In some cases where illegal individuals are exploited and have escaped, they are then at risk of being deported due to their illegal immigration status, rather than authorities acknowledging them as victims of exploitation and protecting them from future harm and abuse.

The danger is that the UK is perceived as a 'hostile state' in the eyes of genuine victims of trafficking, negatively impacting their ability to be rescued by the State and protected from further exploitation. It is argued that "mistrust towards asylum seekers as a group directly contradicts policies to promote community engagement and initiatives to combat human trafficking where trust is an essential component."[15] Furthermore, an environment in which disclosure and identification go hand in hand, it is argued that the people directly affected by exploitation and the identification of victims "will become more difficult within a context of a harsh and increasingly hostile environment."[16] Hostile policy initiatives have resulted in the UK's international reputation for upholding Human Rights values. It is imperative for victims to have and maintain trust in authorities (such as the police). They are vital for victims to have the confidence of self-identifying. Authorities play a significant role in identifying potential victims by referring them to the NRM.

There is a detrimental impact on foreign victims having difficulty in regularising their status. The US TIP Report 2023 recommended that foreign victims should be able to work whilst in the NRM.

I would argue that genuine victims of trafficking and asylum seekers have been caught up inadvertently within the trappings of how two theories of how the role of the State has structured the migrant labour force in response to globalisation. One theory is that the effect of "States' pursuit of neoliberal over the past 30 years to facilitate economic globalisation through privatisation"[17] has led to this to the fact that this had led to a "deterioration in wages and conditions and growing numbers of flexible, low-skilled, temporary jobs routinely undertaken by marginalised groups, including vulnerable migrants."[18] The second theory is that "migrant labour exploitation lies in the rise of 'managed migration' regimes embodying the centrality of national security concerns about terrorism, organised crime and responses to migratory flows."[19] Vulnerable migrants sit in this vacuum between the two theories where the State grapples with maintaining and the pursuit of neoliberal policies consistent with globalisation and consumers requiring lost costs of goods and services facilitated by low skilled labour, whilst organised crime groups are opportunist in nature, seeking to take advantage of this situation. Criminals thrive where States advance hostile immigration policies towards foreign nationals who have been placed in direct competition with their own nationals for State services and support such as welfare and accommodation.

In summary, the practice of the hostile environment is alienating and extremely punitive and continues to be felt by migrants and asylum seekers. The increasing theme of deterrence and detention, especially in the present day where migrants are seeking to arrive in the UK via small boats is another example of the Government following the same trend of excluding a significant number of people within a vulnerable group.[20]

Brexit and Its Potential Impact on Trafficked Victims

The decision of the UK to leave the European Union (EU) was arguably one of the most important decisions in recent decades. There are serious implications for the UK by leaving the largest global economic union and political entity.

There are two ways to look at the impact of Brexit. Some commentators will say that human trafficking and other serious organised crime will increase because of a perceived loss of cooperation with EU neighbours on cross-border collaboration and on a multi-agency approach. Another view is more optimistic as the UK will be able to have more control to implement legislation, as they see fit to combat crime easier. The narrative of 'Taking Back Control' and 'Controlling Immigration' is relevant here and an example can be seen in the introduction of the new Points-Based System (PBS).[21] This section will argue the former view and demonstrate that the UK has experienced a limited loss of cooperation which it depends on other European countries in combatting human trafficking with the impact of Brexit on individuals being susceptible to an increased risk of labour and sexual exploitation a possibility in the future due to other risks on the horizon. This risk has substantially increased as the economic and social dimensions have created a picture of uncertainty, making them vulnerable within the environments where traffickers seek to exploit by manipulating, coercing and controlling victims.

The main impact of Brexit was the loss of free movement of persons which was one of the founding principles of EU law. Citizens of the European Union were requested to register with the Home Office to have their existing rights and entitlements respected in the UK through the EU Settlement Scheme. EU citizens entering the UK after Brexit have lost their automatic rights to work and are now subjected to the new Points-Based Immigration System[22] and treated as Third country Nationals.

Reduced Cooperation with EU Member States, Differencing Relationship with EU Bodies and the Loss of Access to Databases

For many years the UK cooperated, helped and supported other EU States in combatting human trafficking by assisting EU institutions in their aims and objectives. Due to the transnational characteristics, human trafficking remains a significant organised crime which poses a challenge for States and affects many victims because of the actions of non-State actors. To help combat this crime several criminal justice organisations such as Europol[23] and Eurojust[24] play significant roles in investigating organised crime groups, disbanding them and helping to secure successful convictions of traffickers.

As the UK becomes a third country from the perspective of the EU, they will not play the same role that they have played previously. Having said that the EU still requires the assistance of cooperation from the UK on these matters and after all the UK made a significant contribution in establishing Europol and still has some influence. Therefore, it is argued that whilst the political relationship has changed, the practical significant changes to investigations may not be too dissimilar and the negative impact some may have argued in combatting global crime problems within the continent of Europe may not be too great.

Having said that one of the main consequences of Brexit is that the UK will have to re-establish their formal relationships, memberships, arrangements or agreements with law enforcement such as Europol and Eurojust, along with agreeing new extradition treaties especially because of the European Arrest Warrant[25] (EAW) ceasing to apply because of Brexit.

There are a number of challenges which await the UK on resolving these important matters and laying out a path forward to increasing cooperation. One significant issue is the accountability of these bodies to the EU and to recognise the jurisdiction of the Court of Justice of the European Union (CJEU). The UK would need to agree to existing data sharing regulations as Europol is known as a strategic partner who hold personal data. It is suggested that the UK could focus attention on a new bespoke arrangement[26] with partners given that the EU would welcome the continuing contribution of the UK in these matters.

Furthermore, the UK pre-Brexit had access to several EU databases including the European Criminal Records Information System[27] (ECRIS), Schengen Second Generation Information Services[28] (SIS II) and information from Prum Decisions.[29] A new agreement encompassing the above information and agreement to share and have access to data would have to be agreed to the same standard as EU standards to maintain the same effectiveness in combating serious organised crime.[30] One note to mention here is that the UK was never a member of Schengen Area and as the UK is no longer an EU member then they will not have access to SIS II.

Despite the concern that forming new agreements and working relationships with EU bodies taking up to 7 years,[31] there is significant progress in this area. As of 1 January 2021, the Trade and Cooperation Agreement (TCA) forms the basis of the new relationship between the EU and the UK in matters including relating to law enforcement and judicial enforcement. The new arrangement is now set out below:

> Part Three allows the UK to maintain different levels of access to certain databases such as fingerprint and DNA data subject to certain restrictions and preconditions. As a third country, the UK has lost access to the Schengen Information System (SIS II) and will not ne a member of Europol. However, the TCA does enable UK liaison officers to be present in Europol's headquarters to facilitate cross-border cooperation. The UK' access to the European Arrest Warrant is replaced by extradition arrangements.[32]

The National Crime Agency (NCA) has also reached a working agreement as part of the TCA with Europol, meaning that they will still be able to exchange data and work closely on operations on cross-border crimes.[33]

Risk of Dilution of Workers' Rights of EU and UK Nationals Within the Current Environment for Demand for Low Skilled Labour

The aim and objective of the new Points-Based System (PBS) are to reduce the overall levels of migration, prioritise those with the highest skills and greatest talents and shift the focus of our economy away from a reliance on cheap labour from Europe and instead concentrate on investment in technology and automation.[34] As the PBS does not have a specific criterion for low skilled workers, low skilled labour is still required in the UK. This can increase the risks of exploitation.[35] The UK has and still does rely on low skilled labour in the economy within sectors including agriculture, construction, social care, and healthcare and still offers Temporary Seasonal Visas. Agriculture hosts a large number of low skilled workers (40,000) with 99% of them coming from the EU.[36] This situation currently exists within the UK where restrictive immigration policies such as the hostile environment are advanced whilst at the same time the intention is to reduce the numbers of people coming to the UK to lower the net migration figure. Increased migration both legal and illegal will continue and must be balanced with providing international protection to the most vulnerable. If increased restriction to movement continues by limiting the numbers of people claiming asylum, a higher risk of exploitation is possible given the desperation of people to migrate for different reasons and the current lack of safe and legal routes for asylum seekers to access.[37]

It is argued that "a large number of vulnerable people may be targeted by criminal organisations and recruited for the purpose of human trafficking and forced labour because EU citizens may no longer be entitled to live in the UK with the same rights and entitlements."[38] Whilst I agree that vulnerable people are at risk of being trafficked, negotiations at the time between the UK and the EU resulted in EU nationals who were living in the UK prior to Brexit having their rights and entitlements guaranteed. As a result of Brexit, many EU nationals found themselves in the UK and had to register with the Home Office through the EU Settlement Scheme to obtain settled status. Despite having the entitlement to live in the UK, it has been reported that many migrants have been treated less favourably and taken advantage of and have experienced greater hostility, discrimination and hate crime since Brexit.[39] As many workers may not have known their legal employment rights pre-Brexit, it is not inconceivable to assume that they would know what changes, if any Brexit had on their work status. At present, their rights remain the same as they did Pre-Brexit. However, given the pressure on some employers to fill gaps of low skilled people in their workforce, there is a risk that some employers could fail in their duties to ensure the legality of some workers and take advantage of them by insisting that they are illegal or discriminating them by not paying them for overtime, leading to a power imbalance between some employers and EU migrant workers:

> A woman was given additional work within her working hours, so a higher workload that leads you to work extra hours that you don't get paid for. And she was given additional work and told to behave now because she a European. You don't really need to say much more than that, because the employer knows that in the future, they may have more power over them.[40]

It is also argued that "restrictive migration policies, coupled with a labour market that favours deregulation create the ideal environment for modern slavery to thrive."[41] It is difficult for EU nationals and other foreign individuals working in the UK to find work after being made redundant after the Covid-19 pandemic, leading them to having to take riskier forms of employment, exposing them to a higher risk of exploitation:

> There are lots of adverts on websites where you can find job offers with immediate start promising lots of money, and there's no name, just a phone number. People are being kicked out from the job after two or three weeks without being paid.[42]

Two of the most important employment employee protections are the Agency Workers Regulations 2010[43] and the Working Time Regulations 1998.[44] The former provides for the equal treatment of workers on an agency contract as those individuals on regular direct employee contracts provided by an employer, and the latter provides for the capping of a maximum number of hours which employee can work. There is a possibility for the Government to repeal these employment protections or amend them in such a way that they see fit. The UK Government would also not be bound by any decisions from case law arising from CJEU in this area.

Despite the UK favouring deregulation and more unstable forms of employment such as zero hours contracts, it would be reassuring for the Agency Workers Regulations 2010 and Working Time Regulations 1998 to be drafted into domestic law to fully protect workers going forward from unfair working employment practices so that unscrupulous employers can be held criminally liable and punished for breaches of these laws which have protected people in issues concerning sick pay and annual leave. It is hoped that traffickers do not take advantage of a two-tier labour market and where workers are treated more favourably based on their nationality and those who are treated less favourably are at risk of being exploited and pushed into exploitative working environments which they have no choice but to endure and cannot escape from.

Status of EU Law and the Future Loss of Rights Because of the Repeal Act

As a member of the EU victims of trafficking were protected through several Directives including the main Directive relating to victims of trafficking, Directive 2011/36[45] also known as 'The Trafficking Directive,' Directive 2004/80/EC,[46] Directive 2011/99/EU[47] and Directive 2012/29/EU.[48] The Trafficking Directive advocates for States to identify victims and provide them with support as quickly as possible.[49]

'The Trafficking Directive' contains important rights for victims regards support and assistance during the identification process and onwards. These important measures, guarantees and protections have direct effect in the UK and can be relied upon by individuals if taking the UK to national courts.

The new Retained EU Law (Revocation and Reform) Act 2023 ended the supremacy of EU law on 31 Dec 2023[50] and set out the procedure for the Government, but not Parliament to review this body of law and decide which elements it wishes to retain, amend or repeal. This has led to concerns that the Government of the day will have Henry VIII powers allowing the Government to revoke or replace legislation[51] without Parliamentary scrutiny. A further consequence of the Act encourages the role of the Court of Appeal and the Supreme Court to make more use of their powers to overturn previous EU-based caselaw.[52]

As it stands the status of the Directives is still effective and in force, as is the Government's strategy to address modern slavery which includes pursuing offenders, preventing people from engaging in modern slavery, protecting vulnerable people and increasing safeguards and improving victim identification and enhanced support.[53] To fully cement the protection of victims' rights, a domestic law seen in the proposed Modern Slavery (Victim Support) Bill will hopefully be passed to signify a strong commitment to upholding the rights of trafficked victims who are identified in the UK which complements the UK's strategy on this.

The proposed Bill advocated for two main benefits for victims. The first is to amend Section 49 of Modern Slavery Act 2015 to include the provision of support and assistance before Reasonable Grounds Decisions and during recovery and reflection periods and the second benefit is to amend Section 52 of Modern Slavery Act 2015 to provide leave to remain to support adult victim of modern slavery.

The guaranteed protection afforded to victims of modern slavery would be at least 12 months of support and the right to stay in the UK which would greatly enhance the advantages for victims to come forward and self-identify. At the time of writing, the Bill has been re-introduced into Parliament to have its second reading in the House of Lords.

3   Conclusion

It will be some time before the true long terms impact of Brexit will be seen from an economic, social and legal perspective. However, what can be established right now is that there are numerous potential dangers in the short term for workers because of Brexit.

As the climate of hostility against migrants continues, this presents a significant opportunity for traffickers to occupy the vacuum which has presented itself existing because of the gap in protection for this social group to exist within the UK. Consequently, more vulnerable people will be at the mercy of traffickers through debt bondage who either offer a path into the UK illegally or simply exploit vulnerable persons here in the UK because of the restrictive immigration policies of not offering safe and legal routes to entry into the UK. This situation alongside the toxic rhetoric from some politicians is consistently subscribed to as it serves as being politically advantageous to them and appealing to some parts of the UK electorate too.

Workers require protection of existing EU Law on workers' rights to prevent an increased risk of exploitation for both EU and UK nationals. It is hoped that new visa schemes do not tie workers to their employers as a pre-requite of being in the UK which has been shown to encourage the risk of trafficking. Therefore, seasonal workers such as those working in agricultural and also care workers do require some flexibility to change their employer if required to alleviate the risks. Whilst there are restrictive immigration policies there will always be a risk of exploitation and where there is a hostile environment towards migrants, it becomes even more difficult to identify victims and for victims to have trust in the State if they wish to self-identify themselves as victims of exploitation.

Notes

1. See Home Affairs Committee Press Release, 7th February 2023, https://committees.parliament.uk/committee/83/home-affairs-committee/news/185985/new-inquiry-examines-human-traffi cking-in-the-uk/#:~:text=In%20this%20new%20inquiry%2C% 20the,prosecute%20perpetrators%20and%20protect%20victims.
2. J. Kirkup and R. Winnett, "Theresa May Interview: 'We're Going to Give Illegal Migrants a Really Hostile Reception," The Telegraph Newspaper, 25th May 2012.
3. Under Section 95 of the Asylum & Immigration Act 1999, the Home Office has a statutory duty to provide financial support and housing to asylum seekers whilst their claim is being processed.

4. See 2015 Conservative Manifesto at page 29, https://www.the resavilliers.co.uk/sites/www.theresavilliers.co.uk/files/conservative manifesto2015.pdf.

5. See K. Duke, "Refugee Communities in the UK: The Role of the Community Group in the Resettlement Process," Paper presented at the British Sociological Association Annual Conference, Reading, UK, April 1–4 1996, 13.

6. S.N. Hodkinson, H. Lewis, L. Waite and P. Dwyer, "Fighting or Fuelling Forced Labour? The Modern Slavery Act 2015, Irregular Migrants and the Vulnerabilising Role of the UK's Hostile Environment," (2015) Critical Social Policy, 41(1), 8.

7. Home Office, "Managing Global Migration: A Strategy to Ensure and Enforce Compliance with Our Immigration Law" (2007), https://assets.publishing.service.gov.uk/government/uploads/sys tem/uploads/attachment_data/file/243288/7096.pdf.

8. S.N. Hodkinson, H. Lewis, L. Waite and P. Dwyer, "Fighting or Fuelling Forced Labour? The Modern Slavery Act 2015, Irregular Migrants and the Vulnerabilising Role of the UK's Hostile Environment," (2015) Critical Social Policy, 41(1), 2.

9. A. Travis, "Immigration Bill: Theresa May Defends Plans to Create 'Hostile Environment." The Guardian Newspaper, 10 October 2013.

10. House of Commons Home Affairs Committee, "Immigration Policy: Basis for Building Consensus," 15 January 2018, HC 500 of session 2017–19 at 20.

11. House of Lords Library Report, "Impact of 'Hostile Environment' Policy Debate" on 14th June 2018.

12. J. Elgot, "Theresa May's Hostile Environment at Heart of Windrush Scandal," The Guardian, 17th April 2018.

13. United Nations, "End of Mission Statement of the Special Rapporteur on Contemporary Forms of Racism, Racial Discrimination, Xenophobia and Related Intolerance at the Conclusion of Her Mission to the United Kingdom of Great Britain and Northern Ireland." 11th May 2018.

14. People not holding a legal immigration status can also be seen from victims subjected to the Windrush Scandal where members

and their children migrating from post British colonies, arriving in Tilbury docks on the SS Empire Windrush on 22 June 1948 were subjected to hostile environment policies many decades later where they could not access UK services, with some victims deported or refused entry back into the UK.

15. See P. Hynes, P. Burland, A. Thurnham, J. Dew, L. Goni-Yusuf, V. Lenja, H. Thi Tiran, A. Olatunde and A. Gaxha, "Between Two Fires: Understanding Vulnerabilities and the Support Needs of People from Albania, Vietnam and Nigeria Who Have Experienced Human Trafficking into the UK," (University of Bedfordshire and International Organisation for Migration 2019).

16. P. Haynes, "Exploring the Interface between Asylum, Human Trafficking and/or 'Modern Slavery' within a Hostile Environment in the UK," (2022) Social Sciences, 11, 246 at 18.

17. See J. Peck, N. Theodore and K. Ward, "Constricting Markets for Temporary Labour: Employment Liberalization and the Internationalization of the Staffing Industry," (2005) Global Networks, 5(1), 3–26.

18. See B. Barbieri, "Flexible Employment and Inequality in Europe," (2009) European Sociological Review, 25(6), 621–628.

19. S.N. Hodkinson, H. Lewis and L. Waite et al. (1 more author) "Fighting or Fuelling Forced Labour? The Modern Slavery Act 2015, Irregular Migrants and the Vulnerabilising Role of the UK's Hostile Environment." (2021) Critical Social Policy, 41(1), 68–90.

20. This can be evidenced from the Illegal Migration Bill 2023 which will be discussed later in this chapter.

21. The UK's Points Based System, https://www.gov.uk/government/publications/uk-points-based-immigration-system-employer-information/the-uks-points-based-immigration-system-an-introduction-for-employers#:~:text=Under%20the%20points%2Dbased%20immigration,those%20who%20gain%20enough%20points.

22. See UK Immigration Rules—Points Based System, https://www.gov.uk/government/publications/uk-points-based-immigration-system-employer-information/the-uks-points-based-immigration-system-an-introduction-for-employers.

23. Europol is a Europe wide police agency who conduct investigations into serious organised crime which are cross-border in nature.
24. Eurojust conduct joint investigations with 2 or more other EU Member States to focus on an investigation for a limited time and encourage mutual cooperation between judicial authorities.
25. 2002/584/JHA: Council Framework Decision of 13 June 2002 on the European Arrest Warrant and the surrender procedures between Member States.
26. See The Anti Trafficking Monitoring Group, "Brexit & the UK's fight against modern slavery," July 2017 at 8.
27. Access to the criminal convictions of an individual in another Member State.
28. Provides access of live alerts on individuals within a Member State.
29. Access to databases containing DNA profiles, fingerprints and vehicle data across the EU.
30. House of Lords, European Union Committee, 2016 at para 63.
31. House of Lords, European Union Committee, 2016 at para 58.
32. UK Parliament House of Lords Library, "Beyond Brexit: policing, law enforcement and security," 7 February 2022.
33. See National Crime Agency Press Release, 'NCA and EUROPOL Sign Up to a New Working Arrangement,' September 2021, https://www.nationalcrimeagency.gov.uk/news/nca-and-europol-sign-up-to-a-new-working-arrangement#:~:text=NCA%20Director%20General%20Dame%20Lynne,EU%20Trade%20and%20Cooperation%20Agreement.
34. UK Parliament, "Could the UK's New Immigration System Increase Human Trafficking and Human Smuggling?" House of Lords Library, Tuesday 19th January 2021.
35. Independent Anti-Slavery Commissioner, 'Protecting individuals from exploitation by criminal traffickers and unscrupulous employers: Identifying and mitigating risks in the EU Settlement Scheme and the UK's new points-based immigration system,' February 2021 at 6, https://www.antislaverycommissioner.co.uk/media/1563/identifying-and-mitigating-risks-in-the-eu-settlement-scheme-and-the-uks-new-points-based-system.pdf.

36. Department for Environment, Food and Rural Affairs (2020b) Written Evidence (LF0033) submitted to The Environment Food and Rural Affairs Committee.
37. The UK Government is looking to consult in the use of safe and legal routes for refugees by working with local authorities to under the complexities and pressures placed on public services and accommodation provisions with a view to introducing a cap on the number of vulnerable and at-risk people entering the UK based on how much support and services local authorities have. It is anticipated that the cap will be agreed by Parliament and start in January 2025, along with the possibility of proposing any additional safe and legal routes. For further information, please see https://www.gov.uk/government/news/government-consults-on-safe-and-legal-routes-for-refugees#:~:text=The%20UK%2Dwide%20consultation%20will,as%20local%20communities%20can%20support.
38. M. Ventrella, "Brexit and the Fight Against Human Trafficking; Actual Situation and Future Uncertainty," Marmara Journal of European Studies, 26 (1) at 1.
39. See B. France, "Lost in Transition: Brexit & Labour Exploitation," Labour Exploitation Advisory Group Position Paper Flex-LEAG, August 2017 at 5.
40. B. France, "Lost in Transition: Brexit & Labour Exploitation," Labour Exploitation Advisory Group Position Paper Flex-LEAG, August 2017 at 4.
41. Anti Trafficking Monitoring Group, "Brexit & the UK's Fight Against Modern Slavery," July 2017 at 16.
42. B. France, "Lost in Transition: Brexit & Labour Exploitation," Labour Exploitation Advisory Group Position Paper Flex-LEAG, August 2017 at 5.
43. Agency Workers Regulations 2010 which implemented Directive 2008/104/EC.
44. Working Time Regulations 1998 which implemented the EU Working Time Directive 2003/88/EC.
45. Articles 11–17 sets out the help and support individuals are entitled to as victims of trafficking.

46. Victims of trafficking can obtain compensation from their traffickers.
47. Those victims identified in one Member State shall be entitled to the same support in another Member State.
48. This Directive establishes minimum standards on the rights, supports and protection of victims of crime, aims to ensure that victims of crime receive appropriate information, support and protection and can participate in criminal proceedings.
49. Article 11 Directive 2011/36/EU 5 April 2011.
50. Section 3 Retained EU Law (Revocation and Reform) Act 2023.
51. Section 14 Retained EU Law (Revocation and Reform) Act 2023.
52. Section 6 Retained EU Law (Revocation and Reform) Act 2023.
53. The 2020 UK Annual Report on Modern Slavery outlines the UK Government approach to tacking modern slavery and human trafficking.

4

Legislative Developments in Immigration Law Which Make Identification of Trafficked Victims More Challenging

1   Introduction

In 2021, the UK Government launched their 'New Plan for Immigration Policy Statement,'[1] stressing the importance of fairness within the immigration system when people are seeking refuge as asylum seekers or victims of modern slavery. This was launched acknowledging the changes which Brexit has on the UK's ability to control its borders and manage migration to the UK because of free movement ceasing to apply any longer.

At the same time that the UK was seeking policies to manage its borders and control legal immigration whilst combatting the challenges of illegal migration, the issue of small boats crossing the English Channel started to emerge as a phenomenon gaining more attention. This issue continues to be a hot political topic and a constant thorn in the Government's immigration pledges on reducing the net migration figure. It has been in the news and media for many months and continues to play a toxic and emotive role in addressing and combating illegal immigration. Two questions require answering here. Why are people making this journey and secondly, who are the people making this journey?

© The Author(s), under exclusive license to Springer Nature Switzerland AG 2024
M. Davis, *Identifying Victims of Human Trafficking*, Palgrave Studies in Victims and Victimology, https://doi.org/10.1007/978-3-031-61741-6_4

It has been established that "in 2022, 45,755 people entered the UK having crossed the English Channel in small boats and 3,400 recorded detections of people attempting to enter the UK illegally through other routes."[2] In comparison, to previous years, there were just 299 migrants using small boats to reach the UK.[3] With the increased numbers arriving in the UK, there has been a significant financial burden for the Government to bear with the costs of accommodation. The present cost as of May 2023 was £90 per night per person with a total population of 114,000. This is expected to rise with costs expected in 2024 to be £126 and £152 projected in 2025.[4] Looking more broadly and the applications made for protection as victims of modern slavery, "of the 83,236 people who arrived in the UK on small boats between 1 January 2018 and 31 December 2022, 7% (6,210 people) were referred to the National Referral Mechanism. Most of these individuals (5,897 or 95%) had also made an application for asylum in the UK. In 2022, there were 2,691 NRM referrals of people who arrived on small, which accounted for 15% of all NRM referrals in that year."[5] We will now look at how the legislation has impacted individuals coming to the UK seeking protection under modern slavery laws and how they impact on victims already present within the UK.

The Nationality & Borders Act 2022

Whilst the content of this legislation relates to immigration and asylum, there are significant issues for victims of human trafficking. This section will highlight what the main issues are from the provisions and how they impact on the victims of human trafficking.

After many concerns from the House of Lords, The Nationality & Borders Act 2022 was eventually passed into UK law on 28 April 2022. This legislation fits with the UK Government's New Plan for Immigration[6] devised to reduce the numbers involved in illegal migration by setting out punitive consequences for those involved in illegal entry and having a wider deterrence effect, dissuading those from making the journey to the UK illegally.

The legislation deals with a wide variety of issues including nationality, asylum, immigration, victims of slavery and human trafficking. This legislation along with the Illegal Migration Act 2023 (to be discussed later) seeks to combat the small boats issue and attempts to break the business model of people smuggling individuals into the UK. The Government was also concerned about the misuse of the NRM in the UK with non-genuine claims being made and advocated that the legislation would enhance the early identification of victims, enable genuine victims to access support and prevent misuse of Modern Slavery Act 2015. However, it is argued that "given the complexity of both victim identification and the crime of human trafficking, authorities should give the benefit of the doubt to a person claiming to have been subjected to exploitation possibly related to trafficking."[7] The next section identifies the main legal provisions of the Act and their potential impact on the identification of trafficking victims.

The Disclosure of Victims' Experiences

Sections 58 and 59 Nationality & Borders Act 2022 deal with the provision of information relating to being a victim of human trafficking or modern slavery and the impact on credibility because of 'late compliance' where individuals may not have disclosed that they have been or are still a victim of exploitation. We know that there are a host of reasons why victims will not or do not self-identify as victims. The Competent Authority must be made aware of the reasons why disclosure was given late. The Government believes that the intention of this provision is to prevent the misuse of someone using the story of being exploited for a reason to stay in the UK. The Government wishes to identify victims as early as possible so that they can get support. However, it is acknowledged that trauma plays a role in victims not disclosing this and it can be up to 2 years before someone discloses what has happened to them.[8] This view is also acknowledged in the UK Government Modern Slavery Guidance which outlines some of the identification challenges associated with trafficked victims.[9] It is concluded that victims could be penalised for either delayed or non-disclosure. It can also be argued that it is a violation of Article 3 European Convention on Action against Trafficking in Human Beings on the basis that it does not promote or protect the rights of victims. The consequence could be legitimate victims being barred from entering the NRM to be identified as a victim as set out in Section 60.

The Identification of Victims, Recovery Period, Disqualification from Protection and Assistance and Support

Sections 60–67 Nationality & Borders Act 2022 deal with issues which take place during the NRM process.[10] Section 60 deals with the change of the standard proof threshold needed for victims to obtain a RGD, meaning that the victim is required to show that they are a victim of modern slavery. Consequently, there is a greater focus on evidence showing this earlier within the referral process and to a much higher level than before as decision makers will make akin to a decisions being based on the balance of probabilities but falling short of this. The reasoning for such a change has been the argument that the Government believes that the NRM system is being abused and undermined by serious criminals to get into the UK.[11] This view is not supported as it has been seen that NRM statistics show that 87% of all Reasonable Grounds Decisions made in 2022 were positive.[12]

The impact of such measures has been seen to have a negative effect on positive RGD being granted at the beginning of 2023. In the first quarter of 2023, "3,528 reasonable grounds decisions were issued this quarter; of these, 58% of reasonable grounds decisions were positive."[13] Those individuals who were unable to provide objective evidence in support of their applications such as documents to prove that they have been exploited, medical evidence to show physical or mental harm and abuse connected to their exploitation or other witness testimony to corroborate their stories fell foul of the new reasonable grounds test threshold. The Government has even acknowledged that the drop in the number of positive RGD is due to the change in the test for the RGD.[14]

This downward trend of decline in positive decisions continued into the Second Quarter of 2023 between April and June. There were "3,635 reasonable grounds decisions issued this quarter; of these, 48% of reasonable grounds decisions were positive."[15] Unlike the results for Quarter 1, no reason was provided for the further drop in positive decisions. However, the likely reason for a continued drop is the impact the threshold test has had within the decision-making process which has been a difficult hurdle for potential victims to overcome to be identified as victims. Further developments on the threshold test will be discussed later in this chapter.

It has been seen that the impact the Nationality & Borders Act 2022 has had on the identification of foreign victims is significant. Research from the International Organisation for Migration (IOM) states that since the introduction of the legislation and analysing the first 6 months of 2023 showed that "only 40% of decisions were positive compared to 86% of decisions for UK nationals."[16] In conclusion, the nationality of the victim is significant to whether they will be positively identified as a victim of trafficking by the NRM.

Section 13 Council of Europe Convention on Action Against Trafficking in Human Beings (ECAT) states that a reflection and recovery period of 30 days must be provided to victims between the period of the Reasonable Grounds Decision (RGD) and the Conclusive Grounds Decision (CGD). Prior to the Nationality & Borders Act 2022, the UK position was that the UK would offer 45 days or until a CGD was received, and then a further 45 days is provided with additional support if required as a result of *NN & LP*.[17] The previous policy of providing additional support was substantially more generous than what the Council of Europe obligates States to do. However, Section 61 now reduces this period from 45 to 30 days or when a CGD is received (whichever is later). The Government has intended to amend the Modern Slavery Act 2015 and give victims more protection. This bill was announced in the Queen's Speech in May 2022, and it remains to be seen whether enhanced periods of protection will be granted. However, it is unlikely given the enactment of this legislation, with a focus on enforcing reporting within supply chains to prevent modern slavery rather than victim protection in the UK.[18]

A new provision within the Nationality & Borders Act 2022 is the non-entitlement to a secondary recovery period which can be read in

Section 62. Often, exploitation works in a cycle where some individuals fall in and out of exploitation. It can happen where the risk of being re-trafficked is higher if services and support are not available or stopped, leaving some individuals falling back into exploitation because of traffickers coercing or deceiving them back into the same or maybe different exploitative environment. Again, the justification for such a clause is the potential misuse of the National Referral Mechanism (NRM). However, this approach fails to acknowledge the reality of some victims' circumstances where it is common for those dropping in and out of insecure working practices can lead to cycles of exploitation. The NRM can often provide an opportunity for them to remove themselves from. It would be unfair for a victim to have escaped their exploitative condition only to be barred from re-entering the NRM. This provision does nothing to help or persuade the victim from leaving the exploitation. International obligations are silent on the issue of additional recovery periods. Positively, the decision maker has discretion to make an additional recovery period for a victim and optimistically decision makers can be persuaded to offer these to genuine victims.

Section 63 deals with the disqualification of protection towards potential victims based on the person either being a threat to public order[19] or has claimed to be a victim of slavery or human trafficking in bad faith.[20] Between 30 January and 30 June 2023, there have been 256 cases where people have been disqualified from seeking NRM support out of 465 applications. 71% of the cases connected to individuals being forced to commit criminal exploitation included the offences of cultivating cannabis and county lines exploitation.[21] There is no right of appeal against the decision to be disqualified. The list of activities which constitute public order is found in Section 63(3)(a)–(i) and includes terrorism offences or those committed in Schedule 4 of the Modern Slavery Act 2015 or if a foreign person has committed an offence which justifies automatic deportation under Section 32 UK Borders Act 2007.[22] The public order disqualification entitles the State to revoke the right of victims not to be removed during the recovery period, no rights to be granted temporary admission to stay in the UK, no rights to help and support and no right to have a Conclusive Grounds Decision.[23]

As we know, some victims are coerced in committing criminal offences under duress as part of their exploitation.[24] If these offences are of a serious nature, then there is a possibility that they will be deported.[25] A likely consequence is the continued control traffickers can have over victims they have forced to commit crimes for them if they are trafficked after conviction but not deported and still in the UK. It may be that victims they are exploiting presently have convictions for more than 1 year and therefore this provides the trafficker with additional forms of control with both the trafficker and the victim knowing that they are at risk of being deported if found by the State which more likely keeps the victim in an exploitative environment. Section 63(3)(i) states that if the person poses a risk to the national security of the UK, then that person can be disqualified from protection. This is a very wide provision indeed. As seen, it may be that victims are not always identified at the first opportunity, and therefore it is unfair for them to be barred from the opportunity of being identified when information can be disclosed or new information provided.

Section 64 deals with assistance and support for victims. Where victims receive a positive RGD, they are entitled to support. Section 64 reads that "assistance and support is necessary for the purpose of assisting the person receiving it in their recovery from any physical, psychological or social harm arising from the conduct which resulted in the positive reasonable grounds decision in question."[26] Therefore, the support from the State is not automatic, but discretionary and is dependent upon evidence being disclosed in support to justify such assistance. It can be argued that the UK is offering support on condition by placing the burden on victims to justify why they need support. Furthermore, it may be that the type of support must be linked to the evidence showing that they are a victim of trafficking and connecting the means of support to the recovery of what they have said to have experienced in their original NRM application. For foreign victims to start the recovery from their trafficking experience, it is beneficial for them to have their immigration status regularised. This issue will now be discussed.

Temporary Permission to Stay for Victims of Trafficking or Slavery

There is no automatic right for individuals to have a residence permit to stay in the UK on the basis that he or she has been recognised as a trafficked victim and received a positive Conclusive Grounds Decision (CGD). Victims of trafficking can apply for Discretionary Leave to Remain in the UK, but the number of successful applications is relatively low indeed as seen in the period between April 2016 and June 2021 where only 447 confirmed victims were granted leave to remain from 6,066 people who applied for it, equating to just a 7% chance of success.[27] There are no present available statistics on the number of residence permits granted to victims of human trafficking. However, we know that in 2015, there were 123 successful applications, in 2019 there were 70 and during the first part of 2020 there were only 8.[28]

In other circumstances, there are instances where an individual is claiming asylum on the basis that there have a well-founded fear of being persecuted or would be at serious risk of harm on the basis of either their race, religion, nationality, membership of a particular social or political opinion and that the State from which they are from are unable to protect that person, as well as being referred into the NRM to be identified as a victim of human trafficking. The decision on a person's asylum claim will be delayed until either a Reasonable Grounds Decision (RGD) or Conclusive Grounds Decision (CGD) has been made.[29] The case of *R (KTT) v SSHD*[30] confirmed the position of the individual being granted permission to stay whilst their asylum claim was pending.

The case of *R (on the application of SSA) (Ethiopia)) v SSHD*,[31] showed that the fear an individual has of being re-trafficked is merely one of the issues put forward as to why they cannot return to their country of origin, not a determinative one. At this point, it can be argued that the fact that someone who has been trafficked does not automatically require that an application for leave will be successful.

The UK Government Modern Slavery Guidance states that "Non-EEA and EEA nationals will automatically be considered for a grant of leave if they do not already have the right to stay in the UK."[32] However, individuals must be in receipt of a positive Conclusive Grounds Decision.

The decision in *KTT* has now been overturned because of the new policy guidance which took effect on 30 January 2023 and the new Immigration Rules which fall in line with the Nationality & Borders Act 2022.[33] The new Home Office Guidance on 'Temporary Permission to Stay considerations for Victims of Human Trafficking or Slavery'[34] was published on 2 February 2023. This replaced the Home Office guidance 'Discretionary Leave for victims of modern slavery.' The previous guidance dealt with 'leave is necessary owing to personal circumstances.' This reflected Article 14 CofE Convention discussing factors which should be considered when granting leave. These were discussed in *R (on the application of SSA) (Ethiopia)) v SSHD*[35] including, but not exclusive to a real risk that the person may be re-trafficked or become a victim of modern slavery again, assessing whether the risk is greater in the person's home country or the UK, if returned home, would the person face ill-treatment from those who first brought them to the UK, or exploited them in their home country, or leave necessary to cooperate with the police or prosecutors in a criminal case.[36]

The new guidance sets out the considerations of granting or refusing permissions to stay in the UK by Home Office staff where individuals have a positive CGD from the NRM in accordance with the Nationality & Borders Act 2022.[37] The fact that a foreign individual has been positively identified as a victim of human trafficking does not automatically entitle the individual to stay in the UK. The individual must meet at least one of the following criteria to be eligible to be granted a period of stay:

1) To assist the person in their recovery from any physical or psychological harm arising from the relevant exploitation,

2) Enable the person to seek compensation in respect of the relevant exploitation, or

3) Enable the person to co-operate with a public authority in connection with an investigation or criminal proceedings in respect of the relevant exploitation.[38]

Under Article 14(1)(a) CofE Convention on Action Against Trafficking in Human Beings, victims can be given a residence permit by a Competent Authority owing to the person's personal situation.[39] The Explanatory Notes from the Nationality & Borders Act 2022 "clarifies the obligation in Article 14(1)(a) of ECAT which provides for a grant of leave where it is necessary owing to their personal situation."[40] This provides that leave is necessary owing to the individual's personal situation where it is necessary in order to assist with recovery from any physical or psychological harm arising from the relevant exploitation.

It appears that the new guidance refers to the CofE Convention with the domestic legislation seeking to clarify in what circumstances leave can be granted. Nevertheless, there are significant challenges for victims to overcome to be granted leave which will be discussed shortly.

For the purposes of this discussion, the focus will remain on the first consideration given the psychological and harmful impact the trauma of exploitation has on victims through exploitation connected to the difficulties of foreign nationals who have irregular status in the UK trying to obtain leave in the UK.

Despite the guidance making it clear that "a victim-centred approach should be adopted,"[41] in deciding whether a grant of stay of up to 30 months[42] is necessary, there are a number of potential barriers for foreign nationals with irregular immigration status in the UK who have been positively identified as a victim of human trafficking. For example, the UK may believe that the individual can have their needs met elsewhere outside of the UK. "Section 65(4) Nationality and Borders Act 2022 makes it clear that permission to stay is not necessary if the Secretary of State considers that the person's need for assistance can be met in either a country of which the person is a national or citizen or a country."[43] The person will also have the burden of proving that they require assistance on a balance of probabilities, meaning that they will require help and support from healthcare professionals and professionals working in the field of helping asylum seekers and specialist anti-trafficking organisations which are stretched in terms of their resources as the demand outstrips supply due to austerity from the past 13 years, meaning that charitable and non-profit organisations have had their funding reduced and access to legal help diminished. Secondly, the words linking the harm to the relevant exploitation potentially exclude historical victims of trafficking, individuals who have been exploited and are moved from exploitation but not formally identified through the NRM and are living a life in the UK without coming to the attention of the State. It appears that historical victims will be outside of the remit of this guidance and further illustrates the reluctance of an individual of this case coming forward to self-identify knowing that the individual may be prosecuted for immigration offences given the nature of having no legal immigration status, leaving them invisible and potentially at risk of re-trafficking.

The duration of this leave is up to 30 months and in some cases, can be less. This is not long enough given the harm inflicted on some victims and the specific care and support required by victims to help them recover from their traumatic experiences. The supply and demand of these services by trafficked victims competing for the same services and support from UK nationals to healthcare and mental health support is a continuous social and political issue.

The consequences for trafficked victims in the UK will be that is more difficult for them to have their immigration status regularised by the State. This will make them less trustful of authorities for the fear of being identified as illegal immigrants rather than victims of crime, making them less likely to self-identify.

The Relationship Between the Nationality & Borders Act 2002 and the EU Trafficking Directive and the Changes to the Sandard of Proof in Determining a Victim of Human Trafficking

The EU Trafficking Directive has been in force since 2011. It has many aims including setting out minimum standards to be applied throughout the European Union in preventing and combating trafficking of human beings and protecting victims and "raising awareness, reducing vulnerability, supporting and assisting victims, fighting the root causes of trafficking and supporting those third countries in developing appropriate anti-trafficking legislation."[44]

As discussed earlier, all EU Directives continue to be in force unless the Government chooses to use its powers under the Retained EU Law (Revocation and Reform) Act 2023. However, the Government believes incorrectly in Section 68 that the Trafficking Directive no longer applies but in fact it does under Section 4 Withdrawal Act 2018 which states that:

> Any rights, powers, liabilities, obligations, restrictions, remedies and procedures which, immediately before [completion day]—(a) are recognised and available in domestic law by virtue of section 2(1) of the European Communities Act 1972, and (b) are enforced, allowed and followed accordingly.[45]

If the Government chooses to use its powers under the Retained EU Law (Revocation and Reform) Act, it will dilute the effectiveness of protection measures afforded to victims including the non-prosecution of victims,[46] the support and assistance to victims[47] and compensation to victims.[48] The present position is that the Directive can be disapplied when not compatible with a provision in the Nationality and Borders Act 2022.

As previously discussed, Section 60 NABA 2022 increases the threshold for individuals to show that there are a victim of human trafficking or modern slavery. On 30 January 2023, the UK Government Modern Slavery Guidance was updated showing an RGD must be "based on objective factors but falling short of conclusive proof."[49] It has been clarified that "an 'objective' factor is a piece of information or evidence that is based in fact. Ordinarily, a victim's own account, by itself, would not be sufficient absent objective factors to have real suspicion."[50] As a result of a recent judicial review case involving two potential trafficking victims who had negative Reasonable Grounds Decisions despite credible accounts of their experience, the Secretary of State for the Home Department has agreed to withdraw, reconsider and revise parts of the Modern Slavery Statutory Guidance which required a potential victim of trafficking to produce 'objective' evidence corroborating a credible account of human trafficking in order to receive a positive RGD. The new guidance[51] makes no reference to 'objective factors' which had previously been included in previous guidance in January 2023. It was found that the relevant guidance was unlawful for three reasons:

1. because it breached Article 4 of the European Convention on Human Rights;
2. were irrational at common law (the fact of someone not having objective evidence of their trafficking circumstances at the point of referral into the NRM being not rationally connected to whether that person is a genuine victim of trafficking) and undercut the statutory purpose of the Modern Slavery Act 2015 and
3. the guidance was procedurally unfair.[52]

Conclusion

Due to the implementation of the Nationality and Borders Act 2022, there are a host of reasons which further affect the issue of identification of trafficked victims. There were many implications for individuals wishing to be identified as a victim of trafficking. Individuals claiming asylum based on being trafficked must expressly provide information in a timely manner. Support is being reduced from 45 days to 30 which still satisfies the CofE Convention.

The implications for victims because of the Nationality and Borders Act 2022 are an increased burden on victims to provide evidence and information which may not be practically available and can create additional hurdles for victims to overcome to gain support from the State via positive identification and has the unintended consequence of more legitimate victims mistrusting the NRM and fearing authorities who can refer them.

There is no evidence to support the view that victims are 'gaming the system' by obtaining trafficking status under pretences with the Government's own figures showing that positive decisions have substantially reduced over the past year.

The Illegal Migration Act 2023

The Illegal Migration Bill was first introduced by the Government on 7 March 2023, dubbed as 'The Small Boats Bill.' The then-Immigration Minister, Robert Jenrick argued that "this Bill is vital to stopping the boats and preventing the dangerous, illegal, and unnecessary journeys across the channel. The Bill was passed by this House made it unambiguously clear to illegal migrants and people smugglers alike that, if they come to this country by unlawful means, they will not be able to stay. Instead, they will be detained and swiftly removed either to their home country or to a safe third country."[53] This would cover instances where individuals have arrived irregularly or spontaneously which would include the use of small boats.

The Act gained Royal Assent on 20 July 2023. The aim of this legislation is to criminalise people who make a claim for asylum and who have failed to do so through one of the safe and legal routes.[54] During the reading of the Bill, it was strategically thought that there are four policy objectives:

1. Deter illegal entry into the UK by making it clear that illegal entry will result in detention and swift removal to a safe third or home country;

2. Break the business model of people smugglers and save lives;

3. Promptly remove those with no legal right to remain in the UK;

4. Set an annual cap on the number of people admitted to the UK for resettlement through safe and legal routes.[55]

Clearly, the approach is to deter as many foreign nationals as possible from entering the UK to claim asylum and removing them out of the UK.[56] This is a new idea and one which cannot on effectiveness until fully implemented and the results seen in the years to come on the numbers of arrivals with this legislation in place. Consequently, there is a large degree of uncertainty associated with the desired deterrent outcome proposed by the Government.

Anyone who has entered the UK irregularly prevents them from being able to access the NRM, claim asylum, and is subject to detention and then removal from the UK. However, it has been found "that more than 90% of victims who claim to be trafficked have later been confirmed to be genuine."[57] The impact of detention on the mental health of trafficked victims has been found to be substantial.[58] Detention can raise several psychological issues. The time spent in detention could be time spent recovering from exploitation and being supported and empowered to cooperate with investigations and prosecutions given the important role victims play in successful trials.

For trafficked victims, this will mean that they will not be able to seek protection from modern slavery legislation,[59] or be potentially identified via the NRM.

The Impact on Victims of Modern Slavery

Not all of the sections in the Illegal Migration Act 2023 have not yet come into force until the pending litigation on the Rwanda policy is fully resolved by the Supreme Court. In November 2023, the Supreme Court ruled that the Rwanda plan was unlawful.[60]

It can be argued that the way in which foreign nationals enter the UK is becoming more important than the victim status of an individual. This can be substantiated by how Sections 22–29 Illegal Migration Act 2023 seeks to disapply the legislative provisions offered to individuals of human trafficking because of the method by which a foreign national has entered the UK illegally. In other words, the crossing of the Channel into the UK via a small boat will prevent that person from protection from modern slavery protections granted under the UK Government. This is unfair given how many victims are coerced into travelling to another location and therefore not in full control of their actions. Incidentally, many victims find themselves in debt bondage when they arrive in the UK, forced to pay off their debts of smugglers who have arranged and facilitated their travel followed by traffickers exploiting them at the destination. Individuals finding themselves in this situation will be subjected to a public order disqualification (which will be discussed below).

Public Order Disqualifications

Justification for the removal of protections has been based on the numbers of people losing their lives making the crossing,[61] the pressure on public services by asylum seekers through the large cost of accommodating asylum seekers and the increasing frequency of large numbers of people attempting to cross the English Channel using small boats.[62] There are several public order disqualifications which will be revoked. These include:

(a) any prohibition on modern slavery grounds on removing the person from the UK or requiring them to leave;
(b) any requirement on modern slavery grounds to consider the person for Temporary Permission to stay as a Victim of Human Trafficking or Slavery (VTS) in the UK;
(c) access to a recovery period or modern slavery-specific assistance and support and
(d) where a Conclusive Grounds Decision has not yet been made, a Conclusive Grounds Decision will not be made.[63]

This directly conflicts with Article 13 ECAT which obligates a "recovery and reflection period of at least 30 days, when there are reasonable grounds to believe that the person concerned is a victim. Such a period shall be sufficient for the person concerned to recover and escape the influence of traffickers and/or to take an informed decision on cooperating with the competent authorities. During this period, it shall not be possible to enforce any expulsion order against him or her."[64] The denial of support exposes the risk of the victim being subjected to exploitation as well as being in violation of their international obligations in this area. The other consequence for foreign victims who cannot have their immigration status regularised will be that they stay under the radar avoiding law enforcement but then they will be subjected to the types of examples under the 'hostile environment' which was discussed earlier in this chapter.

There will be an exception to the revoking of the public order disqualification in cases where that person who has arrived illegally in the UK but has a Reasonable Grounds Decision from the NRM. In these circumstances then the condition of stay is dependent upon whether the person cooperates with the investigation related to their exploitation.[65] If this is agreed then the person will not be removed from the UK and has 30 days of help and support from the NRM which in some cases can be extended. The balance is too heavily weighted in favour of the State rather than the victim, given the trust that the victim is expected to have that the State will protect them in exchange for their cooperation. The 'carrot and stick approach' can raise significant issues relating to the relationship between the State and the victim underpinned by trust in the respective rights and obligations of both. This approach creates a situation where the State is separating trafficked victims into two groups, firstly those individuals who wish to cooperate with authorities and those who do not. There are a host of reasons why victims may not want to cooperate with the police such as fear of reprisals or harm (or threats of harm) to their families. Therefore, this approach is somewhat disadvantageous to vulnerable victims in fear of what may happen in the future, and it is fundamentally unfair.

Section 22 provides for the power to remove trafficked victims of foreign nationality before the end of the NRM decision process. In cases where victims have a Reasonable Grounds Decision, but are awaiting a Conclusive Grounds Decision, then under the Statutory Guidance the victim can be removed which is a violation of Article 10(2) ECAT. Furthermore, it violates the State's obligation to protect credible victims who are at real risk of being exploited[66] and undermines the NRM mechanism.

Automatic Disqualification—Criminalisation of Trafficked Victims at the Expense of Low Prosecutions of Offenders

Section 29 sets out the restriction of modern slavery protection for foreign victims[67] who have been convicted in the UK of an offence[68] and have been sentenced to a period of imprisonment for the offence.[69] This provision overlooks the possibility that foreign nationals can be coerced and forced to commit offences under duress and consequently punished by the State at the expense of being protected, identified and have access to services and support under the ECAT. It further distracts from the fact that whilst criminalisation and secondary victimisation against foreign nationals take place, the trafficker remains to exploit victims with impunity.[70] This is supported by the present low numbers of prosecutions and convictions against traffickers in the UK,[71] where victims play a significant role in the criminal justice system by taking risks to give evidence against their traffickers which many are reluctant to do. Where victims are not protected and given the opportunity to cooperate with authorities safely, there is no possibility of the investigation taking place, no charge, no prosecution and no conviction results in the exploiters acting with impunity.

Foreign Nationals 'Gaming the System' Myth and the Impact of Not Being Able to Regularise Their Immigration Status and Being Sent to a Third Country

The Home Office published an impact assessment on the Illegal Migration Bill Impact Assessment.[72] The cost of detaining and keeping migrants in accommodation has estimated costs of £6bn to the UK taxpayer, signifying the urgency and public opinion this has on their electoral intentions at the next General Election.[73] There is significant concern that modern slavery provisions are being taken advantage of by unworthy migrants as a way of staying in the UK. The Home Office believes that the protections afforded by the NRM are being at risk of misuse and act as an incentive for those crossing the English Channel.[74] There is no factual evidence to support such claims that either the NRM is an attractive idea for individuals to take advantage of or the NRM being misused to gain entry and stay in the UK. Consequently, the language used remains rhetoric which has created legislation which directly impacts foreign individuals which are a vulnerable social group, existing in the UK.

It appears that foreign victims do consent to entering the NRM even though foreign nationals are exposed to being put on the radar meaning that the focus shifts from their status as a potential victim of crime but questions whether they are an offender due to the nature of their method into the UK. The mechanism could be argued as an important use by the State to identify those individuals who have made the journey across the Channel and deal with them as an offender rather than a victim of trafficking. It has been suggested that many more victims refuse consent to entering the NRM and choose to stay in an abusive, exploitative environment for the fear of potentially being identified as an illegal immigrant in the current hostile environment.[75]

Conflict with International Law—Article 4 Considerations

The European Convention on Human Rights has been incorporated into UK law through the Human Rights Act 1998. Article 4 of the European Convention on Human Rights states that no one shall be held in slavery or servitude and that no one shall be required to perform forced or compulsory labour.[76] In the case of *Siliadin*,[77] it was held that States have positive obligations "to adopt tangible criminal-law provisions that would deter such offences, backed up by law-enforcement machinery for the prevention, detection and punishment of breaches of such provisions."[78] Therefore, States must make provisions to investigate potential instances of trafficking when one comes to light, punish the perpetrators and protect the victim.[79] This requires a comprehensive legislative and administrative framework to deal with such cases. It is arguable whether the detection of potential victims of trafficking arriving in the UK by small boats is being screened by the Home Office. Authorities in England and Wales who have First Responder status (as the Home Office does) are under a statutory duty[80] to make a referral to the NRM.

Section 22 of the Illegal Migration Act 2023 grants the power for disapplying the modern slavery provisions (from Sections 61 to 65 Nationality & Borders Act 2022) even where a decision has been made by a Competent Authority that there are reasonable grounds to believe that the person is a victim of modern slavery.[81] Again, the justification for the withdrawal or restriction of such protections is based on factors including "the pressure placed on public services, the large numbers of irregular and dangerous journeys, including via small boat Channel crossings."[82] This has a negative impact on victims being able to either access support or have support continued by providers. It also will have a negative impact on identification levels as genuine victims who have been exploited because of arriving in the UK via a small boat will be dissuaded from self-identifying and wanting to be referred into the NRM. If a person is cooperating with an investigation or criminal proceedings,[83] if it is necessary for the person to be present in the UK to provide coopera-tion,[84] then victims will not be subject to Section 22(1(b). Consequently, traffickers will be able to manipulate and exploit victims and keep them hidden knowing that victims will be at risk of being deported if found by authorities. They will also be wary of victims going to the police and wanting to disclose their identities to law enforcement although in many cases victims will not want to do this out of fear and reliance upon the trafficker.

The legislation removes or limits help to potential victims of traf-ficking which may contravene the European Convention on Action Against Trafficking of Human Beings[85] and the UK's positive obligations under the ECHR. It will be interesting to see how if an action is brought by an individual the ECHR would deal with this issue and rule whether this section in the Illegal Migration Act violates Article 4 obligations.

Conclusion

It is clear to see that the Illegal Migration Act 2023 has the potential to have a detrimental effect on identifying foreign nationals in the UK who are victims of human trafficking. The impact will be largely seen through how the UK Government seeks to treat foreign nationals of traf-ficking differently by placing them in detention and removal alongside not allowing them access to the NRM or stopping support as part of the Mechanism based on the method of their entry into the UK which has been characterised as illegal. The NRM has not been previously discrim-inatory against the nationality of victims in the past, but now this is being brought into question because of how the Illegal Migration Act is drafted. UK victims continue to be unaffected by the new legislation, however it can be argued that foreign nationals are once again being subjected to a hostile environment due to the withdrawal of support the NRM offers or indeed the lack of access to the referral process which genuine victims have. A further impact of the legislation seeks to put the treatment of UK victims in direct contradiction against foreign nationals despite the same type of exploitation and abuse being suffered by both foreign nationals and UK victims.

2   Conclusion

As it has been shown, the impact of Brexit alongside the domestic legislation which the Government has brought through over the past few days has had serious implications on individuals seeking protection and support from the State. Whilst the true effects and consequences of Brexit will not be seen for a least a decade, the consequences from the enacting of the Nationality & Borders Act 2022 and the Illegal Migration Act 2023 will be seen far soon. The effectiveness of the laws will depend on the self-identification of victims and the efficient processing of migrants through the Home Office so that the vulnerable can be quickly identified and directed to appropriate services and support.

It has been shown that domestic legislation has made the hostile environment more aggressive and can be traced back to before the hostile environment policy was created in the early 2010s. There needs to be changes at the legislative, policy and practical levels to help maintain the balance of deterring illegal migrants to the UK with protecting victims of trafficking and exploitation by identifying them in a positive manner so that they can receive the help they are entitled to under international law.

What we have seen is that any proposals to criminalise migrants whilst protecting genuine victims cannot succeed given the thin distinction between a legitimate and illegitimate applicant. This is why screening processes are vital and why more resources are required to catch up on the backlog of asylum claims and process them in a timely manner alongside making NRM decisions. The current approach is neither succeeding nor productive given the increasing numbers of people.

The impact on the issue of identification of trafficked victims who are foreign nationals is potentially substantial. The fear of detention and deportation remains a significant reason why trafficked victims find it difficult to self-identify. There will be less incentive for foreign nationals who enter the UK illegally for the purpose of claiming asylum to self-identify if they know that they will not be referred into the NRM. In effect what the State has done through the legislation is to victimise their status as illegal immigrants at the expense of identifying more victims and taking them out of exploitative environments. Foreign nationals will be more wary and less trusting of the State, which is present at a low level. Consequently, the Illegal Migration Act 2023 will make self-identification even harder and create a vacuum whereby traffickers in the UK can continue to take advantage of vulnerable foreign nationals who enter the UK and keep them in an exploitative situation for longer. All the above measures can be seen to disadvantage genuine trafficked victims. Furthermore, they amount to distractions which favour traffickers acting with impunity. It is therefore safe to assume that the UK is a safe environment for traffickers to thrive in at the expense of trafficked victims who find themselves subjected to a hostile environment when it comes to being positively treated as a victim of crime and deserving of protection. This current dynamic requires to be flipped so that the attention remains on the protection of victims and prosecuting the offenders.

The next chapter examines the impact Covid-19 has had on the identification of trafficked victims. It will discuss the issues, barriers and challenges the pandemic posed for victims and authorities who had less contact and interaction with potential victims during the pandemic.

Notes

1. UK Government, "New Plan for Immigration: Legal Migration and Border Control," 21 May 2021, accessed at https://assets.pub lishing.service.gov.uk/government/uploads/system/uploads/attach ment_data/file/988518/FBIS_Strategy_Statement_-_Web_access ible.pdf.

2. Home Office, "Impact Assessment on the Illegal Migration Bill," 26 June 2023 at 1, accessed at https://assets.publishing.service. gov.uk/government/uploads/system/uploads/attachment_data/ file/1165397/Illegal_Migration_Bill_IA_-_LM_Signed-final.pdf.
3. Home Office, "Impact Assessment on the Illegal Migration Bill," 26 June 2023 at 6, accessed at https://assets.publishing.service. gov.uk/government/uploads/system/uploads/attachment_data/ file/1165397/Illegal_Migration_Bill_IA_-_LM_Signed-final.pdf.
4. Home Office, "Impact Assessment on the Illegal Migration Bill," 26 June 2023 at 7, accessed at https://assets.publishing.service. gov.uk/government/uploads/system/uploads/attachment_data/ file/1165397/Illegal_Migration_Bill_IA_-_LM_Signed-final.pdf.
5. M. Gower and G. Sturge, "Modern Slavery Cases in the Immigration System," House of Commons Library, Research Paper, 8 March 2023 found at https://researchbriefings.files.parliament.uk/ documents/CBP-9744/CBP-9744.pdf.
6. UK Government New Plan for Immigration, accessed at https:// www.gov.uk/government/publications/new-plan-for-immigr ation-legal-migration-and-border-control-strategy/new-plan-for-immigration-legal-migration-and-border-control-accessible#:~: text=At%20the%20heart%20of%20our,who%20arrive%20in% 20the%20UK.
7. OSCE, 'Trafficking in Human Beings: Identification of Potential and Presumed Victims A Community Policing Approach,' SPMU Publication Series Vol. 10, at 50.
8. GLA Conservatives Report, Shadow City 2013 found at http:// www.kalayaan.org.uk/wp-content/uploads/2014/09/Shadow-City.pdf.
9. Sections 13.10–13.3 Modern Slavery Guidance.
10. Sections 66 and 67 on Legal Aid will not be discussed in this book due to the complexity of the issue.
11. Home Office Press Release, "Alarming Rise of Abuse Within Modern Slavery System," 20 March 2021, accessed at https:// www.gov.uk/government/news/alarming-rise-of-abuse-within-modern-slavery-system and Molly Blackall, "Modern Slavery Crime Reports are 11 Times Higher Than in 2015, New Data

Reveals," 28 December 2022, accessed at https://inews.co.uk/news/modern-slavery-crime-reports-higher-new-data-1990343.

12. Official Statistics, Modern Slavery: National Referral Mechanism and Duty to Notify Statistics UK, End of Year summary 2022, published 2 March 2023 at Section 3.1.

13. Official Statistics, Modern Slavery: National Referral Mechanism and Duty to Notify Statistics UK, Quarter 1 2023—January to March 2023, published 4 May 2023, accessed at https://www.gov.uk/government/statistics/modern-slavery-national-referral-mechanism-and-duty-to-notify-statistics-uk-january-to-march-2023/modern-slavery-national-referral-mechanism-and-duty-to-notify-statistics-uk-quarter-1-2023-january-to-march.

14. UK Government Official Statistics, Modern Slavery: NRM and Duty to Notify Statistics, Quarter 1 2023—January to March, published 4 May 2023 at 3, accessed at https://www.gov.uk/government/statistics/modern-slavery-national-referral-mechanism-and-duty-to-notify-statistics-uk-january-to-march-2023/modern-slavery-national-referral-mechanism-and-duty-to-notify-statistics-uk-quarter-1-2023-january-to-march.

15. Official Statistics, Modern Slavery: National Referral Mechanism and Duty to Notify Statistics UK, Quarter 1 2023—January to March 2023, published 10 August 2023, accessed at https://www.gov.uk/government/statistics/modern-slavery-national-referral-mechanism-and-duty-to-notify-statistics-uk-april-to-june-2023/modern-slavery-national-referral-mechanism-and-duty-to-notify-statistics-uk-quarter-2-2023-april-to-june.

16. IOM's Analysis of National Referral Mechanism Data Following the Introduction of the Nationality and Borders Act, 18 October 2023, accessed at https://unitedkingdom.iom.int/news/ioms-analysis-national-referral-mechanism-data-following-introduction-nationality-and-borders-act#:~:text=Only%2053%25%20of%20Reasonable%20Grounds,the%20same%20period%20in%202022.

17. See NN & LP v SSHD (2019) EWHC 1003 (Admin) which stated that withdrawal of support after 45 days was incompatible with ECAT, and a new Needs Assessment process would need to

be followed detailing what type of support a recognised victim would require after a positive CGD.

18. See https://lordslibrary.parliament.uk/queens-speech-2022-home-affairs/.
19. Section 63(1)(a).
20. Section 63(1)(b).
21. IOM UK National Referral Mechanism—Data Analysis Briefing—2023 Mid-Year Review (January–June), 16 October 2023, accessed at https://unitedkingdom.iom.int/sites/g/files/tmz bdl1381/files/documents/2023-10/iom_uk_nrm-briefing_2023_midterm.pdf.
22. Under Section 32, if a person is sentenced to a period of imprisonment of at least 12 months, the Secretary of State can make a deportation order in respect of a foreign criminal.
23. UK Home Office, 'Modern Slavery: Statutory Guidance for England and Wales (under s49 of the Modern Slavery Act 2015) and Non-Statutory Guidance for Scotland and Northern Ireland,' July 2023, Section 14.231 at 169 accessed at https://assets.pub lishing.service.gov.uk/media/651e9cf17309a1000db0a8af/Mod ern_Slavery_Statutory_Guidance__EW__and_Non-Statutory_Guidance__SNI__v3-5_.pdf.
24. The criminalisation of victims will be extensively examined in Chapter 6.
25. Home Office figures accessed at https://www.gov.uk/government/news/over-320-foreign-criminals-and-immigration-offenders-ret urned#:~:text=In%20total%2C%20more%20than%20690,kid nap%20and%20possession%20of%20firearms show that more than 690 people have been removed on 8 charters and multiple scheduled flights since 1 January 2023.This includes over 450 foreign national offenders who were convicted of serious crimes including rape, supply of drugs, kidnap and possession of firearms.
26. Section 64(1) NBABA 2022.
27. D. Taylor, 'Revealed: Just 7% of Trafficking Victims Given Leave to Remain in UK,' The Guardian, 4 January 2022, accessed at

https://www.theguardian.com/uk-news/2022/jan/04/trafficking-victims-leave-to-remain-uk-data#:~:text=1%20year%20old-,Revealed%3A%20just%207%25%20of%20trafficking%20victims%20given,leave%20to%20remain%20in%20UK&text=Only%207%25%20of%20confirmed%20victims,data%20disclosed%20to%20the%20Guardian.

28. Group of Experts on Action against Trafficking in Human Beings (GRETA) Evaluation Report on the United Kingdom, Third Evaluation Round—Access to Justice and effective remedies for victims of trafficking in human beings, 20 October 2021 at 77.

29. As discussed in the previous chapter, there is a substantial backlog in the Home Office in asylum claims and therefore lengthy delays in asylum seekers receiving a decision on their asylum application.

30. R (KTT) v SSHD [2021] EWHC 2722 (Admin).

31. R (on the application of SSA (Ethiopia)) v SSHD 2021-LON-001894.

32. Modern Slavery: Statutory Guidance for England and Wales (under Section 49 Modern Slavery Act 2015) and non-statutory guidance for Scotland and Northern Ireland, 18 May 2023 at 15.194.

33. Section 65 Nationality & Borders Act 2022.

34. Home Office Guidance can be found here at https://assets.publishing.service.gov.uk/government/uploads/system/uploads/attachment_data/file/1161777/Temporary_Permission_to_Stay_for_Victims_of_Human_Trafficking_and_Slavery.pdf.

35. R (on the application of SSA (Ethiopia)) v SSHD 2021-LON-001894.

36. R (on the application of SSA (Ethiopia)) v SSHD 2021-LON-001894 at 16.

37. See Section 65 Leave to remain for victims of slavery or human trafficking.

38. Home Office Guidance, "Temporary Permission to Stay considerations for Victims of Human Trafficking or Slavery," 2 February 2023 at 10–11.

39. Council of Europe Convention on Action against Trafficking in Human Beings Warsaw, 16 May 2005 found at https://assets.pub lishing.service.gov.uk/government/uploads/system/uploads/attach ment_data/file/236093/8414.pdf.

40. Section 641 Nationality & Borders Act 2022—Explanatory Notes.

41. Home Office Guidance, "Temporary Permission to Stay considerations for Victims of Human Trafficking or Slavery," 2 February 2023 at 16.

42. Home Office Guidance, "Temporary Permission to Stay Considerations for Victims of Human Trafficking or Slavery," 2 February 2023 at 20.

43. Home Office Guidance, "Temporary Permission to Stay Considerations for Victims of Human Trafficking or Slavery," 2 February 2023 at 10.

44. Directive 2011/36/EU of the European Parliament and of the Council of 5 April 2011 on preventing and combating trafficking in human beings and protecting its victims and replacing Council Framework Decision 2002/629/JHA.

45. Section 4(1) Withdrawal Act 2018.

46. Article 8 EU Trafficking Directive.

47. Articles 11 and 12 EU Trafficking Directive.

48. Article 17 EU Trafficking Directive.

49. UK Government, Statutory Guidance for England and Wales (under s49 of the Modern Slavery Act 2015) and non-statutory guidance for Scotland and Northern Ireland, 18 May 2023 at Section 7.4.

50. UK Government, Statutory Guidance for England and Wales (under s49 of the Modern Slavery Act 2015) and non-statutory guidance for Scotland and Northern Ireland, 18 May 2023 at Section 14.52.

51. UK Government Statutory Guidance, July 23, accessed at https://www.gov.uk/government/publications/modern-slavery-how-to-identify-and-support-victims.

52. See Matrix Chambers, "SSHD Withdraws New Evidential Test for 'Reasonable Grounds' Decisions in Modern Slavery Statutory

Guidance," published 27 June 2023 found at https://www.mat rixlaw.co.uk/news/sshd-withdraws-new-evidential-test-for-reason able-grounds-decisions-in-modern-slavery-statutory-guidance/.

53. UK Parliament, Illegal Migration Bill, Hansard Volume 736: Debated on Tuesday 11 July 2023, accessed at https://hansard. parliament.uk/commons/2023-07-11/debates/5D96460C-A67B-4782-B74B-89BDD8ACE51A/IllegalMigrationBill.

54. Currently there are only safe and legal routes designed for nationals of Hong Kong, Afghanistan and Ukraine. There was a Syrian Refugee Scheme which was set up in 2015 but this was withdrawn in 2020. See Explanatory Notes—Illegal Migration Act 2023 at page 7 which states that between 2015 and March 2023, the UK has offered refuge to 511,998 people through safe and legal routes, as well as family members of refugees.

55. Home Office, "Impact Assessment of the Illegal Migration Bill," 26 June 2023, accessed at https://assets.publishing.service.gov.uk/ government/uploads/system/uploads/attachment_data/file/116 5397/Illegal_Migration_Bill_IA_-_LM_Signed-final.pdf.

56. The estimated costs incurred to relocate a foreign national of flights and escorts removing individuals arrived illegally in the UK amounts to £169,000 per person, as stated by Home Office, "Impact Assessment of the Illegal Migration Bill," 26 June 2023 at 25, accessed at https://assets.publishing.service.gov.uk/govern ment/uploads/system/uploads/attachment_data/file/1165397/Ill egal_Migration_Bill_IA_-_LM_Signed-final.pdf.

57. Helen Bamber Foundation, ATLEU, Focus on Labour Exploita-tion and Medical Justice, 'Abuse by the system: Survivors of Trafficking in Immigration Detention,' 4 October 2022, at 2 https://www.helenbamber.org/sites/default/files/2022-10/ ES_Abuse%20by%20the%20system_survivors%20of%20traffic king%20in%20immigration%20detention.pdf.

58. UK Parliament, "Written Evidence by the Taskforce on Victims of Trafficking in Immigration Detention," accessed at https://com mittees.parliament.uk/writtenevidence/114294/pdf/#:~:text=4% 20For%20trafficking%20survivors%2C%20immigration,deteri oration%20in%20mental%20health%20and.

59. Modern Slavery Act 2015.
60. R (on the application of AAA (Syria) and others) v Secretary of State for Home Office, Supreme Court judgment, 15 November 23, accessed at https://www.supremecourt.uk/cases/docs/uksc-2023-0093-etc-judgment.pdf.
61. See Home Office Factsheet on Illegal Migration, 20 July 2023, accessed at https://www.gov.uk/government/publications/illegal-migration-bill-factsheets/illegal-migration-bill-overarching-factsheet#:~:text=The%20Illegal%20Migration%20Bill%20will,asylum%20claim%20will%20be%20considered.
62. HM Government (2023) Illegal Migration Bill Explanatory Notes at 5.
63. Home Office, "Modern Slavery: Statutory Guidance for England and Wales (under s49 of the Modern Slavery Act 2015) and Non-Statutory Guidance for Scotland and Northern Ireland," July 2023, in Section 14.231 at 169.
64. Article 13(1) ECAT.
65. Jenrick, R (2023) 'Illegal Migration Bill' HC Deb. Vol. 736 col.207.
66. See Rantsev v Cyprus and Russia at para 286.
67. Section 29(4)(i) Modern Slavery Act 2023.
68. Section 29(4)(ii) Modern Slavery Act 2023.
69. Section 29(4)(iii) Modern Slavery Act 2023.
70. The criminalisation of trafficked victims will be examined further in Chapter 6.
71. See UK Home Office (2023) 'Crime Outcomes in England and Wales, Open Data April–December 2022' which state that between April to December 2022, less than 55 of modern slavery offences in England and Wales had resulted in either a charge or a summons.
72. Home Office Impact Assessment Illegal Migration Bill, accessed at https://data.parliament.uk/DepositedPapers/Files/DEP2023-0535/Illegal_Migration_Bill_Economic_Impact_Assessment_26.6.2023.pdf.

73. See "Illegal Migrants Plan Could Cost £6bn over Two Years, Say Government Projections," accessed at https://www.bbc.co.uk/news/uk-politics-65789136.
74. See Home Office Factsheet on Illegal Migration, 20 July 2023, accessed at https://www.gov.uk/government/publications/illegal-migration-bill-factsheets/illegal-migration-bill-overarching-factsheet#:~:text=The%20Illegal%20Migration%20Bill%20will,asylum%20claim%20will%20be%20considered.
75. See Modern Slavery & Human Rights Policy & Evidence Centre, "Explainer: The Illegal Migration Act Modern Slavery Provisions," 11 September 2023 at 7.
76. Article 4 ECHR. For further analysis of Article 4 see Guide on Article 4 European Convention on Human Rights, accessed at https://www.echr.coe.int/documents/d/echr/guide_art_4_eng.
77. Siliadin v France, Application Number: 73316/01, 25 July 2005.
78. Siliadin v France, Application Number: 73316/01, 25 July 2005 at para 71.
79. Guide on Article 4 European Convention on Human Rights, accessed at https://www.echr.coe.int/documents/d/echr/guide_art_4_eng at 16–21.
80. Section 52 Modern Slavery Act 2015.
81. Section 22(1)(b) Illegal Migration Act 2023.
82. Illegal Migration Act 2023 Explanatory Notes, at Section 147.
83. Section 22(3)(a) Illegal Migration Act 2023.
84. Section 22(3)(b) Illegal Migration Act 2023.
85. See Article 10 Identification of the Victims, Article 12 Assistance to Victims, Article 13 Recovery & Reflection Period and Article 14 Residence Permit.

5

The Impact of Covid-19 on the Identification of Victims of Human Trafficking in the UK

1 Introduction

The impact of Covid-19 left a transformative legacy on individuals, communities, and regions across the UK as well as the rest of the world. Many different types of vulnerable individuals from various social groups were detrimentally affected in many ways. These groups include refugees, undocumented migrants, asylum seekers awaiting decisions on their refugee applications, exploited workers and children and adults requiring safeguarding services and support. A further vulnerable group were trafficked victims who were especially impacted by the social restrictions during the pandemic, occurring at the same time as them being exploited by traffickers.

This chapter examines the impact Covid-19 has had on the identification of trafficked victims. The effect seen during the pandemic was that they had less opportunity to either self-identify themselves as victims or be identified by frontline agencies. Therefore, without individuals being identified, victims were not able to access the support and services required to assist them to initially escape from their exploitation and then start to recover from their traumatic experiences.

© The Author(s), under exclusive license to Springer Nature Switzerland AG 2024
M. Davis, *Identifying Victims of Human Trafficking*, Palgrave Studies in Victims and Victimology, https://doi.org/10.1007/978-3-031-61741-6_5

The pandemic in 2020 severely impacted different groups of people significantly in the UK in different ways, with "evidence showing that the pandemic has increased vulnerability to modern slavery all over the world, as many of the underlying drivers of modern slavery have worsened across many countries during the pandemic, such as poverty, inequality and unemployment."[1] This provided an opportunity for traffickers to profit from illegal forms of migration via lockdowns and to take advantage of restrictions on internal travel within borders. This resulted in many victims being trapped in exploitation. Social restrictions also had a negative impact on the number of trafficked victims being identified. It was found that "the number of detected victims fell for the first time in 20 years as the pandemic limited the opportunities and potentially pushed trafficking underground, while constraining law enforcement capacity to target the crime."[2] Globally, it has been estimated that there was a drop of 11% in the number of victims identified as trafficked in 2020 compared to 2019 with sexual exploitation and cross-border trafficking dropping by 24% and 21%, respectively.[3] These findings can be explained by the hidden nature of sexual exploitation which was driven even further underground during the pandemic alongside countries closing their borders because of the prohibition on international travel and restrictions on social movement. Whilst there was an increase of 3% in the number of male victims identified during the pandemic, there was a drop of 11% in the number of females identified.[4]

Despite the prohibition on travel other forms of illegal migration such as human smuggling continued during this period as the demand for services increased:

Research on specific migratory routes shows that Covid-19 related travel restrictions have not diminished and may, in fact, have increased demand for smuggling services in the medium to long term. Since the beginning of the pandemic, people on the move, including those leaving their countries of origin or stranded in transit, have experienced increasing difficulties in reaching their planned destination, with may resorting to the services of smugglers to cross borders.[5]

The overlap between these two global crime issues heightened the danger that some smuggled persons may have been at a greater risk of being trafficked at a later point as a way of them repaying their debt to their smugglers during this period. If a person had been smuggled during the pandemic, they would have been less visible to society and easier for the exploiter to take advantage of them. The impact on existing trafficked victims would have been the inability for many to access services and support through effective means of identification due to organisations changing their way of work to remote systems and employees being told to 'Stay At Home – Protect the NHS.'[6]

This section examines the impact Covid-19 has had on the nature and scale of human trafficking within the UK. It will identify the key drivers associated with vulnerability of people susceptible to trafficking and examine the consequences for existing victims in accessing specific types of support during the pandemic. This chapter also establishes how a new group of victims have been susceptible to trafficking because of the direct impact Covid has had on the changes of the economic and social way of life which was altered during the pandemic.

2   The Impact Covid-19 Has Had on Existing Victims of Trafficking in the UK

The UK has three distinct levels within its identification and detection policy framework for victims of modern slavery which arose from the UK incorporating its legal obligations under Article 10 Council of Europe Convention on Action against Trafficking (ECAT). The first are charities and organisations that come into contact with potential victims in their frontline work. The second are First Responders such as local authorities and the police who make referrals to the National Referral Mechanism (NRM). As referenced in the book, cases then pass to the third level who is the Single Competent Authority (SCA) or the Immigration Enforcement Competent Authority (IECA) who then make formal decisions as to whether an individual is a trafficked person or not by issuing Reasonable Grounds Decisions (RGD) and Conclusive Grounds Decisions (CGD).

The main impact Covid has had on victims has been the lack of opportunity to identify more individuals of trafficking and for victims to self-identify themselves. The predictable consequences associated with the issue of identification have been for many trafficked victims do not have the ability to escape exploitation and recover from their ordeal:

> The Covid-19 pandemic has created circumstances that may increase the risk of trafficking, inhibit identification of those who are trafficked and those who survive trafficking, and make it harder to deliver comprehensive services to support survivors' recovery.[7]

Given the impact of Covid on this issue, there were several different groups who were directly affected by Covid-19, consequently pushing them into further exploitation. These groups are primarily migrants and existing trafficked victims who were going through the National Referral Mechanism (NRM).[8] The specific impact on these groups will now be examined.

Individuals Exploited Within Specific Sectors of the Economy

Often, traffickers will exploit different types of individuals in various forms of exploitation using different forms of coercion and control methods. There were several exploitative environments within the UK economy where trafficked victims were coerced into working during the pandemic. Research has shown that "the majority of these cases were in labour abuse including a range of sectors including agriculture, factories, construction and also in commercial sex situations."[9] It has been acknowledged that trafficking for sexual exploitation was less detected during the pandemic with a 24% reduction in identifying victims of sexual exploitation.[10]

The Office for UK Statistics shows that 2.2 million people work in the construction industry.[11] It relies on skilled workers, many of which returned to the EU because of Brexit, resulting in a skills shortage in this area as well as other industries such as manufacturing and agriculture. An effect of Covid has been the shortage of workers to complete projects at a time when housing building and other construction projects were allowed to continue despite the pandemic. Many workers are recruited through agencies and have unclear contract terms and conditions, making their rights on pay, and conditions vague or non-existent. This was an issue before the pandemic.

Prior to Covid-19, Operation Cardinas was set up by the Metropolitan Police to investigate modern slavery which was taking place in the Southeast and London from 2009 to 2018. It led to 3 members of a Romanian family being convicted after earning an estimated £2.4 million from 33 businesses that were investigated which had between 300 and 500 victims being exploited.[12]

The Anti-Slavery Commissioner produced a report showing that there continued to be risks of exploitation within the construction sector, trapping many victims for a variety of reasons. These reasons are important to highlight because they explain why it is so difficult for victims of trafficking exploited within this sector to self-identify and why it was easier for traffickers to continue exploiting victims during the pandemic.

Many of the reasons why it is so difficult to self-identify vary according to the different exploitative environments victims find themselves in. The methods of control and coercion often differ too. For example, withholding pay or payments being made into bank accounts in the names of victims, but which the victim does not have access to. Workers can often be threatened with violence and intimidated with their family members at risk of harm if they do not comply with what the trafficker wants them to do. Victims are also often isolated when they are not working so they are prevented from going out in the evening. This makes any potential identification extremely difficult because of restrictions of movement and feelings of isolation.

There has also been evidence of widespread criminality taking place with traffickers able to exploit lapses in security and vetting procedures to ensure safety on construction sites. It has been common for victims to be coerced into fraudulently obtaining Construction Skills Certification Scheme (CSCS) cards showing fake qualifications with people lying that they have passed the required health and safety tests to work on construction sites. Additionally, "perpetrators have added minor qualifications to increase the hourly rate that their victims could earn. As a result, some victims were forced to work in high-risk environments, exposed to toxic materials without the training or knowledge to protect themselves or those around them."[13] Furthermore, it should be acknowledged that some non-UK workers if they are now classed as overstayers have been unable to return home, making them more vulnerable and at risk of trafficking due to the fact that their immigration status is now regarded as irregular.[14] This has made some workers liable to be exploited further for longer periods because of States tightening their sovereign borders, preventing travel, which made victims' situations precarious, illustrating a key driver of vulnerability. Victims were often treated inhumanely by being forced to continue working on construction sites, factories and other locations whilst being kept in sub-standard accommodation.

Moreover, the number of workplace inspections to measure compliance had not been taking place, leading to more instances of exploitation taking place within working environments which were deemed unsafe and did not protect labourers. In cases where breaches of unsafe workplace practices and procedures have occurred, they have not come to the attention of health and safety executives or law enforcement. Traffickers were able to act with impunity by taking advantage of this.

Often with the exploitative nature of trafficking, victims are moved around communities, towns and cities to meet the demand of a particular service. It is very difficult for law enforcement to build intelligence on the whereabouts of victims when their traffickers constantly transport them to another part of the country to other exploitative environment locations where there is significant demand for services provided by exploited people under duress from traffickers. The consistent and frequent movement of individuals being exploited across communities, regions and borders within the UK makes identification of victims by authorities extremely difficult. From the perspective of victims, they continued to be exposed and subjected to repeated harm and abuse in exploitative conditions, making escape extremely difficult.

The Impact on the Health of Migrants in Exploitative Environments and Trafficked Victims During the Pandemic

Victims of trafficking and people from vulnerable social groups having to work in poor working environments continued to be forced to continue working during the height of lockdown restrictions. This had a negative impact on their health if they contracted Covid.

Covid-19 is a serious contagious respiratory infection which spreads easily, requiring protections and precautions being taken by individuals, employees and employers. These safeguards were available to most citizens during the pandemic but were sadly not available to vulnerable groups and were continued to be exposed to the virus.

Their ability to be protected from contracting Covid-19 in the first place was also compromised. It was estimated that between 23 March 2020 and 23 September 2020, workers in labour abuse or exploitative situations were being made to work with a lack of personal protective equipment (PPE).[15] Furthermore, those individuals in exploitative environments were often exposed to the virus as "many had little access to or choice of whether to wear masks or to insist that others nearby do."[16] Testing was vital during this period, but victims neither had the opportunity nor were "reluctant to seek Covid-19 testing and medical support due to the fear that they will be detained and deported."[17] Additionally, victims were not able to access or have a very limited opportunity to become vaccinated despite the exposure to the virus within the high-risk environments that they were being forced to work in.

The Impact Social Distancing Had on Trafficked Victims Which Prevented Identification

Many people required health services during the pandemic placing them under significant pressure. Some health centres were closed or severely reduced their availability due to social restrictions. It has been acknowledged that "the barriers faced in closed settings in accessing services and finding their way in society highlight that some approaches to victim protection may serve to isolate and marginalise people rather than effectively reintegrate them into society."[18] The decline in victims' mental health who had previous experiences of being trafficked or were proceeding through the NRM occurred as "lockdowns and the isolation from friends and family increased anxiety, triggering memories of exploitative situations."[19] This situation has been referred to as an 'immigration lockdown' where victims are awaiting decisions from the NRM as to whether the UK has recognised their status as a trafficked victim or not.[20] Citizens were advised to stay away from hospitals and this narrative further excluded people who required medical attention who would have normally been seen. A direct consequence would have been for more victims to experience repeated and harsher abuse from traffickers during this period where they would have been at a higher risk of being in public and a chance that someone may have spotted that the individual(s) are being exploited.

Returning back to the issue of social distancing, the United Nations Office on Drugs and Crime (UNODC) feared that the restriction of travel as part of the lockdowns during the pandemic would "drive crime further underground and cause traffickers to adjust their business models."[21] As reiterated so far, social distancing has had a direct impact on victims as "there is a risk that they are not identified by first responders and may find it harder to access support."[22]

As a direct response to social isolation, there was a reduced chance and less opportunities for victims to be rescued and identified by First Responders. Police to social workers had fewer opportunities to identify and engage with possible victims, as time and resources were diverted to the Covid-19 response. Furthermore, there was a distinct lack of legal enforcement and criminal proceedings during the pandemic. This impacted the number of prosecutions being brought. Victims who wanted to obtain accountability from the offenders of traffickers via the criminal justice system were prevented from doing so as there were significant delays in the number of trials due to the closure of courts during the pandemic. This led to a backlog of trials which needed to be heard by courts after Covid social restriction measures had been relaxed.

One further consequence of social isolation was the inability of victims to have legal advice or continue to be advised on their cases. It has been stated that "without proper legal representation, victims of human trafficking might not gain formal recognition."[23] Victims need to prove their case and they rely on quality legal support to achieve this. The areas of advice victims require help and support on are welfare benefits, housing, debt advice as well as immigration and asylum advice.

Prior to the pandemic there have been issues with victims having access to legal services. The advice work is not covered by the existing legal aid regulations. The type of legal work required for victims is pre-NRM advice, where individuals are advised of what this process is about, advice about trafficking identification through the NRM, and advice on obtaining compensation as a victim of crime through the Criminal Injuries Compensation Scheme.[24]

The impact of social distancing from the pandemic has been that some victims (and indeed other vulnerable groups such as asylum seekers) have missed deadlines to submit evidence and appeals to challenge decisions. This would have affected their immigration status and/or being recognised as a victim of trafficking.[25] Moreover, many victims were unable to have contact with their advisers during this time meaning that their best interests were not being safeguarded and their cases progressing in the usual way. This was because of digital poverty and/or the unavailability of accessing/using the internet. The result has been intense anxiety which "can be extremely traumatising and survivors without the necessary support will often fail to recall the information that is essential to get the right NRM decision."[26] Restrictions to access of legal representation and delays in support had a detrimental impact on victims. It represents a negative environment for victims to live in, it stops their ability to recover from their ordeals from the exploitation and makes them vulnerable to being re-trafficked.

For foreign nationals who have been identified as trafficked, it is imperative that they regularise their immigration status. A positive Conclusive Grounds Decision (CDG) facilitates this opportunity. Foreign victims require a positive CDG so that it entitles victims to apply for the possibility of obtaining Discretionary Leave to Remain (DLR) to stay in the UK. This issue has been clarified in *R (On the application of K) v Secretary of State for the Home Department*:

With conclusive status, there is no automatic grant of discretionary leave for one year and one day, although this may be granted if the individual is co-operating with the Police or owing to their personal circumstances.[27]

The changes to obtaining temporary permission to stay in the UK were examined in Chapter 4. There have been several barriers to legal representation which have existed before Covid-19 but have since exacerbated because of the pandemic. Namely, these are the lack of access to the internet, and the unavailability of advisers to physically see victims face-to-face to obtain testimony to help prove that they are victims. This issue has been specifically detrimental to those victims in the early stages of proceeding through the NRM process.

Not only have trafficked victims been compromised by the restriction of advisers assisting them, but quite often other groups also rely on legal representatives to lodge appeals and review of decisions within specific timeframes. For example, "an appeal of an asylum decision must be made within 14 days and a judicial review of a negative Conclusive Grounds decision must be made within 3 months,"[28] giving rise to a heightened risk of asylum seekers becoming vulnerable to being trafficked during this period. Asylum seekers remain a vulnerable group to being trafficked whilst their cases for refugee status are being considered and decided upon. As part of any Asylum Screening certain questions are meant to be asked to ascertain the basis of their claim as a minimum requirement. These were as follows:

Question 3.1 "Why have you come to the UK?" and Question 3.3 "Please outline your journey to the UK."[29] The case of *DA v Secretary of State for the Home Department*[30] was brought as these two questions were omitted from the screening process by interviewees and was argued by the claimant was contrary to law as the risk of not identifying a potential victim of trafficking was higher. Due to the pandemic, the interviews were being conducted via telephone and due to last between 15 and 18 minutes. The responses to the two questions above would have meant that interviews were taking a lot longer, hence why these two questions were omitted. However, despite the adjustment to the operational measures which would have resulted from longer interviews, "the burden was held to be necessary and justified."[31] Furthermore, it was held that:

There was a serious risk of injustice and irreversible harm from those questions continuing to be unasked and unanswered. In particular, there were real risks through the absence of the asking of those questions, potential victims of trafficking who would otherwise be detected at the early stage of the screening interview would not be.[32]

In conclusion, the omission of the two questions from the interview was held to have been unlawful. This is also a question of what happened to many asylum seekers during this time. If they went missing. In November 2023, the Home Office were unaware of what happens to asylum seekers if they had their asylum applications disqualified for non-compliance.[33]

The Impact on Victims Seeking Help and Assistance During the Pandemic

The previous section examined the impact Covid-19 had on existing victims of trafficking. This section discusses the impact the pandemic has had on trafficked victims who were in difficult situations challenging decisions to withdraw support from the NRM. Discontinuation of support would make victims vulnerable to re-trafficking.

In the case of *NN & LP v SoS HD 2019*[34] it highlighted the necessity of ongoing needs-based assessments for victims. The case concerned applications for asylum made by two victims of human trafficking. One victim was from Albania who was trafficked to the UK, was held captive and repeatedly raped before being rescued in March 2017. The second victim was from Vietnam who was trafficked into the UK and was made to work on a cannabis farm. The UK Government had promised to remove the amount of time victims would have access to services and support, often known as the 45-day rule originating from the EU Trafficking Directive below:

Article 11 of the EU Trafficking Directive[35] requires States to provide support and assistance to victims of trafficking. Furthermore, Article 12(1) of the Council of Europe Convention on Action against Trafficking states that:

Each Party shall adopt such legislative or other measures as may be necessary to assist victims in their physical, psychological and social recovery. Such assistance shall include at least:

a. standards of living capable of ensuring their subsistence, through such measures as: appropriate and secure accommodation, psychological and material assistance;
b. access to emergency medical treatment;
c. translation and interpretation services, when appropriate;
d. counselling and information, in particular as regards their legal rights and the services available to them, in a language that they can understand;
e. assistance to enable their rights and interests to be presented and considered at appropriate stages of criminal proceedings against offenders;
f. access to education for children."[36]

In the UK, victims are entitled to £65 per week, accommodation (usually provided for by the Salvation Army) and access to a support worker. The 45-day rule was brought in by the Home Office in 2017 which increased the length of support from 14 days after a positive CGD. It was judged by charities and those working with victims that having only 14 days after receiving a positive Conclusive Grounds Decision was not enough and could indeed lead to a higher risk of persons being re-trafficked. This led to the change in policy.

So, it was argued by the claimants in *R (on the application of NN & LP)*[37] that the removal of the 45-day rule was in breach of the Trafficking Directive and the Council of Europe Trafficking Convention. More time was needed to recover and 45 days were not enough. In rebuttal, the Government advocated that there is a process of requesting an extension to the 45-day rule. However, during proceedings, the court found no evidence of a policy assessing what the criteria is to judge such extension and one is not forthcoming from the defendant, leading to the court being unsure of what the result would be for the claimants if they were to apply for such an extension.[38] The claimants responded by referencing evidence from support workers who outlined the benefits of continued support:

The 45-day deadline is very daunting for victims. Having built a relationship with their key worker, having felt safe and secure. Having received support to access the care that is needed, the prospect of that support no longer being there is a blow.[39]

The impact on the victim's progress to their mental recovery was also cited for justification of support to be continuous and consistent because victims experienced anxiety and 'complex trauma' meaning that progress does not always happen alongside a specific timeframe. There were important financial and practical considerations which must be considered if provision of support and services would continue, including the availability of support workers and the provision of accommodation. These would include the cost to the taxpayer of continuing financial resources to consistently provide care after the 45 days balanced with the risk of harm against the victim if support were to cease.

Nevertheless, it was held that removing help support after 45 days would be prejudicial to victims and is incompatible with Article 12 of the Council of Europe Convention on the basis that it would cause "a serious risk of irreparable harm to victims of human trafficking who received positive Conclusive Grounds determinations"[40] if support ended after this time. Consequently, the Government was forced to drop the 45-day limit on supporting trafficked victims, reassuring victims that care would continue after this time which would be a positive result knowing that help would be available and provide continuity with their support and service providers, enabling victims to continue their recovery from their previous exploitation and lessen the risk of them being re-trafficked or falling into less secure environments where exploitation could re-occur.

The implications of the judgement meant that the present system would be replaced with a needs-based assessment[41] detailing what services and support are required for the victim to start their recovery. The consequences resulting from this change meant that victims were entitled to specific services but were unable to have access to them because of the Covid-19 lockdown restrictions. Now that Covid has receded, focus needs to re-apply to the individual needs assessments and then follow up with practical support for victims. This is difficult given the additional pressures on social care and the NHS seen since the reopening of society and through the lenses of Brexit where we are starting to see decreased labour in low wage environments such as the care and health sector.

Other Social Issues

Victims with existing mental health issues often rely on daily routine and predictability to ensure their mental wellbeing. As a result of the persistent lockdowns, this meant that "individuals were not able to employ their usual coping strategies and were at risk of developing negative coping strategies, such as substance abuse."[42]

Moreover, the pandemic was likely to affect certain racial and ethnic minority communities disproportionately. This could be seen through higher unemployment, lower incomes and higher housing costs compared to the majority population.[43] In severe cases people had been made homeless. This is a factor associated with the higher chance of being vulnerable to trafficking.[44]

Homelessness remains a massive social issue in the UK. According to Shelter, there were 276,000 people who were homeless in the UK and there are 126,000 children.[45] Victims of human trafficking are not often regarded as a being a group in priority need. Under the Homelessness Code of Guidance for Local Authorities,[46] victims will not be seen as in priority need even though they have a positive grounds decision. The weight attached to a positive Conclusive Grounds Decision bears no significance to whether they should be prioritised as in need of housing. What is required is a more detailed analysis of what makes a particular victim of trafficking vulnerable to be persuasive to local authorities with the assistance of legal assistance, demonstrating a positive need requiring victims to have safe and secure housing, provided by councils. As discussed, the availability and accessibility of legal representation during the pandemic have been severely restricted, marginalising this type of vulnerable group and heightening the risk of existing victims rescued or out of exploitation being pushed back into exploitation. Section 8(3) Homelessness Reduction Act 1996 Homelessness Code of Guidance law on preventing homelessness should be amended to include victims of modern slavery (regardless of whether victims are UK Nationals or Non-Nationals) to recognise their vulnerability to local authorities.

The availability and accessibility of not-for-profit law centres have diminished over the past decade.[47] Victims require quality legal representation so that they know their rights. The nature of this work requires time for the adviser and the victim to build a level of trust due to the vulnerability of the victim. Due to social restrictions either interviews or case work could take place denying victims from having the representation they require.

The ongoing cost of living crisis presents a significant and real risk to many people who are economically marginalised in the UK. These groups include those on benefits, those with disabilities and those in low paid work and receiving in-work benefits such as Universal Benefit. Survivors of human trafficking who have been positively identified through the National Referral Mechanism are entitled to £35 per week and those survivors who have an existing asylum seeker application are entitled to £65 per week. With the increasing costs of inflation and the downturn in the economy, people in vulnerable groups are finding it difficult to buy essentials. Consequently, they become more vulnerable to being drawn to riskier forms of employment which are less secure or are exploitative in nature.

Victims who have been identified as trafficked are still compromised because of less services being available. The impact is that this slows down the recovery period for victims to recover from their ordeal and may retraumatise them with the interruption of services provided to them before the pandemic or if they have been recently identified the start of their treatment and services as part of their needs assessment.

Even where prosecutors are seeking criminal convictions of those offenders involved in exploitation during this period, there are substantial delays in conducting trials which is hampering victims being able to see justice being done through successful prosecutions during these delays.

In conclusion, it is argued that the situation we are left in is that as a result of Covid-19 more victims found it more difficult to be rescued or indeed self-identify during the pandemic meaning that more victims are being hidden and continue to be exploited.

Not only has the pandemic had a negative impact on existing victims, but it has also been seen that a new group of individuals have been pushed into being exploited because of the pandemic. This issue will now be examined.

3   The Impact Covid-19 Has Had on Vulnerable Individuals, Pushing Them into Exploitation

As we know, human trafficking is a crime which takes place in the shadows of society. The business model of traffickers is to target and take advantage of vulnerable people by exploiting them for profit. The World Bank approximates that between "40 to 60 million people will be pushed into extreme poverty due to the pandemic."[48] This signifies the challenges going forward to combat a growing phenomenon prior to the pandemic.

Due to the pandemic, traffickers have had to adjust how they commit this crime and facilitate the continuation of exploiting vulnerable persons. The way traffickers recruited victims and operated during the lockdown period will give clues on the types of people most vulnerable to being trafficked and exploited. For instance, the use of online technology has been a huge facilitator for criminals with the greater utilisation of the internet through social media and communication to reach people in the absence of social contact and take advantage of the restrictive and isolated environment in which social contact took place. Furthermore, the dark web has been used by "cyber-sex traffickers to utilise the COVID-19 pandemic to target vulnerable children especially as many are not in the safe environment of schools. It is also possible that abuse at home may increase where people try to make money to fill the gap created by the economic impact of COVID-19."[49] There is a nexus between the need for exploiters to continue making money during the pandemic and the facilitation of finding new ways to exploit victims can be clearly seen here. The UK National Crime Agency, Europol and Interpol have all identified crime diversification which has focussed on cannabis cultivation in private homes or business premises and online fraud.[50] The lack of face-to-face contact has meant that it has been extremely difficult for more victims to be clearly seen and be rescued from exploitative conditions and for victims to have the trust and confidence to self-identify themselves to those authorities who can keep them safeguarded. There may have been instances where this has happened, and suspects have come to the attention of law enforcement. However, even where some offenders have been arrested and charged, there would have been a high risk of suspects absconding from bail, hampering the prospect of successful prosecutions taking place during the pandemic.

Many people (both UK nationals and those with irregular status) may have been suffering from a host of societal pressures prior to the onset of Covid including issues such as inequality and poor opportunities to work and employment, mental health issues and homelessness. It has been acknowledged that the pandemic has created significant additional inequality between groups arising from a combination of social, structural and other factors.[51] For some the pandemic served as a pretext to exacerbate and intensify these sociological issues. The themes of vulnerability (of individuals within disadvantaged communities), accessibility of support (through State structures such as the NRM) and safeguarding (from local authorities) are relevant to the following discussion. Without acknowledging and understanding them in detail, it will be difficult to fully comprehend how Covid has impacted society in various ways, increasing the risk of re-trafficking and exploitation amongst individuals within vulnerable groups across communities, towns and cities in the UK.

Consequently, it is not inconceivable that more people have become more vulnerable to trafficking because of the impact of Covid-19. It has been argued that "Covid-19 highlights what we already knew to be true: that economic, social and structural inequalities render some people more vulnerable than others."[52] These issues represent wider consequences for not only victims and those vulnerable to trafficking during the pandemic but also in the medium and long term as society will have a greater understanding of the effects of Covid-19 in the exploitation of people during this period.

The direct impact of the pandemic on individuals and groups can be seen through two perspectives, the economic aspect (where there were redundancies, shutdowns of factories and offices) and from the social perspective (because of the social distancing rules and movement restrictions). Economic and social consequences arising from the pandemic have been the key drivers of vulnerability. The economic impact of Covid may have led to more persons becoming vulnerable during this period. Many factors are present which can lead to vulnerable people being exploited. Despite the UK Government bringing in the Furlough Scheme for UK businesses, some people lost their jobs or were unable to find employment during this time, providing them with either with no other means of income, or severely reduced income. Additionally, many people who were reliant on specific health, education and housing support which had stopped during the pandemic would have put some individuals at a disadvantage in adapting to the lockdown. Consequently, some individuals would have become members of marginalised groups living in the UK who are at more risk of becoming exploited during this period, specifically because of their vulnerability. The many marginalised groups include (1) the unemployed, (2) those recently unemployed, (3) the homeless and those people made homeless as a direct consequence of the pandemic (i.e. because of the loss of their job), (4) children in the care system and those children not having formal education because they are not in school, (5) vulnerable adults (such as the disabled or handicapped, people with mental health issues, drug and alcohol issues), (6) asylum seekers and refugees, (7) irregular migrants (who were unable to return home) and (8) sex workers who may have either been coerced or felt as if they had no choice but to take more risks accepting clients who pose a risk to them physically or may have Covid-19.

The legacy of Covid-19 was the lockdowns encompassing the widespread social restrictions. This limited our ability to continue our normal social and economic way of life. The pandemic presented a unique and ideal opportunity for traffickers to continue their criminal activities with impunity and capitalise on the restrictive environment to entice more vulnerable people into exploitation through a variety of means which are often hidden from law enforcement.

The methods employed by traffickers had a direct impact on the ability of people in marginalised groups who were pushed into exploitation because of Covid-19. It also has an impact on those victims who presently remain exploited and continue in a cycle of exploitation now that societies have once opened again socially and economically.

A further consequence is the negative impact Covid-19 played on the ability of more individuals to come to the attention of First Responders who can make an NRM referral so that they can be recognised as a trafficked victim and able to access specific services and support. These will now be discussed in terms of the impact on adults and the impact on children.

The Impact on Adults

The impact of the pandemic has affected individuals as well as communities. A significant need and service for anyone in any well-ordered society is the ability to access healthcare. During the pandemic, access to NHS care was severely restricted due to the priority of the NHS treating patients of Covid. Surgery appointments, consultant appointments and cancer care were compromised due to the focus on tackling Covid of patients entering hospital with the condition and existing patients contracting the virus whilst in a hospital setting. The UK Government's slogan from January 2021 of 'Stay At Home, Protect the NHS, Save Lives' across radio, TV and social media impacted those people who were in dire need of such services, leaving them with no access whatsoever, leading to a higher risk of alienation and not engaging with society.

As a result of the lockdown in the UK, many people were excluded from society. Social exclusion was a substantial challenge for people to deal with. Fear of contracting the virus along with other people not wishing to be near other people led to some people losing the physical connection some people required to maintain a healthy lifestyle. The effect of social distancing impacted some individuals who valued social interaction was distinctly discouraged during the pandemic. The need to have conversations with people or meet up physically could have led to vulnerable people seeking out people who were harmful to them. They could take advantage of them, many of which they would never have interacted with them previously during normal societal times. But for the pandemic new associations may have been damaging for people pushed into exploitation may never have occurred.

One impact on communities because of Covid-19 has been on social groups where young people would have been disbanded and suspended for months, taking away the enjoyment of the structure some people relied upon. The loss felt by individuals within these communities because of Covid should not be underestimated as they impacted negatively on thriving communities becoming less outward and engaging and rather inward and cautious. This effect would have damaged the social fabric of how the communities existed and, in some ways, fragmented the strong bonds held by individuals and groups collectively working together to provide safer communities for individuals and families.

Charities would have done their best but were overwhelmed because of increased demand not being met by the State. Often non-profit groups do bridge the gap which the Government cannot fill but were placed in different situations where they did not have the capacity to help as demand outstripped supply for their help, advice and support. Not only would new people wish to access already inundated services, but this also raises the risk of re-exploitation as "diminished and overwhelmed state and non-state organisations will place victims at risk of not being identified and, even if identified, there are challenges in accessing front-line services, including longer term support."[53]

Many women and some men would be subjected to a further risk of domestic violence or the continuation of increased violence at home. A second group of individuals who would have also been severely compromised and affected by the lockdown would have been children who will now be examined.

The Impact on Children

It was observed that children were less likely to become seriously ill because of contracting Covid-19 than adults. Nevertheless, it has been said that children had been severely affected by the societal measures imposed by the Government to combat the virus. Specifically, this can be evidenced by the decision to close schools, affecting the majority of students during the pandemic. Children of key workers and those deemed at risk and safeguarded were still attending school during this period. However, many thousands of children were home-schooled during the pandemic. Not only did some children miss out on their education, but the restrictions meant that they missed out on the opportunity to play and socialise with friends, associate at youth clubs and enjoy hobbies and activities, impacting their social, emotional and psychological development.

It has been estimated that at the peak of the pandemic, some 1.6 billion children globally were out of school. Some of those "children and teenagers were particularly at risk of becoming victims of e-trafficking due to a combination of poverty, the closing of schools and an increase of time spent online."[54] Children are often identified as a vulnerable group because they are reliant upon someone to keep them safe and satisfy their basic needs.[55] Those children already receiving support were judged to have been at risk, leading to the possibility of more children going missing from care. Prior to the pandemic, "NGOs and scholars had raised concerns about the number of trafficked or potentially trafficked children going missing in the care of local authorities."[56] The disruption in services during the pandemic would have had an adverse consequence for some vulnerable children not being able to receive previous services and support.

The closure of schools during the early stages of the lockdown significantly impacted the development of children's education. Despite the best attempts of the Government to roll out initiatives for laptops for families who could not afford them, not every child had the access to digital forms of technology to facilitate their education. In some cases, third sector organisations assisted to ensure children were not left behind in their learning. Digital poverty increased the possibility of poorer children becoming excluded from their education, leaving them exposed to becoming vulnerable, which in turn gave rise to an increased likelihood of young children falling into exploitation alongside already vulnerable children falling into deeper cycles of exploitation. In summary, it has been acknowledged that "whilst the full impact of the pandemic on the exploitation of children remain an incomplete picture, research identified already marginalised children as a population at an elevated risk of online exploitation or re-exploitation."[57] One such area of child criminal exploitation is county lines exploitation.

The Home Office has described the phenomenon of 'county lines exploitation' as 'gangs and organised criminal networks involved in exporting illegal drugs into one or more importing areas within the UK, using dedicated mobile phone lines. Exploited victims of this crime often use various modes of transport to move drugs from dealers to purchasers. Despite the reduction of rail commuters and travellers during the pandemic, British Transport Police reported that they had not seen a reduction of activity involving juvenile drug runners on trains.'[58] Due to being visible by authorities, traffickers have adjusted their tactics by forcing exploited victims to move drugs using other forms of transport including cars especially to specific deserted towns:

> ...the supply of drugs from metropolitan centres to provincial or seaside towns now more commonly involved medium bulk deliveries in cars rather than sending boys down on empty trains and buses where they would be more likely to be spotted by authorities.[59]

They are likely to exploit children and vulnerable adults to move and store the drugs and money and "they will often use coercion, intimidation, violence (including sexual violence) and weapons."[60] From a victimological perspective we have two types of victims. The first is the person trafficking the drugs around regions and the second are victims of 'cuckooing' where criminals run their operation from the house of a vulnerable person.

It can be difficult to detect this crime due to how the harm starts from the onset, affecting people with drug and/or alcohol issues, those with mental health or physical health issues and those vulnerable within society such as those with prior experience of abuse. The process of 'cuckooing' is where criminals take over a property and then run a drugs operation from there, after either starting an emotional relationship with them or deceiving them into using the property in exchange for some benefit, usually alcohol or drugs. Not only is it difficult to detect but in the same way trafficked victims often find it difficult to self-identify, victims of county lines are often scared of reporting this issue to the police for fear of repercussions.[61] Additionally, vulnerable victims are easier to control and manipulate, keeping them hidden from law enforcement.

In 2021, "2,053 county lines referrals were flagged, a 23% increase from last year. County lines referrals accounted for 16% of all referrals received in the year. The majority (76%; 1,551) of these referrals were for male children."[62] Furthermore, it has been shown by the Office for National Statistics that "boys who received a positive Reasonable Grounds Decision (RGD) were most likely to have been criminally exploited (62%) while girls were most likely to have been sexually exploited (42%)"[63] making males more exposed to the risk of being exploited by county lines opposed to females were more likely to be exploited sexually. Having said that, it has been reported that females were being recruited to obtain hire vehicles with clean driving records and used as a preference over boys to avoid suspicion from police, many of which had been victims of sexual exploitation.[64]

Different children were affected by the pandemic in different ways depending upon the affluence of their parents. When schools closed, they lost many things which schools provide including "emotional support and life skills to, for some, regular meals."[65] Children from more financially stable backgrounds were able to adapt better than those who encounter poverty and inequality, especially in terms of affecting their ability to access digital technology to facilitate their learning. Affluent children were less compromised by the disruption the pandemic caused to their education and in most cases less reliant upon State services. In contrast, Covid-19 impacted those families with children who were already living in poverty and with low living standards. This reflects that there was a need to provide for themselves and lending themselves to county lines exploitation where "victims were argued to have agency and can in itself be seen as rational behaviour because they were being rewarded socially and financially"[66] for the crimes they were committing under duress, making it difficult for them to see themselves as exploited and consequently self-identify as victims of crime.

Children of key workers still attended school, but many groups of children were not at school and identified as vulnerable may be at risk of being dragged into exploitation as they were alone and isolated for long periods. This can often be fair to say especially if a child lost a parent from Covid-19, making the impact of bereavement a significant challenge for children not to be taken advantage of during this disruptive period. As so many schools were closed or partially closed during the pandemic teachers were unable to safeguard vulnerable children and identify those children potentially at risk, especially to child criminal exploitation.

It appears that conditions were very favourable so that the crime has been able to be committed with impunity during the pandemic. Consequently, the way in which the UK wishes to punish this type of offence and protect victims must start with drafting a specific law to make it a criminal offence to exploit children. This would illustrate a positive obligation to guarantee children from being subjected to slavery and forced labour. Presently, there is no statutory criminal law offence of child criminal exploitation. Currently, child criminal exploitation is basically covered under existing similar type of legislation including the Modern Slavery Act (2015), the Children and Young Persons Act 1933, the Child Abduction Act 1984 and the Children Act 1989. However, a specific stand-alone criminal law provision would be most helpful to distinguish the offence and categorise it sufficiently, due to the forced nature of county lines exploitation.

4   Conclusion

As it has been shown, it has been possible to identify certain themes, patterns and trends as to the impact Covid has had on the identification of trafficked victims in the UK. However, it has been difficult to ascertain to what extent has something really happened to the accurate levels of exploitation within the UK because of Covid-19. This is largely because of the hidden nature of the crime and the lockdown which was the UK Government's response to combatting Covid-19. The extent to whether trafficking has been driven underground and been simply hidden from the view of society will likely not be seen in the short term. As businesses and workers within cities and communities reopen across the UK, a likely measure of the impact Covid has had may be the publication of the numbers of individuals either self-identifying as trafficked victims or the numbers of individuals being formally identified by the State. Consequently, the patterns and trends seen from NRM data remain uncertain to predict. However, what is clear is that modern slavery continued to thrive in some sectors during the pandemic. Certain industries which were kept open still had workers exploited within them. These included industries such as manufacturing, agriculture and construction continued to operate through the pandemic, alongside services such as car washes and nail bars. The sectors which had levels of exploitation attached to them were businesses which require workers who have vulnerable immigration statuses and enterprises which demand a low pay remuneration attached to them. There is evidence to suggest that victims were moved from one sector to another and still being exploited. This shows that there was a shift in the supply and demand in some sectors during the pandemic, prolonging the exploitation of some workers. It always shows how adaptable traffickers are in changing their methods of exploitation and business models to continue their organised criminal networks.

A major health issue for victims is that many would have been exposed to Covid-19 because of a lack of PPE, and the lack of opportunity to be vaccinated. Moreover, critical services such as hospitals and law enforcement were moving resources towards the combatting the impact Covid-19 had on State support, creating a perfect environment for exploiters to continue exploiting people with impunity. This exacerbated the conditions for trafficking to flourish. Consequently, identification of individuals as victims of trafficking became a significant issue. In summary, traffickers have taken advantage of the pandemic at a time when support services and those likely to encounter potential victims have been closed or severely restricted due to dealing with Covid-19. Additionally, resources combatting trafficking had to be moved away to deal with enforcement of Covid-19 laws and guidance.

Whilst the situation remains unclear as to the level of trafficking during the pandemic, there is evidence to show that there have been more people becoming vulnerable to exploitation during this period. The circumstances leading to Individuals being pushed into more precarious work environments presented themselves during this period. With the present cost of living crisis alongside the demand for low skilled workers to fill the gap after Brexit, the combination of these factors may result in more individuals who were previously just about getting by now exposed to being exploited and feeling as if they have no choice.

Notes

1. O. Hesketh & O. Johnstone, "Impact of the Covid-19 Pandemic on Modern Slavery," Modern Slavery & Human Rights— Policy & Evidence Centre, Modern Slavery PEC Policy Brief 2021–2024, November 2021, at 4.
2. UNODC, 'Global Report on Trafficking in Persons 2022,' at III.
3. UNODC, 'Global Report on Trafficking in Persons 2022,' at 17.
4. UNODC, 'Global Report on Trafficking in Persons 2022,' at 18.
5. UNODC, "Covid-19 and the Smuggling of Migrants: A Call for Safeguarding the Rights of Smuggled Migrants Facing Increased Risks and Vulnerabilities" 2021 at 8.
6. Government Guidance on Covid-19—Staying at Home and Away from Others, accessed at https://assets.publishing.service.gov.uk/media/5eb130b4d3bf7f6521c3f6e1/Staying_at_home_and_away_from_others__social_distancing_.pdf.
7. J. Todres, "Covid-19 and Human Trafficking—the Amplified Impact on Vulnerable Populations," (2021), JAMA Paediatrics, Volume 175. Number 2.
8. The National Referral Mechanism is the formal process the Home Office must identify whether an individual is a trafficked person or not. This framework was created in 2009 as a response to the UK's

legal obligation from Article 10 Council of European Convention on Action Against the Trafficking of Human Beings 2005.

9. Unseen, "Modern Slavery During the Covid-19 Pandemic," 2022 accessed at https://www.unseenuk.org/wp-content/uploads/2021/10/Modern-Slavery-during-Covid-19.pdf at 1.

10. See UNODC, 'Global Report on Trafficking in Persons 2022,' at IV.

11. See Office for National Statistics (2021), 'Construction Statistics, Great Britain: 2020' at https://www.ons.gov.uk/businessindustryandtrade/constructionindustry/articles/constructionstatistics/2020.

12. E. Crates, "Operation Cardinas and Beyond: Addressing Exploitation Risk in the Construction Sector," Independent Anti-Slavery Commissioner, April 2022 at 9.

13. E. Crates, "Operation Cardinas and Beyond: Addressing Exploitation Risk in the Construction Sector," Independent Anti-Slavery Commissioner, April 2022 at 12.

14. UNODC, "The effects of the Covid–19 Pandemic on Trafficking in Persons and Responses to the Challenges—A Global Study of Emerging Evidence," at 33.

15. Unseen, "Modern Slavery During the Covid-19 Pandemic," 2022 accessed at https://www.unseenuk.org/wp-content/uploads/2021/10/Modern-Slavery-during-Covid-19.pdf.

16. UNODC, 'Global Report on Trafficking in Persons 2022,' at 17.

17. UNODC, 'Global Report on Trafficking in Persons 2022,' at 39.

18. M. McAdam, "Vulnerability, Human Trafficking & Covid-19—Responses and Policy Ideas," ASEAN—Australia Counter Trafficking at 32.

19. O. Hesketh & O. Johnstone, "Impact of the Covid-19 Pandemic on Modern Slavery," Modern Slavery & Human Rights—Policy & Evidence Centre, Modern Slavery PEC Policy Brief 2021–2024, November 2021, at 6.

20. O. Hesketh & O. Johnstone, "Impact of the Covid-19 Pandemic on Modern Slavery," Modern Slavery & Human Rights—Policy & Evidence Centre, Modern Slavery PEC Policy Brief 2021–2024, November 2021, at 6.

21. N. Newson, "Covid-19: The Impact on Human Trafficking," House of Lords Library, 10 July 2020 found at https://lordslibr ary.parliament.uk/covid-19-the-impact-on-human-trafficking/.
22. Ibid.
23. All-Party Parliamentary Group for Human Trafficking and Modern Slavery Inquiry into the Impacts of Covid-19—Recom-mendations with Explanatory Notes.
24. For further research about the issues and impact surrounding the difficulties trafficked victims face in having legal representa-tion, please see ATLEU (Anti Trafficking and Labour Exploitation Unit) report, "It has destroyed me: A legal advice system on the brink," October 2022. https://drive.google.com/file/d/15xlzaXCp N2eyXSIw7Ubx2Au1lr6mRXRF/view.
25. An asylum seeker has 14 days to appeal an asylum decision and 3 months to challenge a negative NRM decision via judicial review.
26. Issues arising from the inquiry initiated by the Human Trafficking Foundation at the request of the All Party Parliamentary Group found at https://www.humantraffickingfoundation.org/appg-cov id19-inquiry.
27. R (on the Application of K) v Secretary of State for the Home Department [2015] EWHC 3688 at para 53.
28. "All-Party Parliamentary Group for Human Trafficking and Modern Slavery Inquiry into the impacts of Covid-19—Recom-mendations with Explanatory Notes," found at https://static1.squ arespace.com/static/599abfb4e6f2e19ff048494f/t/5ee20e01f150 6573c802453f/1591873026531/APPG+Recommendations+fol lowing+Covid-19+Inquiry.pdf.
29. Home Office, "Asylum Screening & Routing," Version 7.0, 28th June 2022 at 17.
30. DA v Secretary of State for the Home Department [2020] EWHC 3080 (Admin).
31. DA v Secretary of State for the Home Department [2020] EWHC 3080 (Admin) at para 9.
32. DA v Secretary of State for the Home Department [2020] EWHC 3080 (Admin) at para 9.

33. R. Syal, "Home Office 'Loses' 17,000 People Whose Asylum Claims Were Withdrawn," *The Guardian newspaper*, 29 November 23, accessed at https://www.theguardian.com/world/2023/nov/29/home-office-loses-17000-asylum-seekers-registered-in-britain.
34. R (on the application of NN and LP) v SSHD [2019] EWHC 1003 (Admin).
35. Directive 2011/36/EU of the European Parliament and of the Council of 5 April 2011 on preventing and combating trafficking in human beings and protecting its victims, and replacing Council Framework Decision 2002/629/JHA.
36. Article 12(1) Council of Europe Convention on Action against Trafficking of Human Beings, 2005.
37. R (on the application of NN and LP) v SSHD [2019] EWHC 1003 (Admin).
38. R (on the application of NN and LP) v SSHD [2019] EWHC 766 (Admin) at para 17(b).
39. Ibid at para 27.
40. R (on the application of NN and LP) v SSHD [2019] EWHC 1003 (Admin) at para 27.
41. Home Office Modern Slavery: Statutory Guidance for England and Wales (under s49 of the Modern Slavery Act 2015) and Non-Statutory Guidance for Scotland and Northern Ireland, Version 2.10, June 2022 at 66.
42. Above n1 at 6.
43. Office for Democratic Institutions and Human Rights (ODIHR), 'Guidance—Addressing Emerging Human Trafficking Trends and Consequences of the Covid-19 Pandemic,' at 27.
44. Ibid. at 101.
45. Figures from Shelter, "274,000 People in England Are Homeless, with Thousands More Likely to Lose Their Homes," found at https://england.shelter.org.uk/media/press_release/274000_peo ple_in_england_are_homeless_with_thousands_more_likely_to_ lose_their_homes.

46. Chapter 8, Homelessness Code of Guidance for Local Authorities found at https://assets.publishing.service.gov.uk/media/5ef9d8 613a6f4023cf12fc67/current_Homelessness_Code_of_Guidance. pdf.

47. The All-Party Parliamentary Group for Human Trafficking and Modern Slavery Inquiry into the impacts of Covid-19—Recommendations with Explanatory Notes acknowledge that there were only 47 law centres in England and Wales, compared with 94 back in 2013–2014.

48. Office for Democratic Institutions and Human Rights (ODIHR), 'Guidance—Addressing Emerging Human Trafficking Trends and Consequences of the Covid-19 Pandemic,' at 8.

49. "Covid-19 and Potential Implications on Human Trafficking and Other Forms of Modern Slavery Internationally," Hope for Justice, April 2020 at 8–9.

50. See INTERPOL (2020). INTERPOL Issues International Guidelines to Support Law Enforcement Response to COVID-19, available at https://www.interpol.int/News-and-Events/News/ 2020/INTERPOL-issues-international-guidelines-to-support-law-enforcement-response-to-COVID-19.

51. See E. Such A. Gardner, M. Dang, N. Wright, L. Bravo-Balsa, V. Brotherton, H. Browne, N. Esiovwa, E. Jimenez, B/ Lucas, E. Wyman & Z. Trodd, "The Risks and Harms Associated with Modern Slavery during the Covid-19 Pandemic in the United Kingdom: A Multi-Method Study," Journal of Human Trafficking, 8th April 2023.

52. M. McAdam, "Vulnerability, Human Trafficking & Covid-19—Responses and Policy Ideas," ASEAN—Australia Counter Trafficking at 2.

53. "Covid-19 and Potential Implications on Human Trafficking and Other Forms of Modern Slavery Internationally," Hope for Justice, April 2020 at 7.

54. Save the Children, "Covid-19 Crisis Has Pushed Child Trafficking Online and Out of Sight," https://www.savethechildren. net/news/covid-19-crisis-has-pushed-child-traffickers-online-and-out-sight-%E2%80%93-save-children.

55. A. Bagattini, "Children's Well-being and Vulnerability," Ethics and Social Welfare, 13:3 at 211.
56. L. Lundy, T. Kirk, F. Gordon, A. Dunhill & A. Kidd, "Responses to Child Victims of Modern Slavery in the United Kingdom,": "A Children's Rights Perspective," (2020) Child & Family Law Quarterly, 23(2), 119–139.
57. E. Jimenez, V. Brotherton, A. Gardner, N. Wright, H. Browne, N. Esiovwa, M. Dang, E. Wyman, L. Bravo-Balsa, B. Lucas, M. Gul, E. Such, Z. Trudd, "The Unequal Impact of Covid-19 on the Lives and Rights of the Children of Modern Slavery Survivors, Children in Exploitation and Children at Risk of Entering Exploitation," (2022) Children & Society, 00: 1–19 at 13.
58. J. Grierson & A. Walker, "Gangs Still Forcing Children into 'County Lines' Drug Trafficking," The Guardian found at https://www.theguardian.com/uk-news/2020/apr/13/gangs-still-forcing-children-into-county-lines-drug-trafficking-police-covid-19-loc kdown.
59. S. Harding, "How Gangs Adapted to Coronavirus—and Why We May See a Surge in Violence as Lockdown Lifts," The Conversation, found at https://theconversation.com/how-gangs-adapted-to-coronavirus-and-why-we-may-see-a-surge-in-violence-as-loc kdown-lifts-140653.
60. Criminal Exploitation of Children and Vulnerable Adults: County Lines Guidance, Home Office Guidance, September 2018, found at https://assets.publishing.service.gov.uk/government/uploads/system/uploads/attachment_data/file/863323/HOCountyLine sGuidance_-_Sept2018.pdf.
61. A.G. Williams & F. Finlay, "County Lines: How Gang Crime Is Affecting Our Young People," (2019) Arch Dis Child; 104: 730–732 at 730.
62. Figures found from Official Statistics Modern Slavery: National Referral Mechanism and Duty to Notify statistics UK, End of Year Summary 2021, published 3 March 2022.
63. Office for National Statistics, Statistical Bulletin, "Child Victims of Modern Slavery in the UK: March 2022," 29 March 2022.

64. B. Brewster. G. Robinson, B. W. Silverman, D. Walsh, "Covid-19 and Child Criminal Exploitation in the UK: Implications of the Pandemic for County Lines," (2021) Trends in Organised Crime, at 8.
65. D. Gurdasani, C. Pagel, M. McKee, S. Michie, T. Greenhaugh, C. Yates, G. Scally & H. Ziauddeen, "Covid-19 in the UK: Policy on Children and Schools," BMJ, 31st August 2022, at 1.
66. K. Olver & E. Cockbain, "Professionals' Views on Responding to County-Lines Related Criminal Exploitation in the West Midlands, UK," (2021) Child Abuse Review, Vol 30: 347 at 353.

6

The Prosecution and Criminalisation of Trafficked Victims

1   Introduction

The previous chapter examined the impact Covid-19 had on the self-identification of trafficked victims along with the issues, barriers and challenges associated with identification during the pandemic. The following two chapters will examine the way trafficked victims come into contact with the criminal justice system and will evaluate how trafficked victims are being misidentified as offenders and then unfairly charged, detained, prosecuted and punished by the State for criminal offences whilst being coerced and controlled by traffickers into that criminal conduct, rather than recognised as potential victims and referred into the National Referral Mechanism (NRM). This situation where the State sanctions victims through 'secondary victimisation' prevents effective identification and results in traffickers escaping criminal liability.

The two-point approach of punishing modern slavery offences against perpetrators whilst simultaneously detecting and identifying victims of trafficking arising from the exploitation carried out by offenders is often overlooked. Prosecuting traffickers is no more important than identifying victims. Both must occur in order for the State to meet its Article 4 ECHR legal obligation simultaneously to punish instances of

© The Author(s), under exclusive license to Springer Nature Switzerland AG 2024
M. Davis, *Identifying Victims of Human Trafficking*, Palgrave Studies in Victims and Victimology, https://doi.org/10.1007/978-3-031-61741-6_6

modern slavery and forced labour[1] whilst protecting the rights of trafficked victims. Where victims of trafficking are prosecuted for offences committed under duress, it undermines any Government strategy in combatting trafficking as traffickers are simply able to get away with their crimes and commit them with impunity.

The most recent data on prosecutions against traffickers comes from the United Nations Office on Drugs and Crime (UNODC). In 2020 there were 17,635 people investigated, suspected or arrested by Member States. There were 10,257 people prosecuted and 2,858 persons convicted of human trafficking.[2] It has been reported that "since the introduction of the Modern Slavery Act 2015, there has been almost 47,000 modern slavery crimes recorded within England and Wales, and throughout 2022/2023, there are just over 3,700 live investigations."[3]

Trafficked victims often encounter the criminal justice system as suspects who have committed criminal offences under duress as part of their exploitation by their traffickers. This is because they are often misidentified, not as a victim, but as an offender, exposing them to being prosecuted under the law for sexual offences like prostitution, drug offences, theft or offences against the person including murder. They may not have known that they have committed a criminal offence, and are blind to the illegal conduct they have been involved in. Comprehensively, the issues outlined below show that the criminal justice system is ill-equipped to deal with behaviour of individuals who on the one hand are victims of crime (as a result of being trafficked and exploited) and on the other an offender in the eyes of the law and are at risk of being arrested, charged, prosecuted and convicted for serious offences. As crimes are committed intrinsically linked to their exploitation, this raises the question of how the present situation lends itself to protecting and safeguarding victims of trafficking whilst acknowledging that they have committed serious criminal offences (albeit under compulsion and duress).

Despite there being a non-prosecution legal obligation from States against victims of trafficking, there is a large degree of inconsistency within the law and this impacts on how victims are treated differently. Despite there being a statutory defence under Section 45 Modern

Slavery Act 2015 to protect victims from prosecution, there are problems with this defence when applied in practice which fails to adequately protect victims and for trials to continue through to conviction and sentence. Consequently, it is difficult for the UK to demonstrate a consistent victim-centred approach protecting victims from trafficking. Throughout this chapter it is vital to keep remembering that individuals involved in trafficking are both a victim and an offender at the same time. This dynamic is very difficult for the criminal justice to deal with appropriately. Prosecution often leads to victims being punished, rather than being recognised as trafficked victims, preventing survivors from having access to rights and entitlements they are legally obliged to receive as they have been positively identified by the State in the correct way. A failure to observe the rights of survivors through prosecution at the expense of identification amounts to 'secondary victimisation,' compounding the trauma victims experienced at the hands of traffickers.

This chapter will examine the international law in this area of non-prosecution of victims and to what extent the legal instruments instruct States to honour their international legal obligations to prosecute victims.

This chapter will argue that trafficked victims should not be prosecuted because they lack the requisite moral culpability to justify the imposition of the criminal sanction. There are, in principle a number of defences available to survivors if they are charged with criminal offences. However, it will be argued that the statutory defence available (examined in the next chapter) to victims is inadequate in a range of different ways and thus fail to provide such persons with the protection. We will see that the statutory legal defence does not provide victims with sufficient protection against criminal liability.

The following chapter will argue that the best way to protect a trafficked victim is to not be in the position where they have to rely on defences and not be prosecuted in the first place. The chapter will examine how important the decision by prosecutors to prosecute is, and the crucial role prosecutors and defence representation play in identifying trafficked victims before a trial starts. We will see how there is still a lack of awareness of human trafficking within the legal profession, relying on Third Sector Organisations (TSOs) to help protect the interests of victims. I will show how the identification of victims by prosecutors, defences and judges has often occurred too late in criminal proceedings, meaning victims have been prosecuted by the State rather than being referred and identified by the NRM. I will examine existing gaps in the current procedure which could be filled by a trafficking advocate who is available to prosecutors to ensure that the decision to prosecute is the correct one, considering whether an individual is a trafficked victim. Victims deserve to have their criminal liability diminished if they have been exploited and held under duress and coerced to commit criminal offences and therefore, they should not be held morally culpable.

By the end of these two important chapters, it will be clear to see how victims have been prosecuted, whilst the traffickers are able to get away with crimes of great severity. To combat human trafficking—and indeed associated crime committed also by victims—the State must concentrate on prosecuting those traffickers who are truly culpable. Traffickers should be held accountable for their actions via or by way of prosecution. From the perspective of victims, the non-criminalisation of this specific social group is justifiable from a human rights standpoint and persuades more victims to cooperate with law enforcement in the prosecution of traffickers, rather than fearing the State who they rely upon for protection from additional harm. Furthermore, it is not in the interest of the State to sanction a victim, especially when they have already been exploited by a non-state actor. It is neither in the interest of the victim nor the State to have inadequate defences because the fear of prosecution will prevent potential victims from coming forward. Where prosecutions are taking place at the expense of referrals to the NRM shows that the State is not presently adopting a victim-centred approach to identify trafficked victims.

2   Non-prosecution of Trafficked Victims—States' International Obligations

There are a host of existing trafficking offenders and organised criminal groups manipulating and coercing vulnerable individuals into exploitation. These associations are organised groups,[4] business type organisations[5] and less structured such as an individual trafficker(s).[6] Convictions against those in business type organisations and individual traffickers are more common than against organised crime groups. Most traffickers convicted are men[7] and most traffickers are aged between 23 and 36.[8] There has been a drop of 44% in the number of convictions against traffickers globally since 2017.[9] Between 2017 and 2020 of those investigated for a trafficking offence, the conviction rate is only 12% which is much lower now than the period between 2008 and 2012 when the conviction rate was 24%.[10]

As we will see later in the chapter, there is a tendency to overlook the criminal activities of organised groups and place more attention on the specific individual committing criminal offences. In many cases this results in overlooking the status of the individual as a victim and prioritising the criminal liability of what the victim has done rather than understanding the reasons behind why the criminal behaviour by the specific individual has taken place.

There are four sets of international legal obligations relating to the non-prosecution of victims of trafficking committing criminal offences as consequence of the situation they find themselves in. I will look at what the UN advocates from two legal instruments. Firstly, I will look at the *UN Convention against Transnational Organised Crime*.[11] Secondly, I will examine the *UN Protocol to Prevent, Suppress and Punish Trafficking in Persons, especially Women and Children*.[12] Thirdly, I will assess the regional approach set out in the *Council of Europe Convention on Action against Trafficking in Human Beings*.[13] Finally I will examine the European Union's approach to this issue through *Directive 2011/36/EU in 2011 on preventing and combatting trafficking in human beings and protecting victims*. We will see that these instruments do not adopt the same approach to the issue of non-prosecution. The issue of non-prosecution is complicated by the fact that the language used in the legal instruments are different. Non-prosecution is often referred to as non-criminalisation, non-punishment and non-prosecution in different international obligations with varying approaches, demonstrating a vague intent regarding the issue of non-prosecution from a legal perspective.[14]

In this chapter I will refer to the term 'non-prosecution' more than the term, 'non-criminalisation' and 'non-punishment.' I have taken this approach to highlight the risk to victims being prosecuted by the State for offences carried out under duress whilst being exploited. The principle of non-criminalisation is a contentious one and an area which requires greater discussion.

The UN Convention Against Transnational Organised Crime and the UN Protocol to Prevent, Suppress and Punish Trafficking in Persons, Especially Women and Children

The *UN Convention against Organised Crime*[15] does not contain a non-prosecution principle to protect individuals who are forced to commit criminal offences as part of their exploitation. However, UNTOC obligates States to ensure effective protection and assistance to victims and witnesses of organised crimes along with granting witness protection.

The United Nations (UN) Protocol UN Protocol to Prevent, Suppress and Punish Trafficking in Persons, especially Women and Children is also silent on the issue of non-prosecution of trafficked victims but mentions the issue of criminalisation from the perspective of States legislating for domestic criminal law prohibiting the trafficking in persons for the purpose of exploitation. Article 5 states:

> Each State Party shall adopt such legislative and other measures as may be necessary to establish as criminal offences the conduct set forth in article 3 of this Protocol, when committed intentionally.[16]

The Protocol focusses upon the obligation of States to legislate for the criminalisation of human trafficking, rather than offering protection to trafficked victims from the criminal law. The approach in UNTOC is understandable, given a State's main function is to protect its citizens from threats and the obvious way of doing this is to criminalise acts as a means of deterrence. However, the fact that the Protocol offers no immunity from criminalisation is surprising. The forced criminality by victims exposes them to the possibility of States prosecuting and punishing them. This course of action would amount to a misidentification of the individual as a victim of crime and would amount to secondary victimisation by the State. It would have been an opportunity for drafters of both instruments to balance a crime control approach seen in UNTOC with a human rights approach in the UN Trafficking Protocol, showing how each approach could complement one another.

Despite many trafficked victims committing breaching of immigration laws, falling foul of prostitution legislation and violating drug laws during the period of their exploitation, the UN Trafficking Protocol fails to effectively protect victims from detention or deportation. It has been acknowledged that in some situations, trafficked victims are often prosecuted for offences due to their illegal entry in another country.[17] Any victim-centred approach advocated on behalf of victims will be met with resistance from States that will always favour a crime control approach to punishing individuals for offences against other people or against the State, such as the offence of smuggling. The need for victims to be granted protection from criminal liability is evidenced by the UN which issued *Recommended Trafficking Principles and Guidelines for trafficked victims*.[18] These guidelines advocate that victims should not be prosecuted for offences whilst committed as part of their exploitation:

Trafficked persons shall not be detained, charged or prosecuted for their involvement in unlawful activities to the extent that such involvement is a direct consequence of their situation as trafficked persons.[19]

The guidelines are stronger and more explicit in protecting victims than the text in the UN Protocol. A second example of soft law is the *Model Law against the Trafficking in Persons drafted by the UN Office for*

Drugs and Crime (UNODC).[20] Article 10 of the Model Law recognises the criminal offences victims may be involved in but also aims to protect trafficked victims by ensuring that they:

> ...are not prosecuted or otherwise held responsible for offences, be it criminal or other, committed by them as part of the crime of trafficking, such as working in or violating regulations on prostitution, illegally crossing borders, the use of fraudulent documents and so on.[21]

We can clearly see how the victim-centred human rights approach is recognised through soft law instruments by the UN. Furthermore, the Organisation for Security and Co-operation in Europe[22] (OSCE) advocates that "such legislation should take into account a human rights approach to the problem of human trafficking, and include a provision for the provision for the protection of the human rights of victims, ensuring that victims of trafficking do not face prosecution solely because they have been trafficked."[23] Nevertheless, States continue to hold the power as to whether they take a punishable view against migrants who may be trafficked or choose to take moral responsibility to identify them.

The Council of Europe

In 2005, the Council of Europe (CofE) introduced the *Convention on Action against Trafficking in Human Beings*.[24] The UK ratified the Convention on 17 December 2008 and has been in force since 1 April 2009. The Council of Europe Convention explicitly addresses the complex issue of non-criminalisation of victims. Amongst other legal obligations to identify[25] and assist victims,[26] there is an obligation upon States not to prosecute victims of trafficking for offences which they have been coerced into committing.

Article 26 states:

> Each Party shall, in accordance with the basic principles of its legal system, provide for the possibility of not imposing penalties on victims for their involvement in unlawful activities, to the extent that they have been compelled to do so.[27]

The non-prosecution principle is complex because "States have discretion in as much as it does not stipulate that States must not impose penalties."[28] This is shown by the insertion of the word, 'possibility' in Article 26 offering States the discretion to impose sanctions against an individual. It has been argued that the "non-punishment of victims for offences they have committed as a consequence, or in the course, of being trafficked is an essential element of such a human rights approach."[29] However, the provision in Article 26 refers to 'penalties,' but the term has not been defined. Therefore, it is not clear as to what these penalties are or what they are referring to. This is no guidance on what types of offences, committed by victims should be covered by this safeguard. Furthermore, Article 26 neither distinguishes between the terms of non-punishment from non-criminalisation. However, what is clear in terms of its effect is that there is no presumption of immunity from prosecution. This is explained in *R v LM, MB, DG, Betti Tabot and Yutunde Tijani*,[30] which clarified Article 26:

> It does not say that no trafficked victim should be prosecuted, whatever offence has been committed. What it says is no more, but no less, than that careful consideration must be given to whether public policy calls for a prosecution and punishment when the defendant is a trafficked victim and the crime has been committed when he or she was in some manner compelled to (in the broad sense) to commit it. Article 26 does not require a blanket immunity from prosecution for trafficked victims.[31]

It has been argued that "police investigators need to ensure that when they identify potential victims they should take a victim-centred approach and start with the premise that the person in the exploitative situation is a potential victim and not a criminal."[32] Furthermore, if a risk of prosecution remains, it may prevent other potential victims from coming forward to cooperate with authorities.[33]

Regrettably, whilst it does not define 'penalties,' the possibility of a prosecution taking place against a victim exists.[34] It would have been more useful to determine what is meant by penalties and this could have been done within the explanatory notes to the Convention. On the other hand, Article 26 does recognise that trafficked victims are often compelled to commit criminal offences. One final note on this is whether historical victims of trafficking (individuals who have been trafficked but are no longer exploited or have escaped but may be dealing with the trauma of their exploitation) should be regarded as victims who require some degree of protection. In applying this situation, the case of *R v LM; YT; BT; DG; MB*[35] distinguished between a person living a relatively normal life free of exploitation from a trafficked victim who committed offences to escape with the former situation not deserving of having a conviction overturned whereas the latter being more likely to succeed.

The European Union

Two years after the UN Protocol was drafted, the European Union (EU) drafted their first legislation on combatting trafficking. The Framework Decision on Combatting Trafficking in Human Beings[36] focussed on addressing the seriousness of the crime of human trafficking by obligating States to impose criminal sanctions on offenders.[37] This Directive was criticised for not providing effective cooperation between States and agencies. It was subsequently replaced by *Directive 2011/36/EU in 2011 on preventing and combatting trafficking in human beings and protecting victims*. This came into effect in the UK on 6 April 2013. Article 8 of this Directive (which is currently binding in UK law) gives prosecutors discretion in their decision to prosecute or impose penalties on victims. Article 8 further states:

> Member States shall, in accordance with the basic principles of their legal systems, take the necessary measures to ensure that competent national authorities are entitled not to prosecute or impose penalties on victims of trafficking in human beings for their involvement in criminal activities which they have been compelled to commit as a direct consequence of being subjected to any of the acts referred to in Article 2.[38]

The EU Directive recognises the link between advocating a human rights perspective to protecting victims which will encourage them to trust the police and assist prosecutors in investigations. It also advocates that secondary victimisation of victims should not take place:

Victims of trafficking who have already suffered the abuse and degrading treatment which trafficking commonly entails...should be protected from secondary victimisation and further trauma during the criminal proceedings. Unnecessary repetition of interviews during investigations, prosecution and trial should be avoided, for instance, where appropriate, through the production, as soon as possible in the proceedings, of video recordings of those interviews.[39]

In contrast to the CofE Convention, the EU Directive does distinguish between the two issues of non-prosecution and penalties, and requires victims to be protected by Member States:

Victims of trafficking in human beings should, in accordance with the basic principles of the legal systems of the relevant Member States, be protected from prosecution or punishment for criminal activities such as the use of false documents, or offences under legislation on prostitution or immigration, that they have been compelled to commit as a direct consequence of being subject to trafficking. The aim of such protection is to safeguard the human rights of victims, to avoid further victimisation and to encourage them to act as witnesses in criminal proceedings against the perpetrators.[40]

It further recognises that victims should not be prosecuted for offences committed under duress. However, it does not compel non-prosecution, but rather requires that non-prosecution, or the non-imposition of penalties is an option available to the relevant authorities. It has been argued that "the obligation of non-punishment is therefore ultimately tied to the State's obligation to identify, protect and assist victims of trafficking."[41] This can be seen from the case of *Rantsev v Cyprus and Russia*[42] where "the State's human rights obligation includes having in place legislation adequate to ensure the practical and effective protection of the rights of victims or potential victims of trafficking."[43]

Conclusion

As it has been seen from the discussion of the international legislation above, there is a lack of consistency between each legal instrument on the non-punishment principle, making it difficult to adopt an international legal consensus on implementing the right legislative reforms into domestic law. The approach undermines the effectiveness of the non-punishment principle. Furthermore, it contributes to a lack of clarity on this very important issue for trafficked victims regarding them existing in coercive environments. The UN Protocol obligates each State to criminalise the act of human trafficking but does not obligate each State to legislate for the non-prosecution of trafficked victims. Soft law evidenced from the Recommended Guidelines and Principles and the Model Law on Human Trafficking offers victims stronger protection from prosecution if States choose to adopt this guidance.[44] The CofE offers a more victim-centred approach to combatting human trafficking and explicitly provides for the obligation of each State to offer protection from punishment and not impose penalties on trafficked victims. However, understanding what amounts to non-punishment remains problematic. The confusion leads to a lack of distinction between what is meant by non-punishment and how non-prosecution fits in with the CofE's intent. In contrast, the approach seen from the EU Directive is more explicit in their protection of trafficked victims from prosecution, and punishment, but even this measure does not prohibit prosecution or the imposition of penalties.

As far as international law obligations are concerned then it will be appreciated that the relevant measures do not provide a uniform approach, and at best they require the possibility of non-prosecution or the non-imposition of penalties being available. At present, there is a greater need for "clear and specific legislation and policy guidance to support full and effective implementation of the non-punishment principle."[45] There is still plenty of room for manoeuvre for States with a large degree of discretion to draft their own domestic laws whilst still being compliant with their obligations. Thus, a State would be in compliance with its obligations in international law and EU law. In any of the following situations, when a potential trafficked victim comes to the attention of the State, it then has the following options. Firstly, the State can choose not to prosecute a victim. Secondly, they can choose to prosecute and make defences available which may help trafficked persons secure an acquittal. Thirdly, a state could prosecute the person, and upon a finding of guilt, may permit the trafficking context to be taken into account for the purposes of sentencing so as to reduce or negate any punishment which would ordinarily be applied if that context did not exist.

The rationale behind the non-punishment principle is that it does not provide blanket immunity. It recognises that trafficking victims lack real choice in a trafficking situation, where courts should look at whether there is a realistic alternative for the victim but to commit the crime.[46] The justification for victims to have protection from the non-punishment principle by States is that victims can be exposed to further victimisation from the criminal justice system at the expense of them being recognised as a victim of crime. This can lead them to be traumatised after their initial exploitation and criminalisation amounts to a form of 'secondary victimisation.' As can be seen from the next section there are various types of offences committed under duress by victims and the conclusion drawn so far is that where individuals have little or no choice but to commit offences, they are not adequately protected well enough and will be exposed to the risk of prosecution and punishment. These are identified as status offences, consequential offences and liberation offences.

3   Status vs Consequential vs Liberation Offences

A distinction can be made between the three types of offences committed by victims. These require further discussion as it is important to acknowledge the differences and dynamics between them to understand the situation that trafficked victims find themselves at various points of their trafficking journey either at the beginning, during their exploitation, and where they are seeking escape from their trafficker(s). As we shall see, all types of offences can be connected and overlap in some way at various points. Importantly, they need to be acknowledged from the law enforcement perspective that the circumstances surrounding the criminal offences are important to consider.

Where victims are trafficked across international borders, forged or expired visas and passports are often used as a means of gaining entry into a State. These are examples referred to as 'status offences.' They can often be immigration offences and include false statements and disclosure of false documents or certificates to deceive border control officials. The purpose of committing such offences is to gain entry into that country. Victims are then frequently placed under debt bondage and forced to work to pay off these debts through engaging in consequential offences.

Consequential offences are different from status offences because they are committed by victims under duress by their traffickers. As we know, there are several frequent criminal offences committed by victims as part of their exploitation. These include prostitution,[47] theft[48] and cultivation of cannabis plants.[49] Other examples of offences include thefts and burglaries, benefit fraud, handling offensive weapons, money laundering offences and driving offences (vehicles being registered in victims' names). Victims are put under duress by traffickers to commit these acts and it can be said that they take place as a direct consequence of the exploitative situation. The committing of these offences financially benefits the trafficker, although the victim may be given some small material financial reward but in most cases the money is earned to be used to pay off a debt to the trafficker. As acknowledged, "the victims merely serve as agents or instruments while the traffickers are the directing minds behind the offending but without any direct involvement in the commission of individual offences."[50]

In addition, there may be criminal offences committed by victims where traffickers force or deceive victims into moving to a country or in situations where victims are seeking to escape from a current exploitative situation by fleeing to another State. These are known as liberation offences because they are immigration in nature. These acts include possessing and using a forged passport or identification document.[51] An illustrative case can be seen from *R v O*,[52] where a female Nigerian national was trafficked and sexually exploited into the UK but was arrested trying to leave using a false identity card.

Liberation offences have a different dimension and can be more serious in nature. Due to the captative environment victims find themselves in over a long period of time they may resort to using violence and weapons against their exploiter(s). A slow build up of wanting to leave the exploitative environment and improve their situation along with the feeling as if they have no choice but to escape due to their desperation.[53] In other situations, it has been seen that some victims become offenders themselves, carrying out the same behaviours as their traffickers by recruiting, deceiving and exploiting other individuals, a phenomenon which has not been presently researched in much detail.

4   The Illegitimacy of Prosecuting Trafficked Victims

The previous section examined the international obligations which regard non-prosecution of trafficked victims and the types of offences committed by victims as part of their exploitation. This section will examine the illegitimacy of prosecuting trafficked victims to the extent that there has been "a failure to identify a person who has committed a criminal offence as a trafficked victim, which is likely to result in the victim being treated as a normal offender, one who would normally be required to take full legal responsibility, including being sanctioned for their acts."[54]

The rationale for protecting victims from criminal sanctions can be justified for three reasons. Firstly, where victims have committed offences under duress and have also come to the attention of law enforcement, there is an expectation from police that victims will cooperate with them. However, victims may feel less trusting of the police. Victims require fair legal representation to understand and know their rights as trafficked victims to enter the NRM so that they can be safeguarded and provided with care and support. Simply detaining victims after arrest and charge without legal representation is a violation of their human rights. Secondly, some victims are in such dire, exploitative environments where they rely on their exploiter for survival (for housing/accommodation, food, shelter, to feed a substance problem) and consequently commit crimes to meet the demands of the trafficker. This behaviour despite being criminal justifies an empathetic and understanding approach from law enforcement who are willing to acknowledge the circumstances surrounding the criminal actions of a trafficked victim in that situation. In these situations where the victims come into contact with the police, the State is in a very powerful position over the individual where they can be misled into thinking that the individual is a criminal, without acknowledging that they are a victim of crime. Thirdly, when victims are committing these criminal acts, they have lost control over their acts over whether to commit them or not because they are into doing so. They are incapable of making free informed choices because of the physical and psychological threats, harm and retribution threatened or carried out against them for not carrying out these crimes for the benefit of the exploiter. This view is supported by the opinion that "the trafficked person is not a free agent, that they are compelled to commit unlawful acts by those who control and exploit them, that they are victims of crime rather than criminals, that they are acting under duress and are in no position to object."[55] Victims have either lost their autonomy of making good decisions or are compromised because of the duress and coercion exerted by traffickers onto victims. Therefore, it is unfair for the law to prosecute them.

It has been acknowledged that agencies such as the police do not identify victims of trafficking as effectively as they should. As a result, victims are either left in exploitation or they are misidentified as criminal suspects who are arrested and charged for an offence connected to their exploitation.[56]

For example, it has been seen that victims involved in cultivating cannabis are more likely to be prosecuted rather than being seen as a trafficked victim.[57] The moral issue of whether trafficked victims should be prosecuted in the first place is an important consideration and one which requires thought. When the State prosecutes victims, it exposes them to the criminal law which illustrates a less than desirable approach far from the victim-centred one this chapter advocates. Where victims are prosecuted, it also deprives victims of the opportunity to be identified as a victim of trafficking and consequently protected as a victim of crime. Moreover, victims are left without the help and support which may empower them to come to terms with their ordeal. The UK thus fails to in any way adequately satisfy its commitment to victims or to fulfil the moral obligation it has towards human trafficking victims in particular.

A strong argument can be made that trafficked victims should not be prosecuted in any circumstances. This is based on the following reasons:

1. I do not accept that trafficked victims are morally culpable for any type of offence, because of how the high degree of pressure placed upon the victim.[58] Coercion and control methods used by the trafficker may prevent the victim from having free will. These liberties may have been taken away from the victim by the trafficker.[59]

2. I accept that in some cases there will be another victim who may be affected by the actions of the trafficked victim. Notwithstanding the rights of the victim suffering such a crime, we should not be distracted from the fact that the trafficked victim has been deceived or coerced into that situation meaning that the real wrongdoer remains the trafficker.[60]

3. Trafficked victims are often punished by traffickers if they do not consent to being exploited. I do not want the trafficked victim to be sanctioned by the State through the criminal justice system as I believe that this process amounts to secondary punishment.

4. The criminal justice system should spend more time and allocate more resources to prosecuting traffickers, so that the victim can play a significant role in helping the police and bring the trafficker(s) and organised crime groups to justice.

5. The statutory defence available to trafficked victims (found in the Modern Slavery Act 2015) to excuse their liability do not protect victims adequately. This will be examined later in the chapter.

There are many types of situations in which trafficked victims will find themselves being exploited which can result in them being compelled to commit additional criminal offences:

> The increasing global prevalence of human trafficking for enforced criminality can expose victims of trafficking to committing a multitude of offences such as, but not limited to theft, pick-pocketing, drug trafficking, cannabis cultivation and fraud.[61]

Some of the offences will be of the same nature as when they were originally trafficked, whilst other offences which trafficked victims are compelled to do may be different from their original purpose of exploitation. Many of these offences will be less serious in nature, such as cultivating cannabis and obtaining false documents. These offences are often victimless crimes which result in the trafficker benefiting from the crime whilst exposing the victim to an arrest and prosecution. A victim may have been deceived into taking work in the UK, only to find that they are being exploited and forced to work to cultivate cannabis. In these situations where the offence is less serious and is victimless. As long as there is a direct link between the purpose of exploitation and the coercion placed upon the victim, I do not believe that in these circumstances, victims should be prosecuted, and all opportunities to divert from prosecution should be taken. Consequently, in my opinion, a presumption against prosecution, as seen in Scotland must therefore be adopted.[62] Furthermore, I believe that more time and resources should be spent on investigating and tracking down the traffickers as opposed to prosecuting and punishing victims for less serious offences.

In contrast to offences committed as the main purpose of their exploitation, there may be circumstances where trafficked victims in addition to the offences committed as part of their exploitation are then coerced and compelled into committing more serious crimes. In these cases, I argue that it would not be justified for them to be prosecuted even though there is an issue of public interest attached to the seriousness of these crimes. This view is taken for four reasons.

The first reason is that a trafficked victim cannot be held to be morally culpable for the offences that they commit under duress. John Robinson understands culpability to mean:

> ...blameworthiness, and I understand culpability to operate in two distinct, if intimately related, spheres: the moral and the legal. In both spheres paradigmatic culpability involves three elements: wrongful conduct, actual or constructive awareness of its wrongfulness, and a reasonable level of control over one's own conduct.[63]

Where serious and less serious crimes are committed by trafficked victims, there will still often be coercion from traffickers. Where there is coercion, a trafficked victim cannot be held morally culpable. In parallels drawn from cases of domestic violence, the external factor at play is the slow burn of violence which victims experience over a period of time before the victim finally retaliates appearing as a sudden loss of control. Consequently, it will be unfair to judge that the legal culpability of the offence will take priority without acknowledging the lack of moral culpability to the criminal behaviour.

Secondly, during trial the psychological and mental health needs of the victim need to be guaranteed as a trial may expose the trafficked victim to relive the traumatic ordeal that has been endured. It would also make the threat of reprisals more likely from traffickers if the victim were to disclose who was coercing and compelling the victim to commit the criminal offences. Greater forms of witness protection will be required for trafficked victims but this is a paradoxical situation, because the State views and treats the victim as an offender. This is a complicated issue because many trafficked victims do not trust authorities or do not know where to access services to help facilitate the escape.[64] This also adds to the need to correctly identify trafficked victims as the criminal justice system is not designed to recognise recognised the vulnerabilities of victims acting as perpetrators of crime.[65]

Thirdly, the issue of how traffickers use compulsion, coercion and control tactics against victims to force them to commit offences by traffickers and the effects this has on victims has been examined earlier in the thesis. These methods need to be reconsidered here too in light of whether the defences are effective enough for victims to rely upon. If the circumstances are that victims are exposed to lengthy and systematic forms of abuse during exploitation, it will be unfair for victims to be punished a second time, this time, by the State prosecuting them. It has been argued that it is vital that the State recognises the individual as a victim instead of sanctioning the victim:

The criminalisation of trafficked victims may be tantamount to persecution of victims by the State: it fails to recognise trafficked victims s victims and witnesses of those serious crimes and exacerbates their victim-isation and/or trauma by imposing on such persons State-imposed, unjust punishment.[66]

Fourthly, I believe that despite the State arguing that there are suffi-cient defences available for trafficked victims to rely upon, the present range of defences does not offer enough protection from the criminal law. It will be shown shortly that the statutory defence is not specific enough for victims to effectively rely upon it. The statutory defence in England and Wales is not broad enough to rely upon because it has limi-tations in its use based on the nature of the criminal offences committed. It will be shown that the present statutory legal defence places victims at a distinct disadvantage within the criminal justice system. As the next chapter will illustrate, the statutory defence presently offers challenges, not possibilities for victims to be protected adequately from the criminal law.

In summary, I have argued that in a position where trafficked victims are not culpable, criminal liability should not follow.[67]

The Issue of Coercion and Compulsion on Victims by Traffickers

Under present CPS guidelines on Human Trafficking, Smuggling and Slavery, prosecutors should consider "whether the offence committed was a direct consequence of, or in the course of trafficking/slavery, and whether the criminality is significantly diminished or effectively extin-guished because no realistic alternative was available but to comply with the dominant force of another."[68] If no realistic alternative could be evidenced, then this may extinguish the liability of the trafficked victim. The wording of the guidance does not explicitly request prosecutors to consider the effect of coercion and compulsion on the trafficked victim when criminal offences are being committed. The main problem with adopting an objective approach is that it requires the victim to be judged on his or her actions as freely consenting adults, as opposed to acknowledging the difficulty of being manipulated alongside being physically controlled by traffickers, preventing victims from not being able to act freely. The fact that a victim will be also psychologically controlled restricting their escape is significant because it is not so much what the victim has done in terms of committing a certain criminal act, it is rather the background and contextual circumstances around why the person committed the criminal offences by acknowledging and understanding the pressures placed upon the victim in the first place. The objective test does not easily take into recognition the impact of a coercion and control dynamic existing between the trafficker and the victim.

A far more beneficial criterion to establish whether there is a present threat and a fairer method to judge a trafficked victim's conduct can be found from the human trafficking case of *R v Dao*,[69] where the judge requested that the following questions required answering:

1) Whether the accused whose case they were considering had been threatened by someone with death or serious injury if he/she did not cultivate the cannabis plants?
2) Whether the accused in question reasonably believed that the threat would be carried out imminently if he/she did not comply?
3) Whether the threat endured throughout the accused's participation and was it reinforced by incarceration?
4) Whether the threat was the direct cause of that accused's decision to stay?
5) Whether a reasonable person with the characteristics of the accused would have been driven to act as the accused did, considering the opportunities that the accused had to escape?[70]

These questions are broader in scope. The first two questions benefit a trafficked victim who wishes to rely upon a defence of duress because they are more subjective to a victim's thoughts and how they translate into actions as a result of the threats by traffickers, rather than the objective test. The questions also delve deeper into the subjective nature of the victim's circumstances which provides the opportunity for more evidence from the victim to be submitted to justify why the defence should be used. These questions can be used by the CPS at the time when they are evaluating whether a defence is likely to succeed at trial. As far as Question 3 is concerned, however, the threat may not always be present and is a constant one. The victim may, for example, have been threatened once, but will still experience a psychological threat knowing that if the victim does not behave in a given way which is of a criminal nature, the physical threats will constantly remerge which places victims in a prolonged state of fear, compelling victims to continue committing criminal acts. Question 4 regarding whether the threat is the decision that the victim will stay, implies that there is sufficient evidence to prove that there was compulsion. However, the objective nature of Question 5 oversimplifies the harmful psychological experience experienced by victims as there are 'invisible chains' preventing victims from escaping. Feelings of helplessness may exacerbate when victims come into contact with authorities who they do not trust, preventing victims from escaping and opting to stay in exploitative situations. The main issue is the nature and the degree of threats which prevent the victim from leaving. Victims who self-identify as victims of trafficking would be at the mercy of authorities who may misidentify them as another group of migrants. In summary, the questions asked in the *Dao* case should be ones which the prosecutor should ask themselves before a decision to prosecute takes place. If the questions can be answered in the affirmative, then no prosecution should take place.

The present situation is too concerned with the level of coercion placed on the victim to determine whether the criminality can be diminished. As seen in the case of *R v Verna Sermanfure*,[71] the Crown Prosecution Service (CPS) decided that there was insufficient evidence of compulsion which would significantly diminish the criminality of the applicant, as opposed to looking at how the possibility of coercion affected the ability to resisting the act of smuggling drugs. The CPS continued the prosecution because "it was in the public interest to do so given the high level of criminality in smuggling a quantity of cocaine."[72] Even in cases where compulsion has been found to exist, this is often not enough for a prosecution to not take place. The emphasis has been to look at the criminal act(s) which have been committed. If the criminal act is serious, the more likely that the victim's culpability will not be diminished. If both are the same, it is more likely that the victim's culpability will be diminished.

The present situation is also focussed on whether the criminal offence committed by the victim is committed as a result of the victim originally being trafficked in the first place. For culpability of the victim to be diminished, there must be evidence that there is a direct connection between the trafficking of the victim and the next criminal offence taking place.[73] In the case of *R v NTN*[74] the court found that the victim's "culpability was significantly diminished if not extinguished by the direct nexus between the trafficking and the offence whereby it would not have been in the public interest to prosecute him or maintain the prosecution against him."[75] Similarly, the applicant in the case of *Dong Nguyen*[76] argued that he had been brought to the UK to work and it turned out that his employment was at a cannabis factory. It was held that "the offence was committed as a result of compulsion arising from being trafficked into the UK and then re-trafficked internally at such a level that his culpability for his offending was extinguished."[77] This highlights how important identification of the individual as trafficked so that a conviction can be pursued. It also raises the possibility that the individual can be referred to as a potential victim of trafficking and referred to the NRM. However, in this case the victim went missing. This highlights the importance of ensuring that when police intervene and remove victims from the scene of a crime, victims are protected adequately by acknowledging their victim status and therefore not exposed to the risk of being re-trafficked by a failure of referring potential victims to the NRM. In some cases, a trafficked victim may be initially trafficked for one type of exploitation such as labour, but then later becomes exploited for another purpose, such as prostitution. This is not uncommon.

The present situation also places too much emphasis on the degree of resistance from the trafficked victim to determine whether there was a realistic alternative for the victim to commit the criminal act.

Moreover, juries will have differing opinions on whether the victim had a reasonable alternative to committing the criminal act or not. Some jurors may hold the view that a realistic alternative will be to alert authorities or escape from the environment in which victims are placed. However, as Wake advocates, "what may be regarded as a 'realistic alternative' to a juror may appear entirely counterintuitive to a victim of slavery."[78] Wake notes that the challenges for trafficked victims also mirror those of similar victims "like a domestic violence victim, the trafficked victim may fear that alerting the authorities attempting to escape or trying to avoid the situation will put them or their families in great danger."[79] The consequences for victims carrying out a realistic alternative to committing a criminal offence must be weighed against the benefit of staying in the same exploitative position, hidden from view but not exposed to secondary victimisation from prosecutors and other authorities. Therefore, understanding the complexities of these issues is vital to acknowledging the trafficked victim's perspective, and ensuring that the victims' situations are appropriately considered during the criminal justice process.

Positively, the questions asked during the *R v Dao* case offer juries with additional opportunities to consider more evidence, testimony and knowledge surrounding the circumstances of how and why they committed a criminal offence under duress.

The questions asked are more specific to a trafficked victim's situation and provide a clear understanding as to what the victim was experiencing during the time of committing the crime. However, the questions still do not acknowledge the psychological harm placed upon the victim keeping them in the same exploitative environment, making it easier for the trafficker to coerce and control the victim to commit further criminal acts.

As a result of being subjected to repeated abuse, intimidation and violence it is difficult for victims to resist, to not comply with the traffickers' demands and commit crimes. In situations where victims have been broken down emotionally, they may be more likely to accept their situation. Furthermore, the opportunity to inform authorities is not always available and in cases where they may be able to alert authorities, victims may often be held back by a strong mistrust of authorities.[80] The questions posed in the *Dao* case provide sufficient progress to be applied in more cases specific to human trafficking where victims can often be perceived as offenders.

The way in which the UK satisfies its legal international obligations to protect victims from criminalisation can be seen in 4 different ways. These are the common law of duress, prosecutorial discretion, the power to stay a prosecution and the Section 45 defence found in the Modern Slavery Act.

The next chapter will examine the statutory defence presently in force in the UK[81] to establish whether it provides effective safeguards for trafficked victims to rely upon during a criminal prosecution.

Notes

1. Article 4 ECHR relates to the prohibition of slavery and forced labour. No one shall be held in slavery or servitude. No one shall be required to perform forced or compulsory labour. For the purpose of this Article the term "forced or compulsory labour" shall not include: (a) any work required to be done in the ordinary course of detention imposed according to the provisions of Article5 of this Convention or during conditional release from such detention; (b) any service of a military character or, in case of conscientious objectors in countries where they are recognised, service exacted instead of compulsory military service; (c) any service exacted in case of an emergency or calamity threatening the life or well-being of the community; (d) any work or service which forms part of normal civic obligations.
2. UNODC, 'Global Report on Trafficking in Persons 2022,' at 11.
3. 'Modern Slavery and Organised Immigration Crime Programme Annual Report 2022/23,' at 13.
4. Article 2(a) UNTOC which defines an organised crime group as comprising of 'a group of three or more persons that was not randomly formed; existing for a period of time; acting in concert with the aim of committing at least one crime punishable by at least four years' incarceration; in order to obtain, directly or indirectly, a financial or other material benefit.'.
5. Business type organisations operate with three persons or more working together to traffic persons as part of their criminal activities as described in UNTOC, 'Global Report on Trafficking in Persons 2022,' at 48.

6. Court case summaries from the UNODC show that organised crime groups exploit more people for longer periods in more violent environments than non-organised crime groups with organised groups carrying out labour exploitation rather than sexual exploitation. See UNODC 'Global Report on Trafficking in Persons 2022' at 49–50.
7. UNTOC, 'Global Report on Trafficking in Persons 2022,' at 58.
8. UNTOC, 'Global Report on Trafficking in Persons 2022,' at 59.
9. UNTOC, 'Global Report on Trafficking in Persons 2022,' at 64.
10. UNTOC, 'Global Report on Trafficking in Persons 2022,' at 67.
11. UN Convention against Transnational Organised Crime, adopted by General Assembly resolution 55/25 of 15 November 2000.
12. UN Protocol to Prevent, Suppress and Punish Trafficking in Persons, especially Women and Children, supplementing the United Nations Convention against Transnational Organised Crime, 2000.
13. The Council of Europe Convention on Action against Trafficking in Human Beings was adopted by the Committee of Ministers of the Council of Europe on 3 May 2005, to help combat trafficking in human beings by seeking to strengthen protection by considering the human rights perspective. For further information, see https://www.coe.int/en/web/anti-human-trafficking/about-the-convention.
14. For further discussion, see A. Schloenhardt & R. Markey-Towler, "Non-criminalisation of Victims of Trafficking in Persons—Principles, Promises, and Perspectives," (2016) Groningen Journal of International Law, 4(1), International Criminal Organisations, 32–33.
15. Articles 24 and Article 25, UN Convention against Transnational Organised Crime, adopted by General Assembly resolution 55/25 of 15 November 2000.
16. Article 5 UN Protocol to Prevent, Suppress and Punish Trafficking in Persons, especially Women and Children, supplementing the United Nations Convention against Transnational Organised Crime, 2000.

17. The non-punishment principle has also been recognised in the UN Convention Relating to the Status of Refugees under Article 31.1 where "Parties shall not impose penalties on account of their illegal entry or presence, on refugees who, coming directly from a territory where their life or freedom was threatened." It has also been recognised by the General Assembly UN (UN Resolution on Traffic in Women and Girls, A/RES/55/67, 31 January 2001 at para 6, the Brussels Declaration on Preventing & Combatting Trafficking in Human Beings, 14,981/02, 29 Nov 2002 at para 7, and in the Miami Declaration of Principles on Human Trafficking, 10 Feb 2005 at para 28.

18. UN Recommended Principles and Guidelines on Human Rights and Human Trafficking (UN Doc E/2002/68). These are regarded as soft law and are not binding upon any State. However, they do provide guidance for States to consider when looking at promoting and integrating human rights into policies and anti-human trafficking laws.

19. UN Recommended Principles and Guidelines on Human Rights and Human Trafficking (UN Doc E/2002/68) at Principle 7.

20. The 2009 UNODC Model Law against Trafficking in Persons was developed by the United Nations Office on Drugs and Crime (UNODC) in response to the request of the General Assembly to the Secretary-General to promote and assist the efforts of Member States to implement the United Nations Convention against Transnational Organized Crime and the Protocols. It was also developed to assist States in implementing the provisions contained in the Protocol to Prevent, Suppress and Punish Trafficking in Persons, Especially Women and Children, supplementing that Convention.

21. Article 10 Model Law against Trafficking in Persons.

22. The OSCE is an intergovernmental organisation created in the 1950s with 57 participating States to combat security concerns via decision-making bodies. See https://www.osce.org/.

23. OSCE Ministerial Council, Decision No1, Enhancing the OSCE's Efforts to Combat Trafficking in Human Beings, MC (8) DEC/1 (Vienna 28 Nov 2000) at para 9.

24. The Council of Europe Convention on Action against Trafficking in Human Beings was adopted by the Committee of Ministers of the Council of Europe on 3 May 2005, to help combat trafficking in human beings by seeking to strengthen protection by considering the human rights perspective. For further information, see https://www.coe.int/en/web/anti-human-trafficking/about-the-convention.
25. Article 10 CofE Convention.
26. Article 12 CofE Convention.
27. Article 26 Council of Europe Convention on Action against Trafficking in Human Beings, 16 May 2005.
28. OSCE Policy and Legislative Recommendations towards the effective implementation of the non-punishment provision, in consultation with the Alliance against Trafficking in Persons Expert Co-ordination Team, Vienna, 2013 at 12.
29. OSCE's Efforts to Combat Trafficking in Human Beings, MC(8). Dec/1 (Vienna, 28 Nov 2000) at para 9.
30. *R v LM, MB, DG, Betti Tabot and Yutunde Tijani* [2010] EWCA Crim 2327.
31. *R v LM, MB, DG, Betti Tabot and Yutunde Tijani* [2010] EWCA Crim 2327 at para 13.
32. OSCE Resource Police Training Guide: Trafficking in Human Beings, TNTD/SPMU Publication Series Vol 12, Vienna, July 2013 at 126.
33. OSCE Policy and Legislative Recommendations towards the effective implementation of the non-punishment provision, in consultation with the Alliance against Trafficking in Persons Expert Co-ordination Team, Vienna, 2013 at 12.
34. The Council of Europe Explanatory Report at para 274 states that "Each Party can comply with the obligation established in Article 26, by providing for a substantive criminal or procedural criminal law provision, or any other measure, allowing for the possibility of not punishing victims when the legal requirements are met.".
35. R v LM; YT; BT; DG; MB [2010] EWCA Crim 2327.
36. Council Framework Decision 2002/629/JHA.

37. "EU urges higher priority on Trafficking in Women and Children" Europa Press Release IP/01/325, March 7 2001.
38. Article 8 Directive 2011/36/EU of the European Parliament and of the Council of 5 April 2011 on preventing and combating trafficking in human beings and protecting its victims, and replacing Council Framework Decision 2002/629/JHA.
39. Article 20 EU Directive 2011/36 on preventing and combatting trafficking in human beings and its victims.
40. European Recital to Directive 2011/36/EU, European Union, Op. cit at para 14.
41. OSCE Policy and Legislative Recommendations towards the effective implementation of the non-punishment provision, in consultation with the Alliance against Trafficking in Persons Expert Co-ordination Team, Vienna, 2013 at 15.
42. Rantsev v Cyprus and Russia, Application no. 25965/04, Council of Europe: European Court of Human Rights, 7 January 2010.
43. Rantsev v Cyprus and Russia, Application no. 25965/04, Council of Europe: European Court of Human Rights, 7 January 2010 at para 284.
44. See Article 10 UN Office on Drugs and Crime, Model Law against Trafficking in Persons 2009, Vienna.
45. OSCE Policy and Legislative Recommendations towards the effective implementation of the non-punishment provision, in consultation with the Alliance against Trafficking in Persons Expert Co-ordination Team, Vienna, 2013 at 29.
46. See the case of R v L and Other Appeals [2013] EWCA Crim 991; [2014] 1 All ER 113, para 13.
47. Section 2 and 3, Sexual Offences Act 2003.
48. Section 1 Theft Act 1968.
49. Section 6 Misuse of Drugs Act 1971.
50. A. Schloenhardt & R. Markey-Towler, "Non-Criminalisation of Victims of Trafficking in Persons—Principles, Promises, Perspectives," (2016) Groningen Journal of International Law, 4(1): International Criminal Organisations, at 14.
51. Section 6 Identity Documents Act 2010.
52. R v O [2008] EWCA Crim 2835.

53. This situation is very similar to situations of domestic violence where a victim experiences a slow burn of abuse and harm on several levels (physical, emotional, psychological, financial abuse) over a long period of time and then the victim spontaneously inflicts serious harm or death on their partner.

54. OSCE Policy and Legislative Recommendations towards the effective implementation of the non-punishment provision, in consultation with the Alliance against Trafficking in Persons Expert Co-ordination Team, Vienna, 2013, 16.

55. R. Piotrowicz, "The Non-punishment Principle in International Law," (Paper presented at Promoting the Implementation of the Non-punishment Principle for Victims of Human Trafficking: A Workshop for Judicial and Prosecutorial Officials, Strasbourg, 9–10 October 2014), 3.

56. HM Inspectorate of Constabulary and Fire & Rescue Services (HMICFRS), "Stolen Freedom: The Policing Response to Modern Slavery and Human Trafficking," (2017), 60.

57. P. Burland, "Seven: Still Punishing the Wrong People: The Criminalisation of Potential Trafficked Cannabis Gardeners" in "The Modern Slavery Agenda," Bristol, UK: Policy Press, 2019.

58. As the OSCE Policy and Legislative Recommendations report above states at 125, "it is often a deliberate strategy of the traffickers to expose victims to the risk of criminalisation and to manipulate and exploit them for criminal activities.".

59. Also, "the rationale for non-punishment is that whilst on the face of it a victim may have committed an offence, the reality is that the trafficked person acts without real autonomy." OSCE Policy and Legislative Recommendations towards the effective implementation of the non-punishment provision, in consultation with the Alliance against Trafficking in Persons Expert Co-ordination Team, Vienna, 2013 at 10.

60. See OSCE Policy and Legislative Recommendations towards the effective implementation of the non-punishment provision, in consultation with the Alliance against Trafficking in Persons Expert Co-ordination Team, Vienna, 2013 at 10 which argues that whilst victims are prosecuted, the traffickers act with impunity.

61. OSCE Resource Police Training Guide: Trafficking in Human Beings, TNTD/SPMU Publication Series, Vol 12 at 125.
62. See Section 8 Human Trafficking & Exploitation (Scotland) Act 2015.
63. J. Robinson, "Crime, Culpability & Excuses," (2012) Notre Dame Journal of Law, Ethics and Public Policy, Volume 2, Issue 1 at 2.
64. See C. Rijken, Jan van Dijk & F. Klerx-van Mierlo, "Trafficking Victims in The Netherlands an Exploratory Study," (2013), International Victimology Institute, Tilburg University.
65. For example, see S. Fairclough, "'Barriers to Vulnerable Defendants Giving Evidence by Live Link in Crown Court Trials," The International Journal of Evidence and Proof (2017), 21(3) 209.
66. OSCE Policy and Legislative Recommendations towards the Effective Implementation of the Non-punishment Provision, in consultation with the Alliance against Trafficking in Persons Expert Co-ordination Team, Vienna, 2013 at 10.
67. It may be the case that we have to look into circumstances of every given crime and decide to what extent how much of the victims' free will was undermined. There are difficulties where deception, coercion and control are minor, but still result in crimes being committed. This is why examining the circumstances of every crime is required.
68. CPS Human Trafficking, Smuggling and Slavery Legal Guidance, found at http://cps.gov.uk/legal/h_to_k/human_trafficking_and_smuggling/#a20.
69. *R v Van Dao* [2012] EWCA Crim 1717.
70. *R v Van Dao* [2012] EWCA Crim 1717 at 18.
71. *R v Verna Sermanfure* as part of 5 other appeals heard within *R v Joseph* [2017] 1 Cr App R 33 486.
72. *R v Verna Sermanfure* as part of 5 other appeals heard within *R v Joseph* [2017] 1 Cr App R 33 486 at para 60.
73. See R v NTN as part of 5 other appeals heard within *R v Joseph* [2017] 1 Cr App R 33 486 at para 21 where it was held that "it is necessary to assess whether the defendant had been compelled to commit the crime by considering whether the offence was a

direct consequence of, or in the course of trafficking/slavery and whether the criminality is significantly diminished or effectively extinguished because there is no realistic alternative but to comply with the dominant force of another.".

74. *R v NTN* as part of 5 other appeals heard within *R v Joseph* [2017] 1 Cr App R 33 486.

75. *R v NTN* as part of 5 other appeals heard within *R v Joseph* [2017] 1 Cr App R 33 486 at 135.

76. *Dong Nguyen*, as part of 5 other appeals heard within *R v Joseph* [2017] 1 Cr App R 33 486.

77. *Dong Nguyen*, as part of 5 other appeals heard within *R v Joseph* [2017] 1 Cr App R 33 486 at 142.

78. N. Wake, "Human Trafficking and Modern Day Slavery: When Victims Kill," (2017) Criminal Law Review, 658 at 674.

79. N. Wake, "Human Trafficking and Modern Day Slavery: When Victims Kill," (2017) Criminal Law Review, 658 at 674.

80. New European Crimes and Trust-based Policy (FIDUCIA), "Policy Brief on the Findings on Human Trafficking," European Commission, February 2015 at 1 found at https://ec.europa.eu/research/social-sciences/pdf/policy_briefs/policy-briefs-fiducia-02-2015_en.pdf.

81. In England and Wales this is the Modern Slavery Act 2015 and in Northern Ireland it is the Human Trafficking & Exploitation (Criminal Justice and Support for Victims) Act 2015.

7

The Statutory Defence Available to Trafficked Victims and the Role of the Legal Profession in Identifying Victims of Human Trafficking

1   Introduction

The previous chapter discussed the legal issues relating to compulsion and coercion. This section will examine the statutory defence available to trafficked victims in England and Wales, and Northern Ireland.

The purpose of this section is to analyse some of the issues trafficked victims will have in seeking to rely upon the statutory defence when a decision to prosecute has been taken by the Crown Prosecution Service (CPS). This will be done by unpacking definitional issues contained within the Section 45 provision which currently creates obstacles for trafficked victims to convince a jury that because of their compulsion from the trafficker, their criminal liability is either mitigated or extinguished.

© The Author(s), under exclusive license to Springer Nature   **171**
Switzerland AG 2024
M. Davis, *Identifying Victims of Human Trafficking*, Palgrave Studies in Victims and
Victimology, https://doi.org/10.1007/978-3-031-61741-6_7

2   The Section 45 Statutory Defence Under the Modern Slavery Act 2015

The Section 45 statutory defence was drafted to comply with the non-punishment principle from Article 26 CofE Convention giving prosecutors exercised discretion in deciding whether or not to prosecute a trafficked victim for offences as part of their exploitation or not. In England and Wales, under Section 45(1) a person is not guilty of an offence if the act is performed under duress as part of their exploitation as long as:

(a) the person is aged 18 or over when the person does the act which constitutes the offence,

(b) the person does that act because the person is compelled to do it,

(c) the compulsion is attributable to slavery or to relevant exploitation, and.

(d) a reasonable person in the same situation as the person and having the person's relevant characteristics would have no realistic alternative to doing that act.[1]

The defence counsel would raise this statutory defence in circumstances when the trafficked victim is "compelled to commit an unlawful activity,[2] the compulsion alleged is attributable to slavery or to other relevant forms of exploitation,[3] and that a reasonable person in the same situation and having the accused's relevant characteristics, such as his/her age, sex and physical or mental illness or disability,[4] or other personal circumstance[5] would have no realistic alternative to doing the unlawful activity."[6] It was stressed in *R v MK*[7] that "the defendant bears an evidential burden and must raise evidence for each of the four elements."[8] It is for the prosecution to then disprove the defence beyond reasonable doubt. As we will now see, the statutory defence is extremely rigid as to when it can be raised and applied during trials. The Section 45 statutory defence cannot be used if the criminal offence falls within one of the excluded offences. Schedule 4 of the *Modern Slavery Act 2015* lists about 100 excluded offences such as murder, kidnapping and possession of a firearm.[9] Part of the problem with this rationale is that often, the criminal offences that victims are compelled to commit are of a serious nature,[10] and consequently "the statutory defence has the potential to undermine the effectiveness of the defence."[11] It has been found that the Section 45 defence has been used in cases mostly related to drug trafficking.[12] The Organisation for Security and Cooperation in Europe (OSCE) recommends that "States should consider adopting an open-ended list of offences typically related to trafficking in human beings, with regard to the commission of which victims shall be immune from punishment."[13] However, there are no such plans to revise Section 45 of the Modern Slavery Act 2015.

The following sub-sections examine 4 key criteria which trafficked victims must satisfy for a defence to successfully be relied upon. As we shall see, significant words and phrases within the legislation remain undefined.

Section 45(1)(b) offers protection to victims from prosecution by ensuring that a victim will not be found guilty in circumstances in which the victim commits an act where the victim was under compulsion. The term 'compulsion' remains undefined. Despite this, it was stated during the Modern Slavery Bill debate,[14] that "compulsion is a subjective test that does not require evidence of threats, force or any other type of outward action, and that it is submitted that compulsion is intended to be understood broadly."[15] However, as Laird points out, "the breadth of this approach does not sit well with the restrictive nature of the subsequent elements of the defence."[16] The common law of duress requires the person relying on it to be threatened with death or really serious harm, but here "by accepting that compulsion is un-evidenced from a threat of death or serious harm, the new defence constitutes a significant departure from the common law."[17] Therefore, the broadness of the new defence in terms of understanding compulsion here in the statutory defence benefits the victim more than relying upon the common law. The Northern Ireland legislation[18] refers to compulsion by threat from another person and compelled by the circumstances that trafficked victims find themselves in. The Modern Slavery Act of England and Wales does not specifically recognise. The closest the statutory defence recognises duress by circumstance can be found in Section 45(3)(b) which states that:

Compulsion is attributable to slavery or to relevant exploitation only if it is a direct consequence of a person being, or having been, a victim of slavery or a victim of relevant exploitation.[19]

The Section 45 defence does not define the term 'direct consequence' used in Section 45(3)(b). This omission was raised as part of the Modern Slavery Act Review, which questioned whether the statutory defence is consistent with Article 8 of the Trafficking Directive. The Modern Slavery Act review recommended that:

In respect of s45 of the Modern Slavery Act, which provides for a defence for slavery or trafficking victims who commit an offence, consideration should be given to clarifying and/ or enhancing the term 'direct consequence', and to clarifying the process by which s45 is raised and applied.[20]

Whilst some terms remain undefined, the fact that a trafficked victim may have been compelled to commit criminal acts has been recognised. This positive view has been endorsed by Jason Haynes, who states that "courts are now more empowered to take account of the fact that victims may have been compelled to commit unlawful activities by virtue of their own personal circumstances,"[21] and the legislation has at least acknowledged the trafficked victim's personal circumstances. Nevertheless, the issue remains that victims must show that there is enough evidence from the victim to show they were compelled to commit the act. Obtaining evidence by defence counsel from victims is problematic due to mistrust and the effects of trauma.

Having established that showing compulsion is important, the question of what the victims' personal circumstances are when the criminal offence was committed is the next issue. Under Section 45(1)(d) a person will not be guilty as long as a reasonable person in the same situation as the person and having the person's relevant characteristics would have no realistic alternative to committing that act. The three issues consist of (1) 'a reasonable person in the same situation as the person,' (2) 'the person's relevant characteristics,' and (3) 'no realistic alternative to doing that act.' These will be examined separately.

'A Reasonable Person in the Same Situation as the Person'

A person will not be guilty of an offence if a reasonable person in the same situation as the person and having the person's relevant characteristics would have undertaken the same act. A subjective approach is discouraged in favour of an objective test being used by looking at what the reasonable person would do in the same circumstances that the victim finds themselves in. This approach is justified on the basis that "a purely subjective test would allow the defence to be raised in tenuous circumstances because the defendant could argue that they felt compelled by circumstances."[22] The concern is that serious criminals would take advantage of using the statutory defence, escaping criminal liability. During the debates on the Modern Slavery Act 2015 in Parliament, the victim-centred approach appeared to have been overlooked in favour of ensuring that offenders do not take advantage of the law, simply by taking advantage of the defence themselves:

> The reasonable person test provides an important safeguard against this defence being abused and allows all the circumstances of the case to be carefully considered.[23]

Effectively, it is now more difficult for trafficked victims to rely solely on the objective test. The provision in Section 45(1)(d) is a subjective element meaning that the jury must consider 'the same situation as the person,' and 'having the person's relevant characteristics.' These must all be considered together, creating a combination of an objective test and subjective test. The intended effect is that it will not disadvantage the trafficked victim from relying on the defence. The Immigration Law Practitioners Association (ILPA) explains:

> This part of the test is an attempt to import an objective element, that of the "reasonable person", but with a subjective twist – the reasonable person must have the same characteristics as the victim in question.... It would require a member of the jury to attempt to imagine what s/he would have done, if s/he had exactly the same personal circumstances

and background as the person in question and were placed in the same situation. The purported objective test is thus a hybrid: it is so subjective (by importing the need for the 'reasonable person' to be, in effect, the same person as the victim, and in the same situation) that it is unable to achieve the intended objectivity. A judge would have real difficulty in directing any jury as to the correct approach as a result.' The use of the statutory defence needs to be carefully monitored to ascertain whether the inclusion of the 'reasonable person test' forms a barrier to victims accessing protection from unnecessary punishment and prosecution.[24]

This is where a strong justification for a trafficking advocate would be needed here when juries are applying the objective test. The jury would have the evidence from the advocate which the defence counsel can use to outline the circumstances the victim had experienced so that they can examine further the subjective element.

Having the 'Same Relevant Characteristics'

In Section 1(4)(a) "regard may be had to any of the person's personal circumstances (such as the person being a child, the person's family relationships, and any mental or physical illness) which may make the person more vulnerable than other persons."[25] In *R v Bowen*,[26] "the characteristics which can be considered when establishing the nature and extent of duress include age, sex, serious disability and recognised mental illnesses/psychiatric conditions."[27] A trafficked victim may become vulnerable to increased physical and mental harm as a result of experiencing numerous mental health conditions affecting their ability to be coerced to commit other acts because of a decrease in being able to function and make informed choices and autonomous decisions. Victims will be more vulnerable to increased exploitation and more easily compelled to commit further crimes because of the fear of reprisals from traffickers and believe that they have no other choice but to consent and commit repeated criminal offences. Victims may often be broken down emotionally and identified as having a 'learned helplessness' status attached to them. Learned helplessness is a type of characteristic which trafficked victims will experience as part of their exploitation. In the case of *R v GAC*,[28] it was defined as:

> ...the reaction of a victim to chronic and repeated abuse. They have no way of physically or emotionally breaking free from their abuser and the abuse. They cannot extricate themselves from the violent situation no matter how many cries for help they make. They become increasingly passive.[29]

Learned helplessness essentially captures the powerlessness felt by the trafficked victim due to the situation in which they find themselves. Despite the characteristic being recognised in academic terms, it is not recognised as a relevant characteristic for satisfying a defence of duress and not therefore it is not applied.[30] As seen in *R v Hurst*[31] it has a very narrow application where it was held that "it is hard to see how the person of reasonable firmness can be invested with the characteristics of a personality that lacks reasonable firmness."[32] This confirms that a reasonable firmness test is consistently applied by courts without juries considering the impact of learned helplessness on victims. If the law was to recognise the impact of learned helplessness arising from compulsion to committing criminal offences, it would help trafficked victims explain the difficult circumstances they face when they are placed under duress. The present position on disregarding learned helplessness from the process contradicts Section 1(4)(a) which does state that learned helplessness is a factor which makes victims more vulnerable than others, and a main characteristic of being an individual remaining a trafficked victim. Keeping them in exploitation.

A trafficking advocate should be allowed to participate in the criminal justice process such a process where they can obtain more victim testimony and evidence in order to establish the facts and circumstances to their case. It can then be presented in court. Victims may be reluctant to speak with authorities and therefore, advocates with knowledge of what trafficked victims experience can play an influential role by having an opportunity to obtain important information from victims who would otherwise remain silent and remain in exploitation.

'No Realistic Alternative to Committing the Act'

The final element is whether the defendant had a realistic alternative to committing the criminal offence. Section 45(1)(d) states that a victim will not be guilty if the person has no realistic alternative to committing the act. This is an objective test and is included as "a safeguard against unscrupulous use of the defence."[33]

Laird states that the "question is whether a reasonable person of D's age, sex and any physical or mental illness or disability would have thought so, not whether the defendant thought about running away was a realistic alternative."[34] An earlier section mentioned the case of *R v Van Dao*,[35] where the victim had a means of escape, but did not do so because of the fear of being hurt or killed which prevented her from discontinuing the cultivation of cannabis. It must be acknowledged that the fear of escaping can be a reason for not leaving an exploitative situation. The case failed to see that the victims are often fearful of being punished if an escape fails. It is also difficult for some victims to know where to go to get help if they do escape.

As confirmed in the Modern Slavery debate,[36] the test to be applied under s45(1)(d) is an objective one. This approach ignores the feelings of fear from victims in deciding whether to escape or not. If a jury does not fully understand the reasons as to why some trafficked victims feel as if they cannot escape and continue to commit offences, it is more likely to be perceived by some juries that it is easy for victims to leave which is different from what the reality is. Many illegal immigrants may know that they are particularly at risk of being detained. This provides another reason why victims cannot simply leave an exploitative situation.

In the independent review of the Modern Slavery Act 2015 undertaken by Caroline Haughey QC back in 2017, there were concerns that not aware to many practitioners in the criminal justice system were aware of the Section 45 defence.[37] A further review in 2019[38] stressed the need for defence solicitors to be aware of such a defence and to advise clients accordingly. The Independent Anti-Slavery Commissioner's Call for Evidence Report[39] one year later set out specific issues relating to the use of the defence including how late the defence issue is raised in criminal proceeding alongside the negative consequences for victims where they do not benefit from the defence. In conclusion it was said that the "operation of the statutory defence is neither adequately protecting victims of trafficking nor adequately protecting the public."[40]

Analysis

In summary, despite there being a statutory defence which is well intentioned and appears to offer a degree of protection, in practice it offers very little benefit for trafficked victims. It has been highlighted that "there is very limited academic research into the use of Section 45 and no quantitative data on its use is collected, making it extremely difficult to assess how it is working in practice."[41]

The introduction of the statutory defences in the *Modern Slavery Act 2015* and the *Human Trafficking Exploitation Act 2015* should (in theory) provide additional security and protection for trafficked victims from the criminal law. However, the main problem with the statutory defence is that it is extremely restrictive as to when it should be used. This is because of the large number of offences excluded, as set out in Schedule 4 of the Modern Slavery Act 2015, and the type of offences which trafficked victims are compelled to undertake. Despite a statutory defence being introduced, the approach behind the restrictive nature appears to have been the concern that criminals could take advantage by using the defence, rather than adopting an approach which properly gives priority to the position and interests of that of genuine trafficked victims. This again fits into the narrative that not all victims are genuine and laws are being taken advantage of. This was seen earlier in the book when examining the genuineness of migrants and their rights to protection as victims. As long as this concern continues, there is less chance of trafficked victims being able to rely upon the statutory defence which defeats the introduction of a statutory defence being available to trafficked victims in the first place. However, it is acknowledged that:

> ...the CPS is still able to decide not to prosecute if it would not be in the public interest to do so, and the court will also be able to stop an inappropriate prosecution of a victim if the prosecution is found to be an abuse of process.[42]

Additionally, "if new evidence or information supports the fact that the suspect has been trafficked and committed the offence whilst in a coerced situation, there is a strong public interest to stop the prosecution."[43] Therefore, it would be up to the CPS to consider other evidence as to how the victim came to be arrested.[44] It could be complicated by the fact that the person may be scared of authorities and reluctant to disclose information.[45]

There are also issues making it difficult for victims to rely on specific elements of the defence. The objective test of relating to the reasonable man and the subjective test of having the same characteristics further disadvantage the trafficked victim. It has been argued that the combination of both tests may be complex for juries to understand and will be reliant on the direction from judges during trials.[46] This may be more practical than trying to alter the reasonable test by asking "whether the defendant was unable, as a result of exploitation to see any reasonable alternative to acting as they did."[47] The effect is that the onset and impact of mental health issues during their exploitation leaves trafficked victims vulnerable to accepting the exploitative situation they are in and committing criminal offences. The term 'learned helplessness' remains an issue unable to be advanced at trial.

Furthermore, the present law through the statutory defence expects trafficked victims to leave exploitative situations where there is an opportunity of doing so. This is unfair on victims to do so. This is why more evidence from the victim is required to explain what the challenges associated with escaping are. These will usually be the threat of further violence and the fear of the unknown if an escape was unsuccessful. A trafficking advocate would be useful here in these situations.

Unfortunately, the statutory defence does not offer a sufficient degree of protection for offences committed under compulsion. Due to the weakness of both the common law and statutory defence to protect victims effectively, victims should be offered adequate defences. The statutory defence requires changing to reflect how the means of the offence (deception, coercion and control) restricts the free will and autonomy of victims and easier for traffickers to force victims to commit further criminal offences. The defence is a good idea, but the way in which it reads and operates remains very weak and flawed. It is arguable that because the defence fails to properly protect victims of trafficking, there is a strong case against the prosecution of victims of trafficking proceeding in the first place.

In summary, the way in which the defence is formulated is a problematic matter and the responsibility of deciding whether a defendant can rely on the defence is weighed heavily onto a jury even in circumstances where the victim has an NRM decision.[48] The question for the jury is whether there was enough compulsion to carry out the offences by the trafficker and how a victim is made to feel because of the actions and behaviour of a trafficker. The defence is inadequate and therefore there should be no prosecution of trafficked victims. If there is to be a prosecution, then the defence should be amended as explained above. If neither of the approaches above are taken, then at the very least the approach adopted in the *Dao* case should be adopted, since this is an approach which better seeks fairly to assess their moral culpability in a holistic sense, albeit still operating within the limitations of existing law as explained above.

The next section will examine this in greater detail to see how the issue of identification can often be overlooked by people playing roles within the criminal justice process at the time where a decision to prosecute is taken, or when a criminal trial is in progress.

3   The Process and Mechanisms Leading to Trafficked Victims Being Prosecuted

The previous part of this chapter examined the difficulties of relying on the statutory defence for trafficked victims when prosecuted for criminal offences committed under duress. I have argued that trafficked victims should not be prosecuted because the present legal defences do not adequately protect trafficked victims from prosecution. The law should be amended to reflect the modern realities that trafficked victims experience regarding the difficulties victims have resisting demands from traffickers to committing criminal offences. Due to this current situation, an alternative question to ask is whether there are suitable defences available to victims which is not the right question to pose. The question to ask is whether there are adequate mechanisms in place for prosecutors to decide whether a prosecution should take place or not. The evidence presented below indicates that they may not be. Although an argument can be made that where a prosecution does take place, there is the safeguard of the statutory defence, I have already argued that the present defences are not strong enough. Consequently, the decision to prosecute is essentially more important than simply allowing victims to be prosecuted and asking them to rely solely on the statutory defence which in practice does not protect victims well enough.

It has been acknowledged that prosecuting offenders of human trafficking and modern is difficult for several reasons. This contributes to the low number of successful convictions for this crime.[49] Additionally, the cooperation and contribution made by trafficked victims giving evidence against their exploiters is of paramount importance and vital in criminal proceedings.[50] Furthermore, victims may be too vulnerable to assist in investigations,[51] and often viewed as "instruments of law enforcement to cooperate with the authorities in the investigations and criminal proceedings."[52]

Despite the sentiments above, the criminalisation of trafficked victims in the UK has happened regularly despite the international legal obligations in force for many years. As far back as 2011 there were concerns from outside the UK that exploited individuals were unfairly prosecuting victims rather than protecting them from criminalisation:

> While the UK Government has a policy of not penalising victims for unlawful acts committed as a direct result of being trafficked, there are reports of identified trafficking victims being prosecuted for offences they committed while under coercion of their traffickers.[53]

I will show that where victims have not been identified the decision to prosecute has still taken place, exposing victims to criminal trials and convictions. To justify this view, I will examine the role and responsibilities of the prosecutor and the defence who have contributed to the suffering of victims because they have not considered whether the individual is a trafficked victim. I will also show how they rely on TSOs to help victim recognition and referral to the NRM.

For prosecutors to come to an informed decision, a more detailed history on how the trafficked victim became exploited and committed the crimes must be provided by advocates and considered by prosecutors. This could be facilitated through the introduction of a trafficking advocate who would have the ability to obtain and submit evidence from victims. This procedural mechanism is required which would help trafficked victims in the short term to potentially divert them away from prosecution and referred to the NRM.

This section will examine the present guidance and the responsibilities of prosecutors in deciding whether to prosecute trafficked victims. Defence representatives also have an important role in ensuring that individuals who they represent are not prosecuted because of a lack of awareness of human trafficking. It will become clear that an advocate could be introduced to assist in the current decision-making process, meeting the needs of genuine trafficked victims who should be recognised as victims, not offenders, to ensure and protect the interests and rights of trafficked victims.

The Responsibility of the Prosecutor

As Beddoe and Brotherton rightly point out, "the Modern Slavery Act does not make it a statutory duty for prosecutors to identify victims, and does not direct that all such cases where suspects may be victims must be referred to a single lead prosecutor."[54]The CPS has issued guidance to prosecutors on their responsibilities in deciding whether to prosecute a trafficked victim. Presently, there is a four-stage test to arrive at a decision to prosecute:

1. Is there a reason to believe that the person is a victim of trafficking?
2. Is there clear evidence of a credible common law defence of duress?
3. Is there clear evidence of a statutory defence under Section 45 of the Modern Act 2015? 4. Is it in the public interest to prosecute?[55]

In light of the approach above, three main issues will now be discussed which the prosecutor will need to consider when deciding whether to prosecute a trafficked victim or not.

The Identification of the Individual as a Trafficked Victim

Where there is a suspicion that a person may be a victim of trafficking, "prosecutors should have regard to the duty of the prosecutor to make proper enquiries in criminal prosecutions involving individuals who may be victims of trafficking or slavery."[56] As the CofE Explanatory Report[57] notes, "a failure to identify a trafficking victim correctly will probably mean that a victim continues to be denied his or her fundamental rights and the prosecution to be denied the necessary witness in criminal proceedings to gain a conviction of the perpetrator for trafficking in human beings."[58] Therefore, it is an important decision for prosecutors to decide whether to pursue a prosecution or not against an individual. In *R v N*,[59] there was sufficient information presented at trial to show that there was credible evidence of the individual being a trafficked victim and the case being stopped so that an NRM referral could be made.[60] A decision should be taken after the issue of identification has taken place to ensure that there is no failure or breach of duty of the PA to investigate.

Prosecutors will be required to find evidence to establish whether an individual has been referred to the NRM. However, as seen in the case of *R v Joseph*,[61] there is no clear guidance on the cooperation between authorities in terms of accessing documents and statements from victims to evidence that they have been trafficked and it is imperative for processes and guidance to be drawn up to facilitate this.[62] Again, an advocate could complete this work and report back to prosecutors.

In cases where potential victims have not been referred to the NRM, there is a duty upon the prosecutor to advise law enforcement of the need for the individual to be referred to the NRM.[63] The CPS guidance relies heavily on the prosecutor being presented with evidence about the specific trafficking and exploitation situation from either the police or the NRM. Consequently, the nature of the circumstances of an individual's arrest is important to establish the facts behind the behaviour taking place.

Prosecutorial Discretion and the Issue of Compulsion

Prosecutors can exercise their discretion if they believe that it is in the public interest to prosecute. However, States have an obligation to establish an authority to determine who a victim of trafficking, and not to prosecute them unless there are good reasons which have been communicated,[64] after a trafficking assessment has been made by a qualified person.[65] It has also been seen that to continue a prosecution against a trafficked victim may in some circumstances be in conflict with the obligation of a State to protect victims.[66] The issue is whether a trial should go ahead where there is a level of compulsion on a victim of trafficking who has committed a criminal offence as part of their exploitation. In the case of *R v N; Le*,[67] the court held that it was in the public interest to prosecute a victim who had been smuggled into the UK and the other victim was provided with weekly food, there was enough evidence that the two victims had not been compelled to producing a controlled drug and the convictions were safe. In contrast, the case of *R v L, HVN, THN, T*[68] illustrated that where there is strong evidence of compulsion (and the fact that the victims in this case were trafficked children and L was forced into prostitution for some time but then released with what she believed to be a genuine passport and subsequently prosecuted) an appeal is likely to succeed on the basis that an abuse of process had taken place. The level of compulsion was the issue seen in the case of *R v GS*[69] where it was held that it was in the public interest to prosecute as there were reasonable alternatives to the victim agreeing to illegally import drugs for someone else.

Once the evidence has been collated the CPS Full Test Code is applied which is a set of guidelines applied by a prosecutor when determining whether an offender is to be charged with an offence.[70] The prosecutors must then arrive at a decision after considering the following:

> Is there a reason to believe that the person has been trafficked? If so, if there is clear evidence of a credible common law defence of duress, the case should be discontinued on evidential grounds; but even where there is no clear evidence of duress, but the offence may have been committed as a result of compulsion arising from trafficking, prosecutors should

consider whether the public interest lies in proceeding to prosecute or not. (See the judgment in LM & Ors [2010] EWCA Crim 2327)[71]

The case of *R v Joseph*[72] showed that the victim must be under a high degree of compulsion in order for it not to be in the public interest to prosecute. The type of offence committed is also judged to have been an important consideration in this decision to as "a distinction must be drawn between the individual put under some kind of pressure to become involved in drugs smuggling and the genuine victim of human trafficking."[73] The nexus between the compulsion and the offence is seen as relevant to whether the victim should be prosecuted or not based on being in the public interest which appears unfair. It can be argued that a victim in some circumstances does not have any control over the offence(s) they are compelled to commit and this plays into the aspect of fear[74] and the consequences of not committing these offences as part of their exploitative situations.[75]

My argument is that the question of whether to prosecute by answering the questions posed in the CPS guidance cannot be answered before the question of whether the individual is a trafficked person or not has been answered first. Due to the lack of cooperation between the NRM, the police and prosecutors, a decision to prosecute is going to overlook whether the suspect may be a trafficked victim or not. If there is any suggestion of compulsion, then in line with CPS guidelines, no prosecution should take place.

The Consideration of a Relevant Defence by the CPS

Wake reinforces the point that where there is clear and credible evidence of duress, a prosecution should not take place.[76] Evidence to determine duress is vital so that a decision can be made. There is guidance for prosecutors provided by the CPS on the use of the statutory defence under Section 45, and there is further guidance regarding when a prosecutor should use the discretionary 'Public Interest' test in human trafficking and exploitation cases. The Full Test Code can be found in the guidance issued by the CPS.[77] Under Section 4.4, prosecutors must be satisfied that there is sufficient evidence to provide 'a realistic prospect of conviction' against each suspect on each charge. They must consider what the defence case may be, and how it is likely to affect the prospects of conviction. As the guidance states:

> Prosecutors should consider whether or not there is clear evidence of a credible common law defence of duress, as required in the second stage of the assessment. If so the case should not be charged and be discontinued on evidential grounds.[78] This approach was also confirmed in the case of *R v LM, MB, DG, Betti Tabot and Yutunde Tijani*.[79]

A case which "does not pass the evidential stage must not proceed, no matter how serious or sensitive it may be."[80] The prosecutor must decide at this stage the likelihood that the defence used by the victim will be successful or not. If it is judged to have a high chance of success, a prosecution will not take place. Presently, there is no central database to establish the number of cases where the statutory defences have been raised, and the position in Northern Ireland remains vague as there is no current policy guidance on the effect of their statutory defence.

The Significance of an NRM Decision

In deciding whether to prosecute a trafficked victim, the current CPS guidance states that: "if there is a conclusive grounds decision under the NRM that a suspect is a victim of trafficking or slavery; and there is evidence that proves on a balance of probabilities that the other conditions in Section 45 are met, relevant to whether the suspect is an adult or child; and the offence is not an excluded offence under schedule 4 of the Act, then no charges should be brought."[81] However, the CPS are not bound by a positive CGD and can still continue with a prosecution but must provide a rational basis for not discontinuing criminal proceedings.[82] The existence of a CGD decision on its own, obtained through the NRM is not sufficient to divert a prosecution.

The case of *R v Joseph*[83] highlighted that courts are willing to challenge expert evidence and NRM decisions which do not have a binding nature on court proceedings.

Wake correctly argues that "given prior victim status must be established for the purposes of the partial defence, and the CA and the CPS are already charged with making such determinations."[84] The problem is this. Whilst the decision from the CA is not binding upon any court, there is a risk that the NRM decision is not being taken into account. To prevent such risk, it would be useful for the weight of a CGD to be given a greater significant status by becoming a binding decision, on the basis that the decision has been made by an authority of the State. It does appear to be wrong for a decision to be made, but has no relevance to the CPS. The guidance further states that "if there is to be a delay, then prosecutors can take account of the reasonable grounds decision of the suspect but should additionally consider other evidence and the seriousness of the offence when considering the decision to prosecute."[85] Where there is an RGD only, the CPS guidance states that prosecutors should make enquiries about when a CGD is likely to be made which seems reasonable. I believe that the responsibility to follow up on the NRM decisions would fall within a remit of an advocate. It is in the interest of the trafficked victim to have a decision made as soon as possible, and for prosecutors to facilitate swifter decisions.

In circumstances where there is no CGD from the NRM, but there are "other available evidence shows that on the balance of probabilities the suspect is a victim; that is, it is more likely than not that they are a victim of trafficking or slavery, this will satisfy the evidential stage of victim status."[86] This situation may also justify the need for an advocate to act in the best interests of the trafficked victim to establish this evidence to present to the decision maker, and be diverted from prosecution to the NRM to become potentially given an RGD and then a CGD.

As seen from the case of *R v Brecani*[87] (which was discussed in Chapter 2) the jury will no longer have the benefit of a Conclusive Grounds Decision shown to them. Therefore, more reliance will be placed on defence lawyers to find expert evidence and reports in the absence of disclosure of a positive NRM decision which could be difficult to gather.

The Role of the Defence Counsel Representing Trafficked Victims

This section examines the role of defence lawyers play an influential role in identifying trafficked victims and the difficulties that they have in doing so because the issue of identification can be overlooked.

The Failure to Identify Their Client as a Trafficked Victim

The case of *R v O*[88] showed how the prosecution and defence solicitors failed to consider whether an individual had been trafficked. The case concerned a woman from Nigeria who had been arrested for producing false identity documents at French passport control in the UK. The appellant was convicted, but appealed on the grounds that the appellant was a trafficked victim, at risk of physical violence and therefore able to rely upon the defence of duress. The identification issue was overlooked which was acknowledged by the court and "this possibility should have been investigated by the appellant lawyers"[89] in greater detail and should have been raised earlier during legal proceedings. Furthermore, there was an obligation for the prosecution to be proactive in this matter and consider the circumstances in which the individual had committed the offence.

Additionally, the issue of whether the individual may have been trafficked or not was ignored by the defence lawyers during the trial, showing that the quality of representation for the appellant in this case had "fallen below any acceptable standard of competence and well below any satisfactory standard of procedural protection."[90] More specific awareness of human trafficking has become vital, especially when cases have come to court. As Jessica Elliott[91] points out, there is "the need for training for those who may come into contact with victims of trafficking such as legal representatives."[92] Anti-trafficking organisations, such as the Poppy Project[93] who provide support, advocacy and accommodation to trafficked women have also played an increasing role in advocating the rights of trafficked victims by obtaining supporting information concerning the circumstances which led to their trafficking and exploitation. Commonly, they have achieved this by submitting evidence to courts, evidencing that the appellant was indeed a victim of human trafficking. After obtaining information from the appellant in the *R v O* case, the following evidence provided that:

> ...after the trial date of 17 March, the appellant was assessed by a senior outreach worker and was deemed to be a victim of trafficking. A detailed history included showed that she was held in debt bondage, raped and forced to work as a prostitute until she escaped later.[94]

The intervention of the Poppy Project on appeal was instrumental because the victim was able to be referred to the NRM and access her rights as a trafficked victim. During the case of *R v O*, defence solicitors were asked by the court to "make enquiries to establish whether their client is a victim of human trafficking,"[95] especially as the client was young. Without adequate training and awareness of human trafficking, this may be difficult for the defence and places a pressure of resources and time to find this evidence. A failure to be identified represents a missed opportunity for the victim to be diverted away from prosecution which increases the trauma and suffering experienced. If it was not for victims coming into contact with the criminal justice system, victims would not have the opportunity of being identified. The important note is that potential victims are treated as victims, not as offenders, especially where the real wrongdoers (the traffickers) remain free and consequently not held accountable. The advocacy of the Poppy Project illustrated the positive role that TSOs can play in filling the gap between the interests of the State to prosecute, with the rights of individuals to be recognised as trafficked victims and protected from prosecution. It is common practice for a third party to be involved in this process. Therefore, without such an opportunity of third parties being involved demonstrates an inconsistent procedure and ad hoc nature. Presently, those victims fortunate enough to have the help of anti-trafficking organisations will benefit from the possibility of being referred to the NRM, whilst victims without support are exposed to prosecution.

There are issues of victims being sent to prison without the consideration that the person may be a victim of human trafficking.[96] Most cases are raised on appeal as an abuse of process.[97] The Poppy Project conducted their own investigations into a woman from Uganda who may have been trafficked but instead was prosecuted, convicted and sentenced to six months imprisonment for producing a forged passport when she applied for a National Insurance Number. This was the case of *R v L and other appeals*.[98] Whilst the woman was in custody, the Poppy Project enlisted the help of a consultant psychiatrist, Dr Zapata-Bravo who concluded that "there is powerful evidence that the appellant fell to be treated as a victim of international trafficking for sexual exploitation in forced prostitution. She was suffering from complex post-traumatic stress disorder with severe trauma."[99] No previous attempt had been made by her solicitor at the time of the trial to refer her to the NRM. When evidence came to light, she was eventually referred, and the UK Border Agency (UKBA) found "conclusive grounds for believing that she had indeed been trafficked."[100] On appeal, it was held that "if the actual facts had been known at the time when the decision to prosecute had been made, the case would not have proceeded."[101] The same determination was made in two further cases, firstly in the case of *R v THN*[102] where the "Crown accepted that had the evidence which was available at the time when the original decision to prosecute was made, on the basis of the public interest test, there would have been no prosecution,"[103] and secondly in the case of *R v T*,[104] where the National Society for the Prevention of Cruelty to Children (NSPCC) provided the court with a letter indicating that the individual charged with cultivating cannabis, contrary to s6(2) of the *Misuse of Drugs Act 1971* may be a victim of trafficking. It later transpired that the defendant admitted that he had been trafficked a day before, but this was not disclosed during the trial. The CA (in this case the UKBA) concluded that he was a victim of trafficking but "this decision was not provided to the Crown by those representing the appellant"[105] until later in the proceedings.

The issue of whether the accused has been identified as a trafficked victim can arise very late in the criminal justice process. Often, cases are heard on appeal before the issue of identification is raised. Commonly, it has been held that "had these facts been known at the time when the decision to prosecute was made, the appellant would not have been prosecuted."[106] The appropriate time of raising the identification issue is at the decision to prosecute, not on appeal of a conviction. Cooperation is required between judges, prosecutors and defence lawyers who must be informed swiftly of NRM decisions. The failure in communication was evident in *R v HVN*,[107] where it was found that the UKBA made an RGD, but this was not communicated to the court.

The above cases provide a basis for arguing that what is needed is a formal system where third parties with knowledge of human trafficking submit evidence on the victim's behalf to divert a prosecution so that they can be identified as victims of human trafficking. The cases above and the case of *R v N & LE*[108] highlight the importance of the prosecution being made aware that an individual may be a victim of human trafficking and further investigation is required.[109] An advocate at an earlier stage may have prevented victims from being prosecuted and convicted for offences. Disappointingly, it took another organisation to inform the court of the past circumstances of an individual to suggest that the defendant was a potential trafficked person. Imogen Chapman from National Society for the Prevention of Cruelty to Children (NSPCC) saw the defendant with an interpreter. It was found that there were "reasonable grounds for believing that he was a victim of international child trafficking for exploitative work in a cannabis farm."[110] The point is that it took a third party, who were not part of the criminal justice system to educate and inform those within the system (lawyers and judges) of the defendant's past and as a trafficked victim. It is something which should have been investigated by public authorities when the trafficked victim came to the attention of public authorities such as the police and duty solicitor at a much earlier stage. An advocate may minimise the risk of the more trafficked victims being prosecuted in the first place by at least submitting all relevant information to prosecutors.

Where the police make initial investigations about whether individuals who have been arrested could be trafficked victims sometimes, further criminal proceedings continued to take place. The case of *R v LM, MB, DG, Betti Tabot and Yutunde Tijani*[111] involved three women (LM, MB and DG) who were charged, prosecuted and convicted of offences of controlling prostitution under s53 *Sexual Offences Act 2003*. Despite the concerns from the police that they may have been trafficked, they were not referred to the NRM. This was argued by defence lawyers to have been a violation of Article 10 CofE which requires States to provide means by which trained personnel are made available to identify and assist victims. However, this argument was rejected by the court as "a breach of Article 10 does not, by itself render a prosecution unlawful."[112] It was held that the women "ought to have been referred to the identification agencies because other possible measures apart from prosecutions might follow."[113] If this happened, the prosecution would not have occurred and the victims would have been diverted from prosecution to the NRM.

If facts pertinent to an individual's case were presented at an earlier stage, the individual would not be exposed to prosecution proceedings. In the case of *R v N* & LE,[114] defencelawyers were quick to point out that "if the facts had been properly investigated, there would have been, or now following proper investigation after conviction, it has become apparent that there should never have been a prosecution."[115] This illustrates that the correct path for the victim to be guided towards is via the NRM framework at an earlier stage, instead of the victim being taken down the prosecution route, which costs more money, time and resources for the State.

Analysis

As we have seen, the prosecutor and the defence lawyers have responsibilities in establishing whether an individual is a victim of trafficking or not. The prosecutor has the responsibility of ensuring that a referral to the NRM has been made. Proper inquiries should be made before a decision to prosecute takes place. As it has been seen, the question of whether the accused is a trafficked victim has arisen much later in criminal proceedings, after the decision to prosecute has been taken. In some cases, it has been raised during appeals by third parties. An advocate should be introduced to assist prosecutors in making a decision to prosecute, based upon the circumstances of victims, assessing viable defences and questioning whether they should be referred to the NRM, diverting them away from prosecution. Advocates could also work with victims to obtain information to give to the police so that prosecutors can be prosecuted which is in both interests of the victim and the State. Advocates, used within Third Sector Organisations (TSOs) could also work more closely with defence lawyers to advise and support the victim during any proceedings to alleviate concerns and anxieties which victims will have.

A trafficked victim may have more trust in someone involved in the process but not a person in authority given their reluctance to trust authorities. The third party has more knowledge of human trafficking and understand the vulnerability of victims. The prosecutor would have more time to complete other tasks and the delegation of this task to an advocate who can liaise with all relevant agencies will enhance the robustness of the process and protect victims from prosecution.

The defence representatives also have responsibilities but have failed in some cases where individuals have not been referred to the NRM when they should have been. A vulnerable trafficked victim heavily relies on a third party to assist them later in the proceedings. In most cases, a third party has had to raise the issue of identification usually during appeal hearings which highlights the missed opportunities to identify earlier in the process. Missed opportunities in the procedure further justify the need for an advocate to be instructed at an earlier stage before the decision to prosecute is. The advocate would represent the view that a prosecution should be avoided on the basis that there is evidence that the individual is trafficked and as a victim of this kind cannot be held morally culpable.

4   Conclusion

This chapter and the preceding chapter have outlined many different issues and themes relating to the issue of the criminalisation of trafficked victims. The previous chapter began by discussing how the international legislation from the UN, the Council of Europe and the European Union obligates States not to prosecute, criminalise and punish trafficked victims. As I have demonstrated, the international obligations serve a purpose of establishing a basic minimum standard in terms of protecting trafficked victims from prosecution. The legal obligations remain unclear and each State party to each legal instrument continues to have discretion on how to implement the obligations. The lack of clarity gives States wider discretion to decide how to criminalise offenders who may have been trafficked. The non-punishment principle should be widely seen effectively within national responses to trafficking such as the UK's National Referral Mechanism.

However, as we have also seen, the statutory defence introduced under Section 45 Modern Slavery Act 2015 prevents many trafficked victims from relying upon it. It remains to be seen whether more victims will self-identify themselves. There is no classic victim or classic perpetrator of trafficking and a greater emphasis on understanding the crime and the impact of coercion and control more upon victims. Until the defences are more victim centred and framed around the genuine trafficked victim (to appreciate their situation which for example, prevents escape), it remains unclear as to whether more victims will be persuaded to be identified without fear of prosecution without the help of a third party.

A means to safeguard the interests and rights of trafficked victims, ensuring they are not prosecuted in the first place instead of relying on defences, would seem appropriate. This may involve trained trafficking advocates working within the process, crucially at the point of the proceedings where a decision to prosecute will take place. An advocate could be instructed to assist in the process at this point where the opportunity to refer to the NRM can be taken. We have seen that the present responsibilities of the prosecutor to consider whether a suspect should be referred to the NRM have not been met. I have also explained how anti-trafficking organisations have had to intervene to make the victim's defence aware that their client is a trafficked victim, meaning that victims have been punished unnecessarily because they had not been identified earlier in the process.

Often, where defence solicitors and the CPS have allowed a prosecution of trafficked victims to take place, it has meant a missed opportunity for many trafficked victims to be referred into the NRM. This has produced a cost to the taxpayer by the continuation of prosecutions when more resources could be used to investigate, charge and prosecute traffickers with a view to assisting trafficked victims give evidence to help convict more offenders.

Where individuals are incorrectly treated as offenders, rather than victims, it presents gaps in protection for trafficked victims within the criminal justice system, creating barriers for more potential victims to come forward to self-identify. The current system may make victims reluctant to participate in police investigations due to the fear of being prosecuted, rather than being referred and identified.

Notes

Notes

1. Section 45(1) Modern Slavery Act 2015.
2. Section 45(1)(b) Modern Slavery Act 2015.
3. Section 45(1)(c) Modern Slavery Act 2015.
4. Section 45(5) Modern Slavery Act 2015.
5. Section 45(2) Modern Slavery Act 2015.
6. Section 45(1)(d) Modern Slavery Act 2015.
7. R v MK [2018] EWCA 667.
8. R v MK [2018] EWCA 667 at 45.
9. These include Offences against the Person Act 1861, the Sexual Offences Act 2003 (c.42), Domestic Violence, Crime and Victims Act 2004 (c.28) and Anti-terrorism, Crime and Security Act 2001 (c.24) and Terrorism Act 2006 (c.11).
10. These are usually offences associated with drugs and sexual offences.
11. K. Laird, "Evaluating the Relationship Between Section 45 of the Modern Slavery Act 2015 and the Defence of Duress: An Opportunity Missed?" (2016) Criminal Law Review, 395 at 396.
12. See "Evidence Review of Section 45 of the Modern Slavery Act: Background and Context," Modern Slavery & Human Rights—Policy & Evidence Centre, April 2022 at 11, https://modernsla verypec.org/assets/downloads/Section-45-full-review.pdf.
13. OSCE, "Policy & Legislative Recommendations Towards the Effective Implementation of the Non-punishment Provision with Regard to Victims of Trafficking," (2013) at 23.
14. Modern Slavery Bill Debate, col 367 (11 September 2014).

15. Modern Slavery Bill Debate, col 367 (11 September 2014).
16. K. Laird, "Evaluating the Relationship Between Section 45 of the Modern Slavery Act 2015 and the Defence of Duress: An Opportunity Missed?" (2016) Criminal Law Review, 395 at 398.
17. K. Laird, "Evaluating the Relationship Between Section 45 of the Modern Slavery Act 2015 and the Defence of Duress: An Opportunity Missed?" (2016) Criminal Law Review, 395 at 403.
18. Section 22(3) Northern Ireland Trafficking and Exploitation Act 2015 which states that a person may be compelled to do something by another person, or by the person's circumstances.
19. Section 45(3)(b) Modern Slavery Act 2015 and Section 22(4)(b) Northern Ireland Trafficking and Exploitation Act 2015.
20. Recommendation 25 Modern Slavery Act Review, Published in July 2016.
21. J. Haynes, "The Modern Slavery Act (2015): A Legislative Commentary," (2015) Statute Law Review 37(1), at 16.
22. Modern Slavery Bill Debate, col 369 (11 September 2014).
23. Modern Slavery Act, col 371 (11 September 2014).
24. C. Beddoe & V. Brotherton, Anti Trafficking Monitoring Group, "Class Acts: Examining Modern Slavery legislation in the UK," October 2016 at 68, http://www.kalayaan.org.uk/wp-content/uploads/2014/09/atmg_class_acts_report_web_final.pdf.
25. Section 1(4)(a) Modern Slavery Act 2015. See Section 1(4)(a) Northern Ireland Trafficking and Exploitation Act 2015 where the regard for an adult who may be vulnerable should be considered when assessing whether an offence has been committed.
26. R v Bowen [1996] 2 Cr App Rep 157.
27. R v Bowen [1996] 2 Cr App Rep 157 at 166.
28. *R v GAC* [2013] EWCA Crim 1472.
29. *R v GAC* [2013] EWCA Crim 1472 at 26.
30. R v Bowen [1966] 2 Cr App Rep 157.
31. *R v Hurst* [1995] 1 Cr App R 82.
32. *R v Hurst* [1995] 1 Cr App R 82 at 90.
33. B. Simpson, "The Reasonable Victim of Modern Slavery," (2019) The Journal of Criminal Law, 83(6), 508 at 510.

34. K. Laird, "Evaluating the Relationship Between Section 45 of the Modern Slavery Act 2015 and the Defence of Duress: An Opportunity Missed?" (2016) Criminal Law Review, 395 at 402.
35. See the case of *R v Dao* [2012] EWCA Crim 1717.
36. Modern Slavery Bill Debate, col 373 (11 September 2014).
37. Modern Slavery & Human Rights—Policy and Evidence Centre, April 2022 at 7.
38. Independent Review of the Modern Slavery Act: Final Report 2019, accessed at https://www.gov.uk/government/publications/independent-review-of-the-modern-slavery-act-final-report/independent-review-of-the-modern-slavery-act-final-report-accessible-version#acknowledgements.
39. Independent Anti-Slavery Commissioner's Call for Evidence Report," October 2020, accessed at https://www.antislaverycommissioner.co.uk/media/1478/the-modern-slavery-act-2015-statutory-defence-call-for-evidence.pdf.
40. Independent Anti-slavery Commissioner's Call for Evidence Report," October 2020, accessed at https://www.antislaverycommissioner.co.uk/media/1478/the-modern-slavery-act-2015-statutory-defence-call-for-evidence.pdf at 7.
41. Modern Slavery & Human Rights—Policy and Evidence Centre, "Evidence Review of Section 45 of the Modern Slavery Act; Background and Context, April 2022 at 1, https://modernslaverypec.org/assets/downloads/Section-45-full-review.pdf.
42. Greta Group of Experts on Action Against Trafficking in Human Beings, "Report concerning the implementation of the Council of Europe Convention on Action Against Trafficking in Human Beings by the United Kingdom," 2nd Evaluation Round, Council of Europe, 2016 at para 287.
43. OSCE Resource Police Training Guide: Trafficking in Human Beings, TNTD/SPMU Publication Series Vol 12, Vienna, July 2013 at 126.
44. The OSCE states from the report above at 126 that "CPS Guidance Advises Prosecutors to Obtain Further Information from Non-government Organisations that Supports Trafficked Victims."

45. As the OSCE acknowledge, the CPS may be "dealing with a traumatised victim, whose story might change frequently and may not be assessed as credible by the prosecution." OSCE Policy and Legislative Recommendations towards the effective implementation of the non-punishment provision, in consultation with the Alliance against Trafficking in Persons Expert Co-ordination Team, Vienna, 2013 at 29.

46. B. Simpson, "The Reasonable Victim of Modern Slavery," (2019) The Journal of Criminal Law, 83(6), 508 at 511.

47. S. Fouladvand & T. Ward, "Human Trafficking and the State," (2019) JCL, 83(1), 39 at 51–52.

48. R v DS [2020] EWCA Crim 285 at 40.

49. See T. Ward & S. Fouladvand, "Human Trafficking, Victims' Rights and Fair Trials," (2018) The Journal of Criminal Law, 82(2), 138–155.

50. F. Laczko & M.A. Gramegna, "Developing Better Indicators of Human Trafficking," (2003) 10 Brown J World Affairs, 179.

51. HM Inspectorate of Constabulary and Fire & Rescue Services (HMICFRS), Stolen Freedom: The Policing Response to Modern Slavery and Human Trafficking (2017), 60.

52. V. Roth, "Defining Human Trafficking and Identifying its Victims: A Study on the Impact and Future Challenges of International, European and Finnish Legal Responses to Prostitution-Related Trafficking in Human Beings" (Leiden, Martinus Nijhoff 2012) at 187.

53. US TIP Report 2011.

54. C. Beddoe & V. Brotherton, Anti Trafficking Monitoring Group, "Class Acts: Examining Modern Slavery Legislation in the UK," October 2016, http://www.kalayaan.org.uk/wp-content/uploads/2014/09/atmg_class_acts_report_web_final.pdf at 70.

55. CPS Guidance, "Modern Slavery, Human Trafficking and Smuggling" 6 July 2022 at 15.

56. CPS Guidance on Human Trafficking http://www.cps.gov.uk/legal/h_to_k/human_trafficking_and_smuggling/#a23.

57. Council of Europe Convention on Action against Trafficking in Human Beings Explanatory Report.

58. Council of Europe Convention on Action against Trafficking in Human Beings Explanatory Report at para 127.
59. R v N [2019}.
60. R v N [2019] EWCA Crim 984 at 40.
61. R v Joseph & Others [2017] EWCA Crim 36.
62. R v Joseph & Others [2017] EWCA Crim 36 at para 40.
63. CPS Human Trafficking, Smuggling and Slavery Legal Guidance, found at http://cps.gov.uk/legal/h_to_k/human_trafficking_and_smuggling/#a20.
64. See V.C.L v UK (2021) 73 EHRR 9 at 196.
65. V.C.L v UK (2021) 73 EHRR 9 at 161.
66. V.C.L & AN v UK [77587/12 and 74603/12] at 159.
67. R v N; Le [2012] EWCA Crim 189.
68. R v L, HVN, THN, T [2013] EWCA Crim 991.
69. R v GS [2018] EWCA Crim 1824.
70. The CPS Full Test Code are a set of guidelines applied by a prosecutor when determining whether an offender is to be charged with an offence. It has two stages, the evidential stage, followed by the public interest stage. These can be found at https://www.cps.gov.uk/publications/code_for_crown_prosecutors/codetest.html.
71. http://www.cps.gov.uk/legal/h_to_k/human_trafficking_and_smuggling/.
72. R v Joseph (Verna) [2017] EWCA Crim 36.
73. R v Joseph (Verna) [2017] EWCA Crim 36 at 63.
74. B. Simpson, "Modern Slavery and Prosecutorial Discretion: When Is It in the Public Interest to Prosecute Victims of Trafficking," (2019) The Journal of Criminal Law, 83(1), 14–19.
75. S. Edwards, "Coercion and Compulsion—Re-imagining Crimes and Defences" (2016) Crim LR, 12, 889.
76. N. Wake, "Human Trafficking and Modern Day Slavery: When Victims Kill," (2017) Criminal Law Review, 658.
77. CPS Full Test Code found at https://www.cps.gov.uk/publications/code_for_crown_prosecutors/codetest.html.
78. CPS Guidance on Human Trafficking, http://www.cps.gov.uk/legal/h_to_k/human_trafficking_and_smuggling/#a23.

79. R v LM, MB, DG, Betti Tabot and Yutunde Tijani [2010] EWCA Crim 2327 at para 9.
80. Section 4.4 CPS Full Test Code.
81. Human Trafficking, Smuggling and Slavery: Legal Guidance: Crown Prosecution Service.
82. R v AAD, AAH and AAI [2022] EWCA Crim 106 at 120.
83. R v Joseph [2017] EWCA Crim 36.
84. N. Wake, "Human Trafficking and Modern Day Slavery: When Victims Kill," (2017) Criminal Law Review, 658 at 677.
85. Human Trafficking, Smuggling and Slavery: Legal Guidance: Crown Prosecution Service, accessed at https://www.cps.gov.uk/legal-guidance/modern-slavery-human-trafficking-and-smuggling.
86. Human Trafficking, Smuggling and Slavery: Legal Guidance: Crown Prosecution Service, https://www.cps.gov.uk/legal-guidance/modern-slavery-human-trafficking-and-smuggling.
87. R v Brecani [2021] EWCA Crim 731.
88. *R v O* [2008] EWCA Crim 2835.
89. *R v O* [2008] EWCA Crim 2835 at para 17.
90. *R v O* [2008] EWCA Crim 2835 at para 26.
91. Jessica Elliott, Senior Lecturer: Law at University of West England.
92. J. Elliott, "Misidentification of Victims of Human Trafficking: The Case of R v O," (2009) International Journal of Refugee Law, 21(4), 727 at 731.
93. The Poppy Project ran outreaches to prisons to help and advocate for trafficked women. The project started to provide the CPS with information from those in prison as part of their appeals.
94. J. Elliott, "Misidentification of Victims of Human Trafficking: The Case of R v O," (Oxford University Press, 2009) at 731.
95. *R v O* [2008] EWCA Crim 2835 at para 26.
96. See M. Jovanovic, P. Burland, V. Topp, F. Fluhr, 'Tackling the Blind Spot of the UK Anti-slavery Regime,' Modern Slavery and Human Rights Policy and Evidence Centre, November 2023, accessed at https://modernslaverypec.org/assets/downloads/Prisons-modern-slavery-full-report-final.pdf.

97. See DS [2020] EWCA Crim 285, A [2020] EWCA Crim 1408 and AAD, AAH, AAI [2022] EWCA Crim 106.
98. *R v L and Other Appeals* [2013] EWCA Crim 991.
99. *R v L and Other Appeals* [2013] EWCA Crim 991 at para 74.
100. *R v L and Other Appeals* [2013] EWCA Crim 991 at para 74.
101. *R v L and Other Appeals* [2013] EWCA Crim 991 at para 74.
102. *R v THN* [2014] 1 All ER.
103. *R v THN* [2014] 1 All ER at para 45.
104. *R v T from R V L and Other Appeals* [2013] EWCA Crim 991.
105. *R v T from R V L and Other Appeals* [2013] EWCA Crim 991 at para 54.
106. *R v T from R V L and Other Appeals* [2013] EWCA Crim 991 at para 54.
107. *R v HVN from R V L and Other Appeals* [2013] EWCA Crim 991.
108. *R v N & LE* [2012] EWCA Crim 189.
109. *R v N & LE* [2012] EWCA Crim 189 at para 42.
110. *R v N & LE* [2012] EWCA Crim 189 at para 72.
111. *R v LM, MB, DG, Betti Tabot and Yutunde Tijani* [2010] EWCA Crim 2327.
112. *R v LM, MB, DG, Betti Tabot and Yutunde Tijani* [2010] EWCA Crim 2327 at 32.
113. *R v LM, MB, DG, Betti Tabot and Yutunde Tijani* [2010] EWCA Crim 2327 at 32.
114. *R v N & LE* [2012] EWCA Crim 189.
115. *R v N & LE* [2012] EWCA Crim 189 at para 10.

8

Conclusion

This book has examined the difficulties associated with identifying victims of human trafficking and the challenges victims face in self-identifying themselves as victims of crime. The book has extensively highlighted and demonstrated numerous issues, barriers and challenges which have presented themselves and which have intensified during the pandemic. Now that societies are no longer subject to social restrictions; it remains to be seen what really happened during this period. This is extremely important to understand as it will give legislators, policy makers, agencies of the State (such as the police and Border Force Staff, Home Office staff) and third sector organisations a better understanding of what is required to effectively identify more victims to be identified now, and in the future.

The main reason why this book has been written is because the issues examined throughout take place simultaneously within a negative and toxic atmosphere containing a hostile attitude towards migrants and immigration. Migration is different from immigration. The two terms have been conflated and unfortunately confused in the same way that human smuggling is misinterpreted as human trafficking. Both migration and immigration are realities in the modern world and must be

M. Davis, *Identifying Victims of Human Trafficking*, Palgrave Studies in Victims and
Victimology, https://doi.org/10.1007/978-3-031-61741-6_8

managed within communities, at the local level, national governmental level and at the global level. The phenomenon of mass migration flows seen across the world and the way global crimes are carried out by non-state actors and criminal organisations. They take hold because of the lack of forcefulness of Governments to fully understand the nature of problems globalisation over the past 30 years alongside the responses of some Governments to isolate themselves by adopting self-protection policies. The adoption of protectionist policies limits the movement of persons, but forced migration continues which creates a bottleneck where States are unwilling to take in more people fleeing persecution and moving because of war, conflict and climate change. Traffickers can take advantage of this situation and entice them into the world of exploitation, especially where they know that vulnerable people will not be safeguarded or protected well enough within some countries. The language used by some politicians towards immigration and gaming the system has facilitated a fear and hostility towards vulnerable foreign nationals and pitting their interests against their own citizens. This has resulted in much resentment and anger towards migrants which is deep-seated within the political arena and has prevented a rational and measured discussion on immigration. Within communities' discrimination towards low skilled migrants combined with the ongoing xenophobia promoted by loud-voiced influential politicians has become extremely unhelpful for advocates of anti-trafficking to advance the rights of trafficked victims to be identified so that services and support can be provided. It is argued that "fragmented societies with isolated individuals are ideal for creating ideal victims and ideal offenders."[1] This view can easily be agreed with and is likely to continue and able to breed an increased resentment from portions of the electorate listening to xenophobic politicians.

Furthermore, within this hot temperature political environment, victims of human trafficking have been misidentified as other less deserving types of migrants, namely economic migrants who are perceived as taking advantage of the UK labour market and causing increased social pressures on housing, education and health. This is simply untrue.

The steps taken in writing this book have included investigating the issues from a range of standpoints. It has touched on many disciplines.

These have included addressing the political aspects of identification of trafficked victims from the standpoint of immigration. From a legislative perspective, a range of international legal instruments were examined alongside the legal steps taken from the Government enacting new legislation such as the Nationality and Borders Act 2022 and the Illegal Migration Act 2023. The social aspects associated with identification of victims such as the experience of the pandemic were examined to assess the impact associated with the identification of trafficked victims. Conclusively, this approach illustrates the interdisciplinary aspects of the topic, where different realms of consideration are needed to consider giving a comprehensive commentary on the present situation.

Above all, this book has argued that a victim-centred approach is required to instil confidence in the detection, referral and identification process within the UK. Where more foreign victims are identified as victims, they will not be misidentified as other types of migrants, not prosecuted for offences committed under duress, or deported where they could run the risk of being re-trafficked. All of us have a role to play in securing the safety of victims, despite this responsibility taking place within a negative rhetoric towards immigration which has existed since the 1990s and substantially increased in past years. It is hoped that the book advocates for the autonomy of the individual alongside maintaining the identity of the individual. Without increased knowledge, understanding and empathy towards trafficked victims the invisibility of victims of modern slavery will continue. It is hoped that this book shines a light on the plight of trafficked victims and what they experience as part of their difficulties in being positively identified by the State. It is envisaged that the book challenges what the idea of being a free individual should look like, how traffickers harm victims which impacts the freedom and autonomy of victims to make free and informed decisions alongside seeing how traffickers compromise and restrict the lives of so many trafficked victims for their self-interest of making money from the services victims are forced to supply. It is anticipated that the book reinforces the mission of standing up for trafficked victims when needed and helps combat the greatest human rights abuses of our time.

The following sections summarise the main aspects from each chapter.

1   Extent of the Issues, Challenges and Barriers of Identification

As it has been acknowledged, human trafficking remains a formidable global crime issue for States to combat. This is because human trafficking is a fast-paced crime committed transnationally by organised crime groups and internally within countries by non-state actors. It is prevalent across the world violating the human rights of individuals across the globe. In recent decades the issue has drawn increased attention from the United Nations and the Council of Europe as well as the European Union who have implemented international legal instruments for States to adopt a crime control approach as well as consider victim-centred approaches. Striking a balance between these two approaches is exceptionally difficult given the political priorities of Governments.

Despite the advancement of the issue of combatting and preventing trafficking, the successful identification of victims remains a significant challenge for a host of reasons. This is seen through the low numbers of individuals being identified by States across the world. Identification takes place within a migratory environment where the world has experienced significant migrant flows in Syria and more recently in Ukraine arising from conflict and war. The true impact of climate change on people leaving their homes and the effect this has on migratory flows has yet to be seen but will be more evident in the next ten to twenty years.

A leading characteristic of individuals caught up in the web of exploitation is 'vulnerability.' Traffickers thrive on identifying people who they can manipulate, deceive, coerce and control. The more vulnerable a person is, the higher the risk of them being taken advantage of given their precarious circumstances they find themselves in. The effect experienced by victims of trafficking is the loss of autonomy, self-worth and their liberty. This is also exacerbated because of the way in which the experiences of trafficked victims are often hidden and masked over by the negative view and hostility towards immigration, and those seeking asylum. Furthermore, the increasing numbers of asylum seekers and those displaced often dominate the discussions on immigration, and less focus is placed on the exploitation taking place amongst these social groups. Human trafficking victims often get lost within the rhetoric of other groups of migrants, keeping them in shadowy environment and preventing them from being seen and identified. One thing which is evident is that trafficked victims depend on the State for protection and support through an effective identification referral mechanism. The term, 'human trafficking' can often get confused with the term, 'human smuggling,' by the media and politicians often preventing effective solutions from being due to incorrect framing of certain acts such as the 'Small Boats Issue' which is often classed as 'human trafficking' when in fact it is clearly human smuggling. For the intention of clarity, the main difference between the two crimes is the issue of consent, where people consent to be smuggled from place 'A' to place 'B', and in contrast, a trafficked cannot consent to be exploited.

There are a host of reasons why it remains challenging for individuals to self-identify as trafficked victims. This is largely because of the impact that trauma has on them from their exploitative environments. Mental health issues also play a part in non-self-identification. The prevalence of Post-Traumatic Stress Disorder (PTSD) in victims has a material impact on their inability to understand and process what is happening to them.

There are a host of reasons why it is challenging for agencies and organisations to spot the signs that someone may be a victim of trafficking. This is largely due to the onerous task and can result in the misidentification of victims as offenders and being taken through the criminal justice system as defendants. This is often too commonly seen and has been pointed out at various points in this chapter and more explicitly in Chapter 4. The prosecution of victims occurs at the expense of victims being diverted away from prosecution and instead referred to the National Referral Mechanism (NRM).

Self-identification remains a challenging concept and one which requires an understanding in greater detail. The impact offenders have on the mental capabilities of victims should not be underestimated. Mental health conditions such as anxiety, depression and PTSD should not be overlooked and often prevent many victims from acknowledging that they are a victim, let alone disclosing to authorities. This gives traffickers the ability to take advantage of victims and continuously exploit them without much fear of victims going to the police.

Identifying who a victim of trafficking is and what one looks like is problematic as it is extremely subjective and stereotypical attitudes are often at play. The result can be inconsistent identification or non-identification based on judgments of character and the willingness of victims to leave the exploitative situation or not which may determine victim status. The 'why doesn't the victim just leave' narrative is particularly unhelpful here as it shows a degree of naivety and a lack of understanding as to how restrictive victims are in their exploitative environment either preventing them from leaving or not having the empowerment to do so because of the harmful psychological tactics employed by traffickers upon them.

It has also been shown in this chapter how the issue of immigration has been severely politicised largely because of the increased media attention arising from the many migratory flows across the world arising from war and conflict. This has been seen in the displacement and movement of Ukrainian nationals because of illegal invasion by Russia and by people wishing to enter the UK from France using small boats with the help and assistance of human smugglers. This mix of legal migration through the Ukrainian family scheme and sponsorship scheme alongside the illegal forms of migration from the increased boat crossing have been problematic for the UK Government to deal with and has resonated negatively across some pockets of the electorate, hostile to immigration and wanting to take back control of borders now that 'Brexit has been done.' All of this has happened at the same time as asylum cases are backed up at the Home Office and concerns about housing migrants whilst their applications are being processed. Constant delays in decisions happen simultaneously as more boats arrive on the shores of the UK.

The chapter explained the process individuals have to go through to be positively identified, to be supported and assisted as victims of human trafficking in the UK. It has been established that whilst there has been an annual increase in the number of victims being identified, the number of potential victims being referred to the NRM is reducing. This is likely because of the impact the Nationality and Borders Act 2022 and Illegal Migration Act 2023 legislation are having on the genuineness of victims to apply to the NRM, dissuading migrants from meeting authorities for fear of being detained and deported. For those individuals progressing through the NRM, there are significant delays in decisions being made and communicated to potential victims which create backlogs for third sector organisations to accommodate more potential victims. The perception from the previous and present members of the Conservative Government that the NRM system is being abused is particularly unhelpful as it does nothing to advance the empowerment of survivors of trafficking who must have to disclose their exploitative experiences.

The significance of receiving a positive 'victims status' decision has somewhat diminished because of the *Brecani* judgement which held that decision makers from the SCA are not experts and do not meet the expert evidence rules in criminal trials. This is a significant setback for victims wishing to advance their rights as victims when they are being prosecuted for offences under duress. *Brecani* also acknowledged that there may be circumstances where a suitable qualified exert could give evidence to inform a jury to give context to a situation. This could potentially pave the way for a trafficking advocate to be identified as an expert giving a view based on their qualifications, skills and experience in human trafficking to inform the jury as to whether the defendant is a potential victim of trafficking.

It would be particularly useful if the NHS could be added as a First Responder and provide training and awareness to help them identify potential victims by making NRM referrals. An awareness from civil society organisations helping and supporting trafficked victims can bring a risk to professionals working in this area of 'vicarious trauma.'[2] This has been acknowledged as a significant issue and one which should not be disguised, nor overlooked. More support and supervision are required for staff working in this area to prevent the amount of burnout experienced by staff and be aware of negative changes in behaviour[3] whilst working and helping trafficked victims.

2   The Structural and Contextual Issues Associated with Detection and Identification

This chapter examined the impact on individuals seeking to be identified as victims of human trafficking with a negative attitude towards migrants and immigration. No meaningful discussion on immigration within the UK can take place without acknowledging the impact that the hostile environment policies over the past 20 years have had on foreign migrants living in the UK.

The chapter identified the origins of the hostile policy and how it developed and was used by successive Governments as part of party-political manifesto as well as legislative changes such as the *Immigration Act 2014* and *Immigration Act 2016*. The impact is that the hostile environment is now affecting newly arrived vulnerable migrants who are taken advantage of by criminal gangs and pushed into risky and exploitative environments. The hostile environment policy restricts the abilities of these people to disclose their victim status. This, combined with the anti-immigration rhetoric towards migrants through the Brexit referendum, has not disappeared but has been famed against vulnerable people who rely on the services and support from within the UK to help them recover from abuse of non-state actors within the UK. Vulnerable people are placed in limbo where the State makes it very difficult for them to live in the UK and then at risk of being detained or deported if it comes to the attention of the State. This 'limbo' is being exploited by organised crime groups who feed off the realisation that illegality of status is a way to deceive and coerce the vulnerable into exploitation under the radar of the State noticing.

The chapter continued forward by evaluating how the issue of immigration has changed relations between the UK and the rest of the world and how these changes have affected the Government's ability to combat trafficking from a crime control perspective and the likely effect it will have on trafficked victims. The long-term impact of Brexit on immigration in the UK will not be seen for many years. However, one impact of Brexit is the uncertainty some foreign nationals experience due to them experiencing discrimination and being treated poorly by employers. The hostility towards migrants as well as those EU nationals settled in the UK prior to Brexit may push some people into less secure and riskier employment and exploitative environments. For foreign nationals and newly arrived migrants the vulnerability of having a legal immigration status can expose them to the same threats.

From the perspective of the UK combatting organised crime, the loss of cooperation and access to information databases between the UK and the EU remains a legitimate concern. Prior to Brexit the UK and the EU worked closely on operations to disrupt organised crime by participating in this role effectively. Because of Brexit, the role the UK plays will be a lesser one, with an enhanced focus on maintaining and amending existing relationships so that the UK is not taken advantage of by organised crime groups who are able to conduct criminal activities easier now that the UK outside the EU institutions. It remains to be seen how effective the new Trade and Cooperation Agreement (TCA) works out in practice. It is anticipated that the UK will still have a good working relationship, but it remains to be seen whether there are any barriers to accessing information from databases and issues relating to sharing data. There have been concerns whether joint investigations will still take place between law enforcement in the UK and EU counterparts. It was reported that cooperation and activities have continued since Brexit and have been successful.[4]

As the new UK points-based immigration system has no criteria for low skilled workers, the risk of exploitation within sectors such as agriculture, construction, social care and healthcare which rely upon low skilled labour remains a significant one. As discussed in the chapter, some employers may take advantage of low skilled workers by discriminating them and treating them less favourably. Furthermore, people who lost their jobs during the pandemic may force the low skilled into further riskier forms of employment. A way forward to protect the rights of low skilled workers would be for the UK to legislate in domestic form the *Agency Workers Regulations 2010* and *Working Time Regulations 1998*. From a human trafficking legislative protection perspective, the new *Retained EU Law (Revocation and Reform) Act 2023* ended the supremacy of EU law on 31st Dec 2023 which may result in either the repeal or amending of *The Trafficking Directive 2011/36* and other laws which guarantee the rights of trafficked victims to obtain compensation from their traffickers, and the right for victims to ensure that they receive appropriate information, support and protection during criminal proceedings.

As highlighted in the chapter, the bubbling up of resentment towards migrants, combined with the hot political rhetoric arising from issues of immigration within UK society has been decades in the making. The mainstream attention to these issues in the media through newspapers and TV has facilitated an unhealthy behaviour towards the treatment of migrants and asylum seekers. The pushing of negative narrative views of immigration has led to a distinct lack of trust between the electorate and no warmth towards migrants. The notoriety of some politicians to use the immigration issue as a way of political opportunism has been effective and gathered pace and toxicity over many years. This has presented significant barriers to maintaining a meaningful conversation on immigration and along with exposing migrants as scapegoats. This political approach to creating immigration as a threat to the UK during the time of the migration crisis was partly part of a successful Brexit campaign for the UK to leave the EU.

Since Brexit, and because of the focus of the Government to reduce the numbers of net migration into the UK, the UK has legislated for tighter controls on illegal migration which has impacted on the favourable treatment of asylum seekers and refugees. This coincided with the challenges of the UK combatting small boats of smugglers carrying people from France and attempting to cross the English Channel into the UK. The chapter explained the present problem of small boats and the financial cost for the UK to house migrants until their claims can be processed. *The Nationality and Borders Act 2022* seeks to deter people arriving in the UK illegally from relying upon modern slavery provisions under the *Modern Slavery Act 2015*. The chapter examined the impact of the legislation on trafficked victims and seeking to be identified even though some victims are in the UK illegally. The consequences will be they will be disqualified from support through the National Referral Mechanism (NRM) if they have not disclosed that they are victims, but this was challenged by the fact that the impact of trauma and the fear of being deported looms large, making them less likely to self-identify.

The new Temporary Permission to Stay Considerations for Victims of Human Trafficking Guidance, published in February 2023 does not automatically entitle the trafficked victim to stay in the UK, but granted if the period of stay would be to assist the victim in their recovery from any physical or psychological harm arising from the exploitation. This is a barrier for victims who have experienced exploitation to seek help and assistance from healthcare professionals to prove that they require such help which is challenging as they will require assistance from a support worker to do so.

The *Illegal Migration Act 2023* seeks to detain and remove people who have come to the UK illegally via small boats. This, in conjunction with the Rwanda policy is one of the flagship policies that the present Government is focussed on to 'stop the boats,' and break the business model of human smugglers. The indirect effect of this legislation is to prevent as many people as possible from coming to the UK to seek asylum. There are a few provisions which automatically disqualify foreign victims of trafficking who have committed criminal offences. This approach fails to acknowledge that some foreign nationals can be coerced into committing criminal offences under duress. The effect of this provision is to criminalise the victims at the expense of criminalising and prosecuting the offenders of trafficking.

The impression that the Rwanda deal shows is that the UK is seeking to sub-contracting their international legal obligations under the Refugee Convention to a State that is willing to buy the contract for processing asylum seekers. The UK is outsourcing their obligations under the Refugee Convention rather than taking responsibility for their own policy making and implementation. This sets a dangerous precedent for other States looking for an opportunity to do the same. Any such approach will be measured by the reduced number of people seeking to cross the English Channel. Many migrants will simply not be deterred by such threats of deportation and are willing to take the risk of getting to the UK by any such means.

The chapter illustrates that the *Nationality and Borders Act 2022* and the *Illegal Migration Act 2023* represent draconian legislation. There is no doubt that there is an ongoing problem with small boats arriving in the UK issue and smugglers are profiting extensively by facilitating a dangerous journey with a threat to life. There is also no doubt that the present global migration crisis is abating. The question is can it be an effective deterrent for the UK to pass legislation to prevent people from claiming asylum from the method of small boats arriving in the UK? The Rwanda policy along with the new legislation represents a fundamental change in the way the UK views and applies international refugee law through the domestic asylum system. It shows a bad example to the rest of the world looking at the UK trying to combat the issue of smugglers taking advantage of the global migration crisis and confusing it with their dissatisfaction of having to process increased numbers of asylum claims each year. It shows a signal to other international partners and departure from international legal principles and norms observed and applied since the Second World War.

Whilst the UK continues to focus on the people arriving in the UK, smugglers continue their illegal operations with impunity as there are no criminal sanctions for those offering these services. Furthermore, there are no prosecutorial measures in the Act to deter smugglers from engaging in illegal operations.

3   The Impact of Covid-19 on the Identification of Trafficked Victims

As it has been shown, the pandemic had a significant impact on the identification of trafficked victims. The period where Covid-19 presented itself created many issues, barriers and challenges for trafficked victims due to social restrictions, making it less likely that victims would self-identify to authorities or frontline agencies recognise that individuals could be trafficked.

The chapter identified many relevant issues specific to the experiences that trafficked victims were exposed to and had to endure alongside the effects of the pandemic on society. Trafficked victims were disadvantaged during this period given the many issues, barriers and challenges they experienced, making identification less likely to occur. It is difficult to overlook the struggles and plight of victims during the pandemic given the challenges we are all faced in our own lives during this period.

The number of victims identified during this period significantly fell but exploitation in certain industries thrived alongside the increased demand for smuggling services despite the restrictions on international and domestic travel. This meant that whilst society was largely shut down, criminal organisations were still able to continue with their criminal activities, making it extremely challenging for victims to be identified. As police forces were preoccupied with other priorities in enforcing the social restrictions, traffickers were able to continue and in some cases expand their criminal networks, enabling them to continue victimising and recruiting new vulnerable people who could be easily manipulated and deceived.

Certain sectors of the economy such as agriculture, factories and construction were able to stay open and they continued their business operations during the pandemic. These businesses operate profitably because they fundamentally rely on low skilled labour within their business model. It was highlighted how sham employment agencies were able to take advantage of workers on a large scale, and criminality within security vetting procedures allowing workers to be on construction sites safely. Vulnerability of foreign workers increased due to some being overstayers once their visas expired, exposing them to harsher work practices as they could not either leave the country due to international travel restrictions or be able to not have to work. Therefore, they had to work illegally which exposed them to being exploited.

The chapter further acknowledged that victims of modern slavery who were being exploited prior to the pandemic were more easily abused and kept in exploitation far easier during the pandemic. The chapter outlined that some workers in these sectors continued to be placed under increased duress and coercion by traffickers and threatened with more violence. This resulted in many victims continuing to be isolated from frontline agencies, organisations who typically may have noticed that they were trafficked if normal life was continuing rather than the social restrictions being imposed.

In addition to the abuse and harm from their continued exploitation, victims who were not identified during the pandemic were more likely to be exposed to the Covid-19 virus despite the social distancing restrictions placed upon communities by the Government. The chapter acknowledged the mental health impacts of lockdowns on trafficked victims during the pandemic, conditions such as anxiety and depression, and Post-Traumatic Stress Disorder which resulted from isolation and the lack of access to support. These conditions were made worse if victims were battling substance abuse. Consequently, many victims were left in limbo during this period and this exposed them to falling between the gaps of support and safeguarding from organisations closed or severally restricted in offering their services. Many victims receiving support was also affected by either a reduction in support or the withdrawal of support because of the challenges of offering face-to-face support alongside the social restrictions.

One overriding benefit for trafficked victims once identified is the entitlement to legal support. A further consequence of non-identification during the pandemic was the lack of legal support to help them get legal representation on welfare benefits, housing and immigration advice. Furthermore, trafficked victims missed deadlines for submitting evidence to the NRM process and challenged decisions. Applications for leave to stay in the UK (which was discussed in Chapter 3) was also compromised because of the pandemic. Furthermore, victims who also had an asylum decision pending from the Home Office encountered significant delays and added to the existing backlog of cases staff at the Home Office are working their way through.

The chapter identified a new group of social groups of individuals who could potentially be drawn into modern slavery because of the financial pressures associated with the pandemic. The ongoing cost of living crisis presents a real and significant risk to economically marginalised UK citizens, including individuals with disabilities and those in low paid work and receiving in-work benefits. The existing economic, social and structural inequalities which existed prior to the pandemic exacerbated during the pandemic, creating an even wider gap between less well-off people and the providing for people and families to be disadvantaged as part of being impacted by the actions of the Government in combatting the pandemic.

It also examined how marginalised people such as the unemployed and the recently unemployed along with people who had recently been made homeless because of the loss of their job because of the pandemic. This has been occurring at the same time when traffickers are easily adaptable to changing their methods of deceiving and recruiting new victims which has been highlighted through increased social media use rather than social interactions which were curtailed during the Covid-19 lockdowns.

Conclusively, the pandemic impacted how vulnerable people heavily relied on online communication services as a direct consequence of the social restrictions. The chapter explained how cyber criminals were able to take advantage of this unintended consequence of the social restrictions as they were able to target vulnerable adults including those with mental health issues, asylum seekers, refugees and the handicapped and disabled who had less access to support services and especially vulnerable children who would have been in the safe school environment. Inside and outside of the internet and cyber world, the chapter acknowledged how traffickers advertised for offering sexual services and recruited sex workers and existing sex workers continued to be coerced into precarious situations despite the societal restrictions.

Children and young adults are a group who were also significantly affected during the pandemic, primarily because of them missing out on school and them spending more time online. This prevented many children from being socially active and many were socially excluded from friends and peers. The disruption to safeguarding services and support to young people provided by some schools meant that many children became vulnerable. These services especially those children in care who were found to have gone missing were vital. The phenomenon of county lines exploitation was a real threat to vulnerable children in care during this time and a crime which increased during this period. It was found that in NRM statistics where there were positive decisions of modern slavery taking place against a child, gender plays a part in the type of exploitation children were involved in. Male children were more likely to have been criminally exploited and female children were more likely to have been sexually exploited. With no criminal offence of child exploitation being in the UK statute book, prioritising the legislation on prohibiting this behaviour would highlight the seriousness of the offence and the devastating impact it is having on children so that police and prosecutors can prosecute offenders.

As the chapter concluded, the true impact of the pandemic on trafficked victims in the UK will not be seen in the short term. Only in time will academics and researchers learn what really happened to victims during this period once more victims either come forward or are found. Their lived experiences can then be heard and listened to so that lessons can be learnt for any future pandemics which require societal restrictions to be placed upon communities.

4   The Prosecution and Criminalisation of Trafficked Victims

The final chapters of the book extensively examined how trafficked victims are often punished by the criminal justice system, rather than being protected by way of identification through the NRM. As it has been shown, the identification of trafficked victims can often be compromised by the misidentification of the State to criminalise victims for criminal offences committed under duress. The chapter examined how victims can be unfairly charged, detained, prosecuted and punished by the State at the expense of being treated as a potential victim of crime.

The chapter explained that despite the large number of modern slavery crimes recorded in England and Wales, there are very little live investigations which not surprisingly leads to very low numbers of people arrested and prosecuted for modern slavery offences which has been the case for many years. Internationally, there has been a drop in the number of successful convictions against traffickers. This reinforces the view that victims cannot get justice against them and highlights issues and challenges within the criminal justice systems of States to successfully prosecute offenders.

Chapter 6 outlined the international legal obligations of States to the issue of non-prosecution of victims. These include those drafted at the

United Nations level, the Council of Europe and the European Union. It was acknowledged that there is a lack of consistency between each legal instrument, making it difficult for States to adopt a consistent consensus on the non-prosecution of victims in their respective domestic law.[5] To some extent, the lack of consistency on what States should do undermines the rights of victims and does not adequately protect victims from the criminal law effectively enough. Ultimately, the non-punishment principle generally does not provide blanket immunity for victims and therefore States have discretion on how to proceed during criminal justice proceedings where an offence has been committed by a victim of trafficking.

The chapter highlighted that a trafficked victim could commit different types of criminal offences at various points during their trafficking experience and within their exploitative environment. An important discussion to have during this chapter is to investigate what types of criminal offences are committed by victims at various points in their trafficking experience. Where victims are using forged documents and visas to enter a country illegally, these are classed as status offences. In contrast, offences such as prostitution, theft and drug offences are committed as part of their exploitation and classed as consequential offences. They are committed as a direct consequence of them being forced to do so by their trafficker(s). Finally, a victim may commit an offence to remove him or herself from the exploitation, i.e. inflicting harm on someone else or committing an immigration offence such as using false identification to flee a country. These are classed as liberation offences. The distinction between offences is important as a way of understanding the type of behaviour committed by victims at different points of their exploitation and should be better understood by officials to help spot the signs that trafficking may be occurring.

The rationale and justification for protecting victims from prosecution and in return identifying them correctly as a victim of crime was strongly advocated in the chapter. To simply continue the prosecution of victims is a violation of their human rights. It also signals an unempathetic lack of understanding of what abuse victims face during their exploitation and fails to recognise that they are a victim of crime, not an offender. Fundamentally, prosecution represents a failure of the criminal justice system to acknowledge the loss of autonomy victims have because of the duress forced upon them by traffickers. Above all, it is not in the interests of the State to prosecute victims whilst offenders get away with criminal behaviour. It represents a moral collapse of their obligations towards trafficked victims.

The nature of abuse which victims suffer was discussed in the chapter. Coercive and compulsive behaviour imposed by traffickers were examined. It was shown that this behaviour must be better understood and addressed by prosecutors to establish the culpability of an offence, leading to decisions as to whether prosecutions should take place or not. In most cases, trafficked victims are reliant on using the section 45 defence contained in the *Modern Slavery Act 2015*. However, it was highlighted in the chapter that the defence is ineffective as many of the offences victims are coerced into committing under duress are included in the excluded offences listed in Schedule 4 of the Act. This restriction undermines the use of the defence. Furthermore, there is very little evidence on how the defence is being used effectively in practice. This would be useful so that changes to the law can be made within section 45.

The chapter advanced arguments that prosecutors and defence solicitors have a greater role to play in taking steps to identify more potential victims of trafficking during their work within the criminal justice system. This is justified so that less trafficked victims are exposed to secondary victimisation which prosecution amounts to. There is clearly more work to be done to increase awareness of modern slavery within the legal profession and the criminal justice system. The chapter outlined the present responsibilities prosecutors have when deciding to prosecute or not. Case law showed that there were several opportunities for trials to have been stopped at various stages because of the issue that the defendant may be a victim of trafficking. In some cases, it was seen that this issue was only raised upon appeal after frontline anti-slavery organisations raised the point in prisons which then facilitated convictions being quashed. This shows that charities are having to raise issues of a lack of awareness of human trafficking within the legal profession, rather than the legal profession and criminal justice system. Charities are proactive in maintaining the rights of victims and the criminal justice system has been seen to respond too late in trials with their behaviour being reactive to this situation, primarily on appeals.

It was also seen that defence solicitors have often missed the opportunity to identify their client as trafficked and therefore the victim has not only been a victim of crime from modern slavery but then subjected to secondary harm by the State by being prosecuted when in fact the individual should have been referred to the NRM. A failure to represent the victim in this regard falls below the acceptable standard of competence in this area and does not satisfy the procedural protection victims should be provided with. The decision in *Brecani*[6] is disadvantageous to trafficked victims as there is no longer any significance of a positive Conclusive Grounds Decision being shown to the jury. This places more responsibility to gather evidence to prove that the defendant is a victim of trafficking and placed under duress to commit the crime.

The importance of proper enquiries taking place at an earlier stage in the criminal justice system to establish whether an individual is a victim or not and consequently diverted away from prosecution was consistently advocated during the chapter.

5   Conclusion—A Path Forward to Enable More Identifications and Protection of Victims from Further Exploitation

This book argues that identifying more victims of modern slavery is not only in the interest of trafficked victims themselves, but also in the interest of the State. Running through this book has been recurring themes of identification, misidentification, recognition and repression of trafficked victims, the responsibility of authorities, and the moral and legal obligations of the State. These intertwining themes combine to make up a complex picture of what successful and effective identification looks like in the UK.

As it has been shown, there are significant improvements for law enforcement and local authorities to better understand their obligations to identify individuals who may be victims of human trafficking. As updated statutory guidance is released by the Home Office as to how the new legislation will work in practice more work needs to be done to ensure that the guidance is being acted upon and therefore must be better measured. The same issues surrounding a lack of awareness or indeed better awareness amongst police and the courts set out a clear path forward for arms of the State to offer vulnerable people the opportunity to be referred into the NRM. This is a constant throughout the theme of identification of victims and remains a work in progress within this area.

Many issues surround the legislation which allows for the denial of support, detention and deportation of victims who are recognised as victims of trafficking who have arrived illegally in the UK alongside those who have been convicted of offences committed under duress.

Due to the controversy of the *Nationality and Borders Act 2022* and the *Illegal Migration Act 2023,* there is a significant chance of appeals being brought by individuals as to how the State intends to recognise victims of trafficking which have been shown to negatively affect the basic provisions and rights granted under existing international law.

The Home Office Modern Slavery Victim Care Contract is due to be renewed in 2025. It will be interesting to see how the service afforded to existing victims will be either amended, improved or changed considering the issues surrounding the Government's rhetoric towards asylum seekers and other vulnerable people of foreign nationality.

The UK Government through the Home Affairs Select Committee also plans to release their inquiry into Human Trafficking in the UK which will no doubt set a new course for how the UK seeks to combat the crime and offer victim support and protection alongside what its priorities will be for the foreseeable future. It is also envisaged that the new Independent Anti-Slavery Commissioner who has been appointed will continue the important work by encouraging good practice in the prevention, detection, investigation and prosecution of slavery and human trafficking offences and the identification of victims and provide oversight on the Government's legislative approaches in these areas.

It is hoped that more third sector organisations involved in conducting research will continue to present data based on the lived experiences of trafficked victims to help inform policy makers in the future to guarantee the rights and protections under international law. At present, there is no trafficking advocate system in place designed to help and assist authorities. Victims of crime are still directed to Victim Support,[7] the Survivors Trust,[8] Rape Crisis[9] or Migrant Help.[10]

A looming question which requires an answer is whether the NRM is fit for purpose in its current form. Specifically, does the referral mechanism meet the needs and objectives of identification for foreign victims considering the legislative developments trying to address illegal immigration into the UK? The method of how a foreign trafficked victim arrives in the UK remains a pertinent issue and is relevant to whether potential victims are granted access to modern slavery protections including the NRM. The recent Nationality and Borders Act 2022 and the Illegal Migration Act 2023 have both had a devastating impact on the ability of trafficked victims being allowed to be identified and have access to help and support. The legislation has obviously been enacted as a deterrent, but this approach significantly affects the effectiveness of the UK to combat trafficking in the UK because of its lack of focus on the victim, showing a poor victim-centred approach to benefit trafficked victims who could assist authorities in bringing the wrongdoers to justice.

The current points-based system restricting low skilled labour is the type of restrictive immigration policy risks pitting UK workers against foreign workers who could easily be exploited. The fact is that the global economy requires both low skilled and high skilled labour represents a realistic and pragmatic policy on immigration, especially given the demand for low-cost goods and services in the UK which is often provided by low skilled labour. The challenge for the UK Government and all Governments is how they seek to continue to protect the rights and entitlements of workers so neither group are exploited by criminal gangs and individuals profiting from the exploitation of the vulnerable whilst maintaining that they have a strong control of managing migration.

In short, a systematic change to combatting people smuggling and human trafficking whilst preserving and advocating victims' rights by full commitment to services and support is required. This is a difficult balance to achieve but current legislative additions such as the *Nationality & Borders Act 2022* and the *Illegal Migration Act 2023* show that the scales are heavily weighted against victims of modern slavery, presenting significant and insurmountable barriers in being identified. Organisations and charities have been instrumental and extremely effective in advocating for victims of modern slavery found in the UK and this shows no sign of abating. What appears to be lacking is trust from victims to come forward. A significant challenge is individuals who do not have the will, means or opportunities to come forward and trust the State that their rights and entitlements will be observed. This remains a barrier which has yet to be addressed. Recent legislation has shown that this situation remains even more difficult as the gap between victims trusting authorities and authorities treating victims with humanity given the human rights violations they have suffered and States are under obligations to protect is too wide. The UK has even further to travel than before to get to a more understanding and empathetic approach to the identification of victims than before the restrictive immigration laws were passed. The approach of deterring 'illegal' foreign nationals from the UK even where they have legitimate asylum claims remains the priority. So far, this approach from the UK has clearly not worked and is counterproductive to the international legal obligations surrounding identification of potential victims. A more pragmatic starting point to maintain border security is required whilst having a victim-centred approach to the issue of identification which requires more awareness of what human trafficking is and how it operates. More research is required from those victims of 'lived experience' of being trafficked to comprehend what they experienced prior to the pandemic, during the pandemic and since the pandemic to establish what is required from Governments to fully support their recovery from exploitation. A sea-change of attitudes from politicians and Governments is required. We are a very long distance away from a Government which fully understands what modern slavery looks like in the UK and appreciates the plights of trafficked victims. The current situation of demonising migrants is counterproductive to both aims and even more disadvantageous to trafficked victims as they will be hidden even more in the shadows of society. From a social perspective this approach will continue leading to new types of exploitation and further existing exploitation of victims of modern slavery committed by unscrupulous offenders of human trafficking who continue to act with impunity. With the help and assistance of us all, the hope is that more victims of modern slavery will be identified, protected from future exploitation and supported through their journey of recovery whilst traffickers will be prosecuted and held accountable for their criminal actions by the State.

Notes

1. See M. Duggan, "Revisiting the Ideal Victim" (Policy Press 2018) at 22.
2. S.R. Jenkins & S. Baird, "Secondary Traumatic Stress & Vicarious Trauma: A Validational Study," (October 2002) Journal of Traumatic Stress, 15(5), 423–432.
3. Behaviours can include a loss of hope, pessimism and cynicism alongside sadness, and guilt. This can then lead to people avoid listening to victims' stories of traumatic experiences.
4. In June and October 2022, UK and 34 other countries identified 910 potential victims of trafficking and 115 alleged traffickers across Europe. This was referenced in the US TIP report 2023 found at https://www.state.gov/reports/2023-trafficking-in-persons-report/united-kingdom/.
5. As discussed, terms such as non-criminalisation, non-punishment and non-punishment are used in different legal instruments.
6. R v Brecani [2021] EWCA Crim 731.
7. https://www.victimsupport.org.uk/.
8. https://www.thesurvivorstrust.org/.
9. https://rapecrisis.org.uk/.
10. https://www.migranthelpuk.org/.

Index

Printed by Printforce, United Kingdom